RESEAR(HIGHLIGHTS IN SOCIAL WORK 39

Adul Day Services and Social Inclusion

D0336145

Research Highlights in Social Work

This topical series examines areas of particular interest to those in social and community work and related fields. Each book draws together different aspects of the subject, highlighting relevant research and drawing out implications for policy and practice. The project is under the editorial direction of Professor Joyce Lishman, Head of the School of Applied Social Studies at the Robert Gordon University.

Also in the series

Planning and Costing Community Care
Edited by Chris Clark and Irvine Lapsley
ISBN 1 85302 267 5
Research Highlights in Social Work 27

The Changing Role of Social Care
Edited by Bob Hudson
ISBN 1 85302 752 9
Research Highlights in Social Work 37

Social Work
Disabled People and Disabling Environments
Edited by Michael Oliver
ISBN 1 85302 178 4
Research Highlights in Social Work 21

Social Care and Housing
Edited by Ian Shaw, Susan Thomas and David Clapham
ISBN 1 85302 437 6
Research Highlights in Social Work 32

Transition and Change in the Lives of People with Intellectual Disabilities
Edited by David May
ISBN 1 85302 863 0
Research Highlights in Social Work 38

Dementia
Challenges and New Directions
Edited by Susan Hunter
ISBN 1 85302 312 4
Research Highlights 31

Growing Up with Disability
Edited by Carol Robinson and Kirsten Stalker
ISBN 1 85302 568 2
Research Highlights in Social Work 34

RESEARCH HIGHLIGHTS IN SOCIAL WORK 39

Adult Day Services
and Social Inclusion
Better Days

Edited by Chris Clark

Jessica Kingsley Publishers
London and Philadelphia

Research Highlights in Social Work 39
Editor: Chris Clark
Secretary: Anne Forbes
Editorial Advisory Committee:

Robert Gordon University
School of Applied Social Studies
Kepplestone Annexe, Queen's Road
Aberdeen AB15 4PH

The right of the contributors to be identified as authors of this work has been asserted by them in accordance with the Copyright, Designs and Patents Act 1988.

First published in the United Kingdom in 2001 by
Jessica Kingsley Publishers Ltd
116 Pentonville Road
London N1 9JB, England
and
325 Chestnut Street
Philadelphia, PA 19106, U S A
www.jkp.com

Copyright © 2001 Robert Gordon University, Research Highlights Advisory Group, School of Applied Social Studies

Library of Congress Cataloging in Publication Data
A CIP catalog record for this book is available from the Library of Congress

British Library Cataloguing in Publication Data
A CIP catalogue record for this book is available from the British Library

ISBN 1 85302 887 8

Printed and Bound in Great Britain by
Athenaeum Press, Gateshead, Tyne and Wear

CONTENTS

PART I

Policy for Day Services

CHAPTER I

The Transformation of Day Care

Chris Clark

What is day care?

This book is concerned with day services for adults: in particular, adults whose disabilities or other special circumstances lead them to require professional support for some of the activities and attainments of ordinary living. The main groups to be considered are older people including those with dementia; adults with learning disabilities; people with mental health problems; and people without a stable home life. Users of day services are neither entirely dependent on formal services, nor fully able to maintain a satisfactory way of living without professional help. Day services thus occupy an intermediate position in the spectrum between full social care in residential settings and occasional support in the community for independent living. Day care for children is excluded from the scope of this book.

Within these broad generalisations a very wide range of services, centres and activities are subsumed under the label of day care. The conventional idea of day care is based on the concept of the 'centre' to which users must specifically travel in order to benefit. The traditional day centre for infirm elderly people or the adult training centre for individuals with learning disabilities will be familiar to many readers. One of the themes of this book will be the obsolescence of this concept: daytime support is not necessarily, or best, provided within the often institutional structures of 'centres'. Instead, the focus must be increasingly on the diverse needs of users rather than the running of centres – a needs-led rather than a service-led philosophy. For this reason this book adopts the language of day *services* rather than the traditional perspective of day *care*. Day services are no longer provided only in centres. Nor are users now necessarily expected to travel in order to receive the type of support they, and their carers, need.

The user groups identified above represent, perhaps, useful categories for policy and administrative convenience. In reality individuals are not always so readily categorised, and it needs to be especially remembered that administrative categorisations all too easily congeal into agency structures that fail to respond to the diversity and individuality of human need. Institutional and conceptual boundaries should not be allowed to stand in the way of an holistic view of the aspirations of users, or inhibit creativity and innovation in the development of more responsive services.

This book will show that there are important issues common to the different sectors of day services. Day services address a very wide range of needs:

- for physical care and shelter, and the prevention of deterioration of physical and mental health
- for companionship and social stimulation
- for rehabilitation and the teaching of new life and social skills
- for positive experiences and new achievements
- for promoting independence, social integration and employment.

What day services often have in common is a marginal status, corresponding to the marginal social position of their users. Day services are often seen as unglamorous, and receive low priority against more visible acute demands in the broad field of welfare. Day care has often been seen as a long-term palliative for people with insoluble chronic problems. Even where, as for example in the field of learning disability, it has been the avowed intention to use day services as a means of education or rehabilitation with the aim of progression, the result has often been stasis, fixing users and their families in a situation that offers little hope of advance and fails to respond to changing individual circumstances. This book will demonstrate that important advances are now being made to challenge this neglect, and will highlight new thinking by innovative professionals in what has long been seen as something of a backwater of social care.

Issues in day care

While traditional day care has been an important resource for users and their carers, it has attracted regular criticism. The reported comment of users in a recent official review (Scottish Executive 2000, p.54) that what is provided is boring and lacking in direction echoes a familiar theme in reviews of day care. Users want skilled and focused help with coping with their specific problem or disability; they want social contact, acceptance and friendship; they want something interesting to do; they want to maintain or improve their continued capacity for independent life; and they may also be trying more broadly to make or recover the opportunities and activities of an ordinary life, especially the opportunities to participate in paid employment and to have a circle of friends with whom they can share interests.

Traditional services may hold people back from achieving these aspirations rather than promote their development; they may be more oriented to the needs of carers and service providers than to those of users. Services have been insensitive to the different needs of users, including users from different ethnic and cultural backgrounds. However, carers too need more support from day services, which should be aiming not merely to provide a respite from caring but to address carers' wider concerns for the shorter- and longer-term well-being of their relative.

The limitation of day services to set activities in special buildings hinders the effective targeting of help where it is most needed. Several contributors to this book emphasise the role of flexible support activities in the community rather than traditional services based in buildings. One of the disadvantages of traditional centre-based services is that they tend to encourage a mentality of routine and predictability. In such environments it is more difficult to tailor support to individuals' changing needs over time. Day care becomes, paradoxically, a place where progress is suspended, not promoted.

In a similar vein, innovators have questioned the demarcation of 'day care' from other services. New working relationships may be needed with supported employment services or with other areas of health and social care provision. Day care can and should act as a point of access or gateway to other services needed by users. Equally, relying on traditional categories such as 'old people' or 'people with mental health problems' may narrow thinking unnecessarily and unhelpfully.

If there is one development in day services that epitomises all these issues, it is the growth of supported employment. The research has shown that what people with learning disabilities or with mental health problems most clearly want is a job. In Western society the job is not only the key to income security and independence but also the main determinant of social standing, the route to status, worth and recognition, and the means of access to friendship, community and valued recreation. Several chapters in this book therefore focus on supported employment, which represents in some ways the antithesis of traditional day care.

Funding is an issue, as it is in all areas of welfare. But day care typically deals with chronic, long-term needs that may not seem to attract any great priority against situations of more visible urgency and crisis. It is largely concerned with groups that are not highly valued in society, such as elderly sufferers from dementia or adults with recurrent disabling mental health problems. Small changes at the margins in the quality and levels of services may seem to have only minor consequences in terms of improvement or deterioration in users' conditions of life. To achieve real progress for service users it may be necessary to commit the very large inputs per user seen, for example, in supported employment projects.

Day care centres are susceptible to the problem of all group-based provision: costs tend to be averaged out over the user population. This masks variation in the amount of support given to, or needed by, each individual. It also makes attributable costs per individual unduly sensitive to changes in the volume of demand.

Day services and social inclusion

The contributions to this book are addressed to the theme of social inclusion. Enough has already been said to make the point that traditional day care is all too apt to exclude its consumers from wider participation in society. While acting in the name of care and rehabilitation it is liable, in practice, to remove disadvantaged individuals from the mainstream of social provision. Although day care can provide a social focus for people who might otherwise be very isolated, most adult day care environments are rarely visited or seen by ordinary members of the community unless they have a relative who is a user. The goal must be to develop day services that are not exclusionary but inclusionary. The contributors to this book show that day care needs to respond to the following challenges to become:

- *More flexible in time:* day services need to be available at more flexible times of the day, and night. There should be wide scope for different amounts of service per user and per week.

- *More flexible in place:* day services should not be confined to traditional centres and buildings located in main centres of population. They should be delivered in a wide range of settings including in particular ordinary places of resort of the general public, such as workplaces, shopping centres, health centres, etc. Day services should also be more widely available in people's homes.

- *More responsive to individuals' requirements:* the institutional framework of traditional day care encourages a standardised, one-size-fits-all approach to providing help. Users must have choice. Day services need to respond better to the variety of individual needs and interests, and should avoid prior assumptions about the progress or outcomes that individuals may eventually attain. Carers, too, must have choice and not have imposed upon them the preconceptions of professionals.

- *More adaptable to variable and complex needs:* day services should provide more varied activities and services adapted to diverse needs and interests. Services provided should go beyond basic care or warehousing. Again, the needs of carers should be addressed along with the needs of users.

- *Culturally and ethnically sensitive:* day services must recognise the different expectations of the various cultural communities they should properly serve. Minority interests should not be split off from the main body of service provision, since that can easily create another kind of social exclusion.

- *Inclusive of disadvantaged groups:* day care is largely concerned with already excluded groups. Providers of day services should be mindful that in providing a partial community for their users they might unintentionally be exacerbating their users' more general social exclusion. Day services should strengthen links and opportunities within ordinary communities.

- *Supportive of wider social integration:* although day care may alleviate isolation and loneliness, users may be effectively trapped in a narrow range of relationships with professionals and be wanting in real friendships and activities that are personally relevant in the framework of their lives. Day services should foster roles, activities and identities *outside* the care context and aim, where possible, to promote users' eventual independence from the formal service.

Like social work generally, the aim of day care can be conceived as promoting the ordinary life (Clark 2000); this perspective will recur through the chapters that follow. Such a view raises deeper questions than the practices, methods and organisation of day services, important though these are. The official providers of day services focus on structures and systems that will support care by relatives, mitigate dependency, promote rehabilitation and reduce calls on more costly alternatives. Users, however, will probably be more concerned with getting or holding on to opportunities that address their general life aspirations. In this regard the traditional service approach needs to be replaced by a broader understanding of the place of formal services in the lives of users who comprise an excluded minority of the general population.

The argument of this book is that traditional day care provision for adults – which in practice deals predominantly with relatively powerless and socially excluded groups – needs to be replaced by a broader range of day services imbued with a philosophy of social inclusion. Such an approach recognises that for users and carers, day services represent a potential lifeline for disempowered, vulnerable and often forgotten people. It also understands that the community as a whole is impoverished by the exclusion of individuals who do not altogether conform to the culturally valued images of normality – able in mind and body, occupying customary and valued social roles.

Day services need to spread beyond the boundaries of institutional care settings, with their inherent propensity to uniformity and unresponsiveness. They need to develop new kinds of help, and deliver it in new and more flexible ways. Only by doing so can services hope to meet the legitimate demands of users and carers. The contributors to this book recount practical innovations underpinned by what is probably even more important – a new philosophy for services that will reach excluded people in the community.

Synopsis of the book

In the context of a series called *Research Highlights* it is particularly noteworthy that the absence of a systematic base of research and evaluation on day care is remarked on by most of the contributors to this book. Here it is possible only to speculate on the reasons for the lack of research. The low priority it receives perhaps reflects assumptions that the value of day care is largely self-evident. It seems plausible that if day care is actually treated mainly as a means of keeping users either out of full-time institutions or off the streets, then insofar as it succeeds in these limited aims it might not seem to raise pressing issues for research.

The chapters that follow nonetheless reveal that although patchy, interesting pockets of useful research do exist. They also demonstrate very clearly the kinds of research question that urgently need to be more widely addressed in day care. Innovations have been introduced by committed practitioners; what is urgently needed is research-based information about their effects, both intended and unintended, so that useful lessons can be applied in policy and practice elsewhere. As is common in social services, it tends to be the innovatory projects that receive what scant research effort exists. Routine services of established types tend to receive very little evaluation. This makes it very difficult to compare the relative values of traditional and innovative services, and consequently inhibits change.

The chapters are arranged in two parts. Part I has a policy focus. The authors have each discussed the policy environment in relation to one particular user group, commenting on current provision and the relationship of day care to other services. Available research has been drawn on to discuss evidence for effectiveness. All have reflected on the role of day services in promoting social inclusion.

Susan Tester (Chapter 2) builds on her extensive earlier work on day services for older people. Demonstrating the crucial significance of the 1990 NHS and Community Care Act, Tester draws together a wide range of evidence showing clear directions for necessary developments in this large field of social services. However, the pace of change in day services for older people has been slow, and the value of the services for the direct recipients often questionable. Tester proposes areas for future research and argues for broader strategies to promote social inclusion.

Kirsten Stalker (Chapter 3) reviews the field of services for people with learning disabilities, where by contrast there have been far-reaching changes in recent years. Policy and service development have responded to radical critiques of the old, institutionally-based provisions, and attitudes and expectations have been realigned around the ideas of normalisation and the social model of disability. The emphasis in day services has moved away from occupation in traditional centres towards supported employment in the community; but this is not the solution for everyone.

Anne Connor (Chapter 4) looks at services for people with mental health problems. Drawing on the experience of an innovative project in south west Scotland, Connor also focuses on supported employment as a key intervention with people aiming to build or rebuild a normal life after mental ill health. She analyses a range of service models, draws the lessons of experience and shows the implications of the new projects for service development and evaluation.

Abi Cooper (Chapter 5) discusses day centres for people described – not always meaningfully – as homeless. This is a neglected service for a marginalised and often stigmatised group. In contrast to the established sectors of old age and learning disability, services are led almost entirely by the voluntary sector and are often dependent on insecure short-term funding. The government's initiatives on social inclusion have particular relevance for the floating population who depend on such day centres.

Part II of the book highlights case studies of innovation and development. The authors share experiences of a number of projects and initiatives, emphasising useful lessons for practitioners and policy makers in other places.

Jo Moriarty (Chapter 6) analyses patterns of service provision in day services for older people. Using a number of colourful examples, Moriarty shows that day services for older people need not, and should not, be limited to the familiar, safe and dull, confined to traditional hours and premises. While day care is often aimed primarily at providing relief for carers, there is much to be done to improve support for them. Day care has unrealised potential for combating social exclusion but it must develop in ways that respond better to cultural diversity and to the varied interests, needs and wishes of users.

In Chapter 7, Susan Hunter and Glenda Watt offer further insights into the pattern of service provision for older people. They demonstrate the shifts in thinking that have begun to take place but need to develop much further, including moving from a service-led to a person-centred approach and from thinking about care to thinking about empowerment. Hunter and Watt provide further illustrations of innovative and inspiring practice that embody some of this new thinking, and suggest models that can be replicated.

Julie Ridley (Chapter 8) draws on her own research on supported employment projects for people with learning disabilities. Supported employment in some form or other is widely seen as the way forward for integrating affected individuals into the wider community in order to achieve better quality of life, normalisation and inclusion. Ridley's work shows that despite much development in the USA, the ideals are often difficult to put into practice. Her study raises fundamental issues about the aims and philosophy of supported employment, and powerfully illustrates the influence of project leaders' methods and principles.

Ann Lloyd and Angela Cole (Chapter 9) are also concerned with services for people with learning disabilities. They describe the struggle to develop and sustain in their local area a ground-breaking new form of day service, described as 'non-buildings based' – a complete contrast to traditional day care. Lloyd and Cole show how their approach promotes social inclusion. Practitioners and managers will find their story invaluable for the insights it gives into how such a new service can be made to work. The resourcefulness and commitment of the project staff in the face of daunting challenges is strongly communicated.

Finally, in Chapter 10, Bob Grove and Helen Membrey take a primarily research-based approach to draw together the evidence on effective mental health day services – again, much of it American. Supported employment once more emerges as the crucial development of recent years. Grove and Membrey analyse the factors that conduce to success in occupational rehabilitation services and appraise tested strategies for intervention. They show, as several other contributors have also done, that fixed assumptions about alternatives to employment can be dangerously limiting.

References

Clark, C.L. (2000) *Social Work Ethics: Politics, Principles and Practice.* Basingstoke: Macmillan.
Scottish Executive (2000) *The Same as You? A Review of Services for People with Learning Disabilities.* Edinburgh: Scottish Executive.

CHAPTER 2

Day Services for Older People

Susan Tester

Introduction

Day services form an integral part of community care for older people, alongside residential and domiciliary services. Why, then, are day services rarely visible in the policy and research literature on community care? This neglect of day services is long-standing; as noted in an earlier policy study, day care services have 'kept a very low profile in the sphere of health and welfare provision for older people' (Tester 1989, p.1). This chapter takes up key issues raised in that study: the diverse aims and objectives of day services; the assessment of need for the services; coordination between day services and other services; and monitoring and evaluation. These issues are examined in the context of changes in the policy environment during the 1990s, particularly the implementation of community care reforms under the National Health Service (NHS) and Community Care Act 1990.

The stated policy aims of community care usually include the goal of supporting people to live as independently as possible in their own homes. Key principles underlying community care, discussed in the policy and practice literature, include social integration, participation and empowerment of older people. The diverse, and sometimes conflicting, aims and objectives of day services are examined in this chapter in relation to such principles. Major objectives identified by Tester (1989, pp.40–41) include:

- helping people remain independent in the community
- social care and company

- rehabilitation and treatment
- assessment and monitoring
- providing support for carers.

The key objective of providing company and social contacts for older people to compensate for their lack of such contacts may be seen more broadly in the context of social exclusion, defined by Barry (1998, p.1) as: 'multi-dimensional disadvantage which severs individuals and groups from the major social processes and opportunities in society...'. In the case of older people, this exclusion may result not only from individual transitions such as retirement and widowhood, but more broadly through ageism and society's negative attitudes to later life (Bytheway 1995), and the need for older people to secure an identity in the postmodern world (Phillipson 1998). Within the framework of the principles and ideologies on which community care is based, it is sometimes assumed that day services can contribute to the goals of social inclusion, defined by Barry (1998, p.1) as: 'the attempt to re-integrate, or to increase the participation of, marginalised groups within mainstream society'. However, by taking people out of their normal environment and providing special segregated services for them, day services may be contributing to the social exclusion of older people. This paradox is explored further below.

This chapter reviews the range of day services offered to older people with physical or mental disabilities or health problems, using the definition:

> A day care service offers communal care, with paid or voluntary care givers present, in a setting outside the user's own home. Individuals come or are brought to use the services, which are available for at least four hours during the day, and return home on the same day. (Tester 1989, p.37)

However, in exploring the role of day services in promoting social inclusion, the focus is on social day care services rather than on the mainly health care services of day hospitals or on the purely social and educational facilities which are readily accessed by older people or the general population.

Since the major day care studies of the 1970s and 1980s (for example: Brocklehurst and Tucker 1980; Carter 1981; Tibbitt and Tombs 1981) and policy and research reviews of the late 1980s (Horobin 1987; Tester 1989), little empirical or policy research has been undertaken specifically on day services. Government policy documents and community care research and policy literature have minimal content on day services. This chapter draws on the secondary sources available in order to:

- review the aims and provision of current day services in the context of policy changes since 1990

- consider the assessment of need for day services in the broader context of community care and coordination with other services

- review the monitoring and evaluation of day services and the evidence on outcomes for users and carers

- draw conclusions on the role of day services in promoting social inclusion and on future directions for policies on day services for older people.

Policy environment, aims and provision of day services

Day services were established in the United Kingdom earlier than in other European countries. Day hospitals began to develop from the 1950s and their numbers increased rapidly in the 1960s and 1970s; day centres in the statutory and voluntary sectors expanded rapidly in the 1970s. These developments were not explicitly planned. The range of day services is broad, comprising day centres and day hospitals with various sub-categories of each. The main types of day service provision for older people identified in the late 1980s were: NHS day hospitals (geriatric or psychogeriatric); statutory social services community-based day centres and day care in residential homes; and community-based day centres run by voluntary organisations (Tester 1989, p.49). Bacon and Lambkin (1997, pp.43–44) identified six types of day centres and three types of day hospitals; the main types were day care centres (30% of units), geriatric day hospitals (26%) and psychogeriatric day hospitals (17%). They point out that 'the range of unit types identified was greater than that reported in earlier studies' and that the newer types developed mainly since 1980 were psychogeriatric day hospitals, mixed day hospitals, resource centre units and day centres for elderly mentally ill people (Bacon and Lambkin 1997, pp.43–44).

In other north west European countries day care developed later and in different policy contexts. Alber (1993, p.115) commented that: 'given the recent policy emphasis on community care…it is noteworthy that day care centres which serve as flexible integration mechanism [sic] between domiciliary care and residential care are almost everywhere in very scarce supply'. In the early 1990s Denmark had the highest level of available day care places, followed by the Netherlands whereas day care was very limited in Belgium and Germany, compared with countries such as France, Luxembourg and the UK. In the Netherlands day hospitals, first established in the late 1960s, developed rapidly in the 1980s, following planning guidelines issued in 1979, so that 'within a decade the day hospital became a well distributed and firmly established service within the health care system' (Nies, Tester and Niujens 1991, p.250); day centres, however, developed rapidly in the 1980s in an unstructured way. The available evidence suggests that up until the early 1990s, through periods of rapid development in some countries but not others, day services in the UK and more broadly in Europe were generally characterised by a lack of clarity in policy and planning. Policy changes in the 1990s, focused on promoting community-based rather than institutional care, led to a greater diversity of day services.

Reforms under the NHS and Community Care Act 1990 were developed in the context of unplanned changes which occurred in the UK, in conflict with government-stated policies in favour of older people remaining in their own homes. The availability of social security payments for private and voluntary sector residential and nursing home care led to an escalation in independent sector care homes and a large reduction in NHS beds (Audit Commission 1997, p.12). A new system of paying for social care and of assessment of care needs by local authorities was implemented under the NHS and Community Care Act from 1993.

Of the six key objectives set out in *Caring for People*, those most relevant to day services are: 'to promote the development of domiciliary, day and respite services to enable people to live in their own homes wherever feasible and sensible'; 'to ensure that service providers make practical support for carers a high priority'; and 'to make proper assessment of need and good case management the cornerstone of high quality care' (Cm 849 1989, p.5). The other three objectives also impact on day services: the promotion of the independent sector; the clarification of responsibilities between agencies; and the new funding structure for social care. The expected changes under the reformed system and evidence of the effects of the changes in the 1990s are reviewed briefly below in relation to day services.

First, an expansion in day services would be expected, including an increase in provision by the independent sector. Local authorities would commission day services from the private and voluntary sectors under contracts in addition to providing them directly. Statistics show an increase in the number of day centre places purchased or provided for people aged over 65 by local authorities in England from 207,500 in 1996 to 253,900 in 1998; this increase was mainly accounted for by the inclusion in the statistics of places for day care in residential homes (Department of Health 1999b, Table 3.6). In Scotland the number of day centre places for people aged over 65 decreased from 8336 in 1995 to 7309 in 1997 (Scottish Office 1998b, Table 2.19, p.30); in 1998 there were 8398 places, although these differences should be treated with caution as data analysis methods had changed (Scottish Office 1999, Table 1).

The expansion of the independent sector has only been achieved 'to some extent' (Warburton and McCracken 1999, p.27). Evaluation of a Department of Health (DoH) funded initiative showed that there were difficulties in stimulating the social care market even through an initiative with special funding and staff (Perkins and Allen 1997, p.122).

For NHS day care facilities in England there was a gradual decrease in the numbers of total attendances at geriatric medicine facilities from 1,454,867 in 1992–93 to 1,132,058 in 1996–97, to 982,568 in 1998–99; whereas for old age psychiatry facilities there was an increase from 1,364,323 in 1992–93 to 1,574,836 in 1996–97, then a slight decrease to 1,515,199 in 1998–99 (Department of Health 2000b, Table 1, p.1). In Scotland, total attendances at geriatric medicine day facilities increased from 191,627 in 1990–91 to 196,971 in 1996–97, then decreased to 192,838 in 1997–98; at old age psychiatry facilities total attendances increased from 160,358 in 1990–91 to 207,670 in 1996–97, then decreased slightly to 207,165 in 1997–98 (ISD Scotland 1999, Table M7.1, p.207). In general it seems that the main trend has been towards increasing importance of the old age psychiatry day facilities and a decline in those for geriatric medicine.

The Royal Commission on Long Term Care (Cm 4192-I 1999, paras. 2.5–2.7) estimated that 260,000 people aged over 65 were receiving day care in the UK at a total cost of £380 million at 1995–96 prices (£125m funded by NHS; £235m by personal social services, net of charges; £20m by private charges). This, however, represented only 3.4 per cent of the total expenditure on long-term care services (£11,065 million).

With an emphasis on needs-led services, another expectation was that older people's needs for day services would be assessed and, if appropriate, services would be provided as part of an individual package of care, taking account of the user's and carer's views. For example, day services could provide bathing and chiropody as part of a package. This would necessitate a greater diversity of services tailored to the needs of, for example, older people with mental health problems or from minority ethnic groups, as well as to the needs of carers. Bacon and Lambkin (1997, p.45) found evidence of changing patterns of day services, with the development of needs-led models and of innovative services. Day services for older people with mental health problems were a specific area of service development and innovation during the 1990s.

A further expectation was that the division of responsibilities for day services would be clarified and published in local community care plans. By 1992 Bacon and Lambkin (1997, p.45) noted a 'sharpening of boundaries between providers' with statutory social services focusing on those with greatest needs, voluntary organisations catering for more social day care, and NHS agencies providing rehabilitation and treatment. Reviewing the objective of clarifying responsibilities, Henwood and Wistow (1999, p.107) found that the main progress in collaboration had been in the policy area of hospital discharge and continuing care. However, the process of producing community care plans had led to a strengthening of working relationships between social services and health authorities; many had published joint community care plans.

In the late 1990s Government policy documents pointed out that there were still difficulties with the community care system, although the general policy of caring for people in the community was confirmed. For example, *Modernising Social Services* (Cm 4169 1998, para. 2.2) points out that the changes in the 1990s 'concentrated largely on structure and on process, rather than on outcomes. Serious problems remain'. The emphasis was to shift to 'the quality of services experienced by, and outcomes achieved for, individuals and their carers and families' (para 1.7). The White Papers (Cm 4169 1998; Cm 4288 1999) have little specific content on day services but set a new philosophy and context in which services are to be provided. Similarly in Cm 4818-I (2000) and Cm 4818-II (2000) day services are not mentioned specifically, even though there is an emphasis on the development of 'intermediate services' which might be expected to include day services.

The broad aims of social care services for older people, as expressed in policy documents of the late 1990s and early 2000s, are: promoting independence; prevention and rehabilitation; and coordinated services providing individualised care. However, there is little mention of day services in relation to these aims. Social inclusion is considered a key value by the Royal Commission, among others: 'A more positive and inclusive climate should be created and nurtured, so ensuring the development of more opportunities which can be taken up by older people' (Cm 4192-I 1999, para. 1.18). Day services, where mentioned, are included as one of a range of care settings. *Aiming for Excellence* considers day care 'an important part of community services' but 'particularly valuable to people with learning disabilities' (Cm 4288 1999, para. 5.19).

It seems that day services are briefly referred to as services that exist, but are not considered adequate for the promotion of social inclusion. Instead a broader strategy is emphasised, for example by the Royal Commission which argues that independence and social inclusion will be achieved by 'improved access to some of the components of normal life' (Cm 4192-I 1999, para. 8.2). The Royal Commission emphasises the wider interests of older people (para. 10.8) and recommends that 'opportunities for education and access to leisure opportunities for older people should continue to be a high priority in all aspects of public provision' (para. 10.9). This was also a conclusion reached in the earlier day care study (Tester 1989, p.169).

The aims of day services are discussed in this chapter mainly in relation to the older users themselves. Day care, however, also serves the needs of carers by providing important relief from caring. This purpose of day care is mentioned in policy documents at least as often as social inclusion for the older person. Indeed, in a government charter for long-term care in England, the only mention of day care is as a type of break for carers 'arranging for the person being cared for to spend time in a day centre' (Department of Health 1999a, p.14). The different and sometimes conflicting needs for day care of users and carers are discussed further below.

Working together: Assessment of need and coordination of services

The assessment of need for day services for older users and carers and the allocation of services were identified as problematic in the 1980s and early 1990s. The systems did not 'ensure that day care services respond to assessed need in a locality, nor that they reach those who need them most' (Tester 1989, p.20). There were wide variations between areas in assessment criteria and the availability of day care places (Brearley and Mandelstam 1992). New responsibilities for local authorities under the NHS and Community Care Act 1990 were intended to alleviate these difficulties. Overall local need would be assessed in community care plans, individual users' needs through the assessment and care management system, and carers' needs through the Carers (Representation and Services) Act 1995. Although the local authority was given lead responsibility, health authorities and other agencies were involved in assessment and care planning. However, there was often poor co-ordination between professionals and coordination was difficult to achieve (Audit Commission 1997, p.24).

The community care reforms of the early 1990s were intended to produce needs-led rather than service-led flexible care packages designed to meet the needs of individuals and their carers. The social services authority's assess-ments 'should apply both to people seeking domiciliary and day care, and to people seeking admission to residential or nursing home care' (Cm 849 1989, p.18). Day care was seen as part of a package of 'domiciliary support provided to people in their own homes, strengthened by the availability of respite care and day care for those with more intensive care needs' (Cm 849 1989, p.9). It could therefore be expected that day care units would tailor the services they provided to meet the requirements of individual users' care plans. Bacon and Lambkin (1997) found that new approaches were being de-veloped:

> For example, greater flexibility in day unit organisation was seen not only as a way of meeting the changing needs of users, but also as a means of coordi-nating day unit attendance with other parts of an individual's package of care. (p.46)

However, the implementation of the care management and assessment system was found to be variable; although progress had been made, the system did not always produce effective individualised care packages (Audit Commission 1997, p.27; Challis 1999). There was also wide variation in local authorities' policies for charging users for non-residential packages of care including day care and transport to day care (Audit Commission 2000; National Consumer Council 1995), whereas users of NHS day services received them free of charge. The Government intends to issue 'binding stat-utory guidance' on charges from April 2001 (Cm 4818-II 2000, para. 2.24).

One of the reasons for concern about local authority care management processes was that they were insufficiently integrated with the NHS systems: 'the precise contribution of health care and of particularly secondary health care services such as geriatric medicine and old age psychiatry to this process were not clearly specified and are subject to local arrangements' (Challis 1999, p.82). The reformed NHS system of the early 1990s required health authorities or boards to assess local health care needs and purchase services from NHS or independent sector providers, including day hospital units (National Audit Office 1994, p.4). Earlier studies showed a lack of coordination between these services, particularly between day hospitals and day centres, and overlaps between characteristics of their users (Tester 1989, p.63). Those older people who were referred to day hospitals received multidisciplinary assessment of their health care needs, and rehabilitation and maintenance therapy (National Audit Office 1994, p.9). Social care was not an aim in itself although the day hospital provided opportunities for social contacts. Joint planning, provision or purchasing of day services by health and social services and/or voluntary organisations offer an opportunity to overcome these difficulties as users can share some activities and meals but also receive the health and social care services for which they are individually assessed. Bacon and Lambkin (1997, p.45) found 'examples of different providers working together using joint finance to provide new, and in some cases innovative, day units'.

Evidence of the difficulties of coordination of needs assessment and service provision led to proposals for further integration of the health and social care systems in policy initiatives of the late 1990s and early 2000s, which could help to produce multidisciplinary assessment for a care package in which appropriate day services contribute to meeting individuals' assessed needs. Partnerships between health, social services and housing authorities were encouraged in order to improve local joint planning and service provision (see, for example, Cm 4169 1998; Department of Health 1998; Scottish Office 1998a). Specific new powers to facilitate partnership working were proposed by the Scottish Office (1998a) and Department of Health (1998).

These were pooled budgets, lead commissioning and integrated care service providers, which were legislated for in the Health Act 1999. Health Improvement Programmes were introduced from 1999 (Department of Health 1998, p.12), to be produced by health authorities in cooperation with local authorities and other agencies. Joint investment plans and joint commissioning were encouraged and primary care groups and trusts were established. New care trusts proposed in the NHS Plan 'will be able to commission and deliver primary and community healthcare as well as social care for older people and other client groups' (Cm 4818-I 2000, para. 7.10).

Guidance on improving the systems of assessment and care management was introduced by the Scottish Office (1998a, para. 2.12); this included joint assessments. Greater consistency in assessment procedures and the development of guidance on 'Fair Access to Care', to be in operation by April 2001, were planned (Cm 4169 1998, para. 2.36). The Royal Commission (Cm 4192-I 1999, para. 8.12) proposed 'a single point of contact through which the process of assessment is arranged and the necessary care commissioned' and emphasised multidisciplinary assessment for people with complex needs. These suggestions were taken up in *The NHS Plan* which proposed a single assessment process for health and social care by April 2002: a personal care plan agreed by the older person and carer which will 'document their current package of health and social care' (Cm 4818-I 2000, paras. 15.9–10).

As with the documents of the early 1990s there was little direct reference to day services in these new systems and proposals; they do, however, address long-standing problems in assessment and care management, and if implemented successfully would increase the effectiveness of day services as part of a care package. The implementation of new assessment, care management and commissioning procedures with specific relation to day services would provide a fruitful area for research.

Monitoring and evaluation of day services

In the 1980s monitoring and evaluation of day services were found to be inadequate at all levels (Tester 1989, p.181). This section considers the impact of community care reforms in the early 1990s, and the implications of proposals in the late 1990s and early 2000s for the formal monitoring and evaluation of services by providers and government agencies at different levels.

The White Paper *Caring for People* (Cm 849 1989) set out the responsibilities for monitoring and evaluation for the reformed system under the NHS and Community Care Act 1990. At individual level, the care management system would monitor quality of care and review the user's needs (p.21). At day care unit level, the statutory sector would include monitoring independent sector units and ensuring that quality was specified and monitored through contracts (pp.22–23). Local area monitoring of performance would be achieved through community care plans. National and regional level monitoring would be the responsibility of the Social Services Inspectorate (SSI) and DoH (p.41); guidance was issued for setting local standards for quality in day services (Department of Health and Social Services Inspectorate 1992).

However, difficulties in implementing these monitoring systems were reported by the Audit Commission (1997, p.74). These included care managers having inadequate time for individual monitoring and the tendency for authorities to rely on service specifications and complaints procedures to monitor individual units. A review of DoH inspections similarly found that: 'little progress seems to have been made in developing satisfactory systems of monitoring and reviewing the implementation of care plans or service delivery' and expressed 'concerns about the need to enhance the quality of day care and respite services' (Warburton and McCracken 1999, p.30).

Proposals for reform of quality systems are mainly approached from a national perspective through the Government's 'Best Value' approach, performance indicators to assess local authority performance, the National Service Framework for Older People (Department of Health 2001) and, more specifically, through new systems of regulation, inspection and care standards, and improved training for care workers (Cm 4169 1998, Cm 4288 1999). A National Care Standards Commission was established for England under the Care Standards Act 2000 to regulate services and enforce new minimum standards (Cm 4818-II 2000, p.20); and a quality strategy was proposed (Department of Health 2000a). A Scottish Commission for the Regulation of Care is to be set up. Although these systems are mainly for residential and nursing homes and domiciliary care, in Scotland day care for adults will eventually be regulated by the Commission (Cm 4288 1999, para. 5.19). The Scottish Executive issued the first tranche of draft National Care Standards for the care of older people and other groups, focusing on care homes; day services will be covered in subsequent tranches (Scottish Executive 2000).

There has thus been little change in the effectiveness of monitoring and evaluation of day services since the 1980s, although new systems are now proposed or being implemented, initiated at national government level, with consultation of stakeholders involved. The Audit Commission (1997) recommended 'a cohesive approach to quality that brings together all those involved in the care process' (p.74) and suggested that 'the greatest safeguard is likely to be achieved by encouraging service providers to conduct self-assessment procedures and monitor and improve their own services' (p.75). This approach is used in the Netherlands where the Quality Act 1996 'requires care providing organisations to monitor, manage and improve quality of care systematically' (Tester 1999, p.13) and 'quality systems had been developed through a corporatist model through close interaction between the government and all the stakeholders at a series of conferences' (p.32). Perhaps this type of system could improve the effectiveness of monitoring and evaluation of day services in the UK. Further research is needed on the implementation and effectiveness of different methods of formal monitoring and evaluation of day services.

Outcomes of day services for older people and carers

Commentators on day services frequently emphasise that there is little evaluation evidence available on which to base opinions of the effectiveness of services, and that it is difficult to measure outcomes without clear statements of the aims of the services. Most research on day services is small scale and/or relies on secondary sources. This section focuses on key issues identified in discussions of day services in the 1990s: access to particular settings, depending on locality; day services for older people with mental health problems; day services for older people from minority ethnic communities; and day services as support for carers of older people.

Ideally the day services received should depend on relevant referral and assessment followed by allocation of the most appropriate service. However, in spite of the 'sharpening of boundaries between providers' noted above (Bacon and Lambkin 1997, p.45), considerable overlap between services persisted during the 1990s (Collier and Baldwin 1999, p.590; Levin, Moriarty and Gorbach 1994, p.71). The role of day hospitals was the subject of ongoing debate. Day hospitals were considered appropriate locations for assessment, rehabilitation and treatment of older people, particularly those with dementia. However, some commentators argued that day hospitals were in fact mainly providing respite for carers and that the functions of assessment and rehabilitation could easily be undertaken in day centres or other settings with support from day hospital staff (Collier and Baldwin 1999; Fasey 1994, pp.519, 521).

There is now a greater diversity of day services than in the 1980s. The availability of day services and the type of service received by older people vary according to the area in which they live (Tinker *et al.* 1999, p.41; Warrington and Eagles 1995, p.99). Levin *et al.* (1994, pp.64–66) found that day services varied by area in terms of the amount of services available; the sector providing the service; the setting in which the service was provided; and the frequency of attendance. Transport remains a key issue (Levin *et al.* 1994, pp.77–78). In rural areas mobile day centres have sometimes been used (Tinker *et al.* 1999, p.57); another solution has been to provide more localised services through diversification of existing residential care homes, day centres, sheltered housing and village halls (Brown 1999, p.1.21).

People with dementia have been found more likely to use day services than other older people (Philp *et al.* 1995). In a sample of people with dementia living at home, 58 per cent received day care as part of a care package. Day care was used particularly by those with severe dementia and those with co-resident carers (Moriarty and Webb 2000, pp.57–59). Day services for people with dementia are often provided in old age psychiatry day hospitals, whose main users are people with dementia, and tend to be those with the highest levels of dependence (Fasey 1994, p.519). There is, however, increased diversity in services for people with dementia, in both generic and dementia specific community-based day centre settings (Curran 1996a). Although research on day care for people with dementia mainly focuses on the benefits to carers, studies have found that the users themselves benefit from attendance through enjoyment of the company (Moriarty and Webb 2000, p.62) and improved mood and well-being (Levin *et al.* 1994, pp.73–74; Wimo *et al.* 1993). Curran's study of a new day centre suggests that 'women living alone with milder degrees of cognitive impairment derive most direct benefit from attendance' (1996b, p.816).

Responding to a need for small-scale provision geared to the needs of in-dividual users with dementia, home-based day care is an innovation available in some areas. For example, in central Scotland the Joint Dementia Initiative, a partnership of social work, health care and voluntary agencies, developed the 'Home from Home' day care project. Trained and approved local carers, working in pairs, open their homes to groups of three to six older people once or twice a week, providing company and activities in a domestic envi-ronment, with an emphasis on person-centred care (Mitchell 1999, pp.78–79). Unlike in traditional day care, 'in these settings, people with dementia seem to feel more in control and are more likely to believe that they can make things happen' (p.80). The project has been positively evaluated and replicated in other countries.

Research in the UK and other European countries shows that day services for older people cater for the majority population and do not meet the cultural and other needs of people from minority ethnic groups, which tend to provide their own community day services (Tester 1996, p.144). Perkins and Allen found that innovative services had been developed, for example 'specialist day care facilities for the African Caribbean community and day care provision in partnership with a housing association for Asian elders in sheltered accommodation' (1997, p.111). Comparative analysis of findings from studies of needs and provision of services for older people from the majority and minority ethnic populations in Glasgow and Edinburgh shows that only 9 per cent of the majority population used day centres and lunch clubs, compared with 58 per cent of the South Asian sample (Bowes and Macdonald 2000, p.4). The 'multi-cultural' day centres which provided support for South Asian users were purchased by social work departments from voluntary sector community based groups; these providers considered mainstream services inappropriate for minority ethnic groups (Bowes and Dar 2000, pp.44–48). Research for the Royal Commission (Cm 4192-I 1999, p.92) found, however, that older people from minority ethnic groups wanted 'more responsive and culturally sensitive mainstream services' rather than special services.

The aims of day services, whether in day centres, day hospitals or other settings, include providing respite for carers. The benefits to carers, identified in research in the United States, were reduction in care-related stressors, depression and anger (Zarit, Gaugler and Jarrott1999, p.167). Day services are particularly beneficial for co-resident carers of very frail older people, including those with dementia, who require high levels of care and whose carers experience stress. Carers of people with dementia were found more likely to express unmet need for day services than other carers (Philp *et al.* 1995). Research shows that a key benefit for carers is the opportunity for a regular break in which to carry out everyday activities (Curran 1996a, p.113; Levin *et al.* 1994, p.73). Warrington and Eagles (1996, p.255) found little difference between day hospitals and day centres in relieving the stress experienced by co-resident carers of people with cognitive impairment. In some cases day services were introduced too late, when the carer had already been caring for some time and could have benefited from the service earlier (Curran 1996a, p.117; Levin *et al.* 1994, p.75).

According to carers' views, the majority of the people they cared for enjoyed their time at day care (Farrow 1992, p.320). However, the interests of users and carers are sometimes in conflict. In cases where carers did not take up day services which could have benefited them or discontinued the services, the older person had refused to take up day care or had disliked it (Farrow 1992, pp.321, 323; Levin *et al.* 1994, p.80).

The groups discussed above are not mutually exclusive and there are wider issues of balancing the interests of different groups and giving careful consideration, for example, to the needs of black and ethnic minority carers, or minority ethnic older people with dementia.

Day services and social inclusion

Users of day services and their carers may be socially excluded in that they are 'shut out, fully or partially, from any of the social, economic, political and cultural systems which determine the social integration of a person in society' and may be unable to enjoy 'the civil, political and social rights of citizenship' (Walker 1997, p.8). The marginalised groups most likely to be socially excluded are very frail older people and their co-resident carers, especially people with dementia or those from minority ethnic groups, with poor access to financial or social resources. To promote their social inclusion would mean enabling them to participate in society and enjoy citizenship rights. This section considers the extent to which the aim of social inclusion is or could be met by day services.

Day services operate within the context of community care services for older people. The aims of community care are expressed in policy literature in terms of reducing marginalisation, exclusion and loss of autonomy by promoting the social integration or inclusion, independence, participation and empowerment of service users. Barnes (1997, p.155) proposes that: 'the objective of community care should be to enable those previously excluded from community to participate within it'. This goal seems unlikely to be met through the more restricted aims of day services in relation to providing opportunities for social contacts, activities and company. These aims do not necessarily mean that day services provide the 'opportunity to participate in some form of socially meaningful activity' which Doyal and Gough (1991, pp.184–185) consider essential for human autonomy.

There are various aspects to the widely advocated but rather vague concept of empowerment. The key aims of this principle in relation to community care for older people are encapsulated by Hughes as:

> changing the relative power between the older person, professionals, family if necessary and other significant people to ensure that the older person continues to have, or acquires, control over his or her own life and all that goes with power and control – freedom, autonomy, dignity and feelings of personal self-worth. (1995, p.47)

Where day services are concerned, the extent to which older people could have such power and control is likely to be limited, for example, to access to social contacts and information or activities which enhance their self-worth. The contribution of the settings and activities of day services to promoting goals such as social inclusion and empowerment is examined below.

For day services to be integrated within the community, they need to be in or near to buildings used by the general public and to promote links with the everyday life of the mainstream community, for example by being on a shared site, and by presenting an image of accessibility (Bacon and Lambkin 1997, pp.59–62). Such integration could be achieved more easily in day services held in local community centres or resource centres than those offered in hospitals or nursing homes. Many day services, however, are set in premises that are separate from the daily life of the society in which users and carers live, and as such are unlikely to promote social inclusion and, further, could be seen as a form of social exclusion. A notable exception would be day care in carers' homes (Mitchell 1999).

Turning to the users of day services, for most people in need of this type of support, access to services depends on a referral being made, then on an assessment by social or health care authorities. Although there may be consultation with older people and carers, the balance of power in these processes lies with the professionals conducting the assessment. If day services are offered as part of a care package, there may be little choice for the user as to which day service is attended and the hours and days offered. There are further considerations concerning the availability and operation of transport services that reduce users' and carers' power over their own daily routine. Some frail older people with severe physical or mental disabilities, those who most need social inclusion, may be excluded from day services that do not have the facilities to care for them (Tester 1989, p.57). On the other hand, older people may exercise a negative choice and exclude themselves by refusing day services or exiting from them.

A further consideration is the extent to which groups are integrated or segregated in the day care units, and the implications of this for social inclusion. First, there is the question of whether people with dementia receive day services in specialised settings or services that are integrated with other users. Curran (1996a) found that in generic day centres people with dementia were often not accepted or were marginalised, and that insufficient attention was given to their needs. There were, however, examples of generic day centres which also catered specifically for people with dementia by allocating places for them and addressing their needs, as well as dementia-specific day centres with staff trained in dementia care (Curran 1996a, pp.114–115). Culbert stressed that:

> The main consideration is not whether mixed centres are more economically viable or specialist centres more expert, but how the needs of confused elderly people with behavioural difficulties can be provided with day care in a manner which promotes their dignity and acknowledges their worth. (1993, p.11)

Second, where older people from minority ethnic groups are concerned, Bowes and Dar (2000, pp.54–55) noted the tendency for provision of separate services which had been promoted by the communities themselves and welcomed by the statutory sector. These specialist day services were culturally appropriate and responded flexibly to needs; however, there were problems arising from short-term funding and unqualified staff, as well as the 'tendency for mainstream services not to change, and therefore to remain inaccessible'. Bowes and Dar stress that: 'Mainstream services need to be able to respond to the needs of a diverse client group' (p.58). As with services for people with dementia, the key issue is that quality services are provided, by trained staff, to meet the specific needs of the older individuals from minority ethnic groups. However, if social inclusion is a key aim, consideration must be given to how minority ethnic older people can best be integrated with other day care users, whether in mainstream or in separate services.

Another concern is whether the increasing provision of day services in residential and nursing homes is integrated or segregated. Pickard (1999, p.74) comments that if the older person attending for day care merely joins the other residents in the lounge, the service is of poor quality. Where day centre care is provided separately, as in multi-purpose residential homes, there is evidence of users' reluctance to identify with residents; residents' reluctance to use the day centre; and of tensions between residents and day centre users (Wright 1995, pp.53, 102–103). The goal of social inclusion could thus be difficult to achieve for either group by providing separate day centres within residential homes.

Thus the complex issues concerning integrated or separate provision for people with dementia, those from minority ethnic groups, or those in residential or nursing homes are difficult to resolve. It seems that the main consideration is the quality of individual care rather than the goal of social inclusion. These would be fruitful areas for further research.

For people who do attend day services, irrespective of the type of setting, crucial issues include the extent to which the activities during the day can promote social inclusion and/or empowerment, the extent to which they have choices in and power over their activities during the day, and the extent to which the activities are provided on the basis of person-centred care and individualised care plans. Traditional models of day services for older people tended to make the assumption that providing social contacts, a meal in company and social activities would relieve 'isolation and loneliness', without recognising that these services would not necessarily produce close intimate relationships and meaningful activities, roles and identities (Tester 1989, p.168). Models based on principles of inclusion and empowerment would take more account of the diversity and complexity of individuals' lives, needs and choices. The examples below illustrate the implementation of such models.

The 'Home from Home' model (Mitchell 1999, pp.79–80) could be seen as inclusive because day care was set in a domestic environment rather than a formal service setting. Users took part in normal daily tasks such as helping to make lunch and were included as part of a family group, having contact with the carer's children and pets. In small homogeneous groups they were able to choose their activities for the day and take part in projects such as creating a garden or sharing past experiences that helped to maintain or re-construct their identities. The model was empowering in that people with dementia felt more in control (Mitchell 1999, p.80). Stevenson and Parsloe (1993, pp.39–40) cite examples of practice in two day centre settings for older people where managers had introduced new systems that gave staff the opportunity to empower users and to work creatively and tailor activities to individual users' choices and abilities.

Evidence suggests, however, that inclusive models of day services for older people are in the minority and that day care is 'still being provided in very traditional ways' (Moriarty and Webb 2000, p.69). Comparisons with community care and day services for younger groups show that they are more likely to be based on principles of inclusion than services for older people (Harding 1999, p.43; Henwood and Wistow 1999, p.9). Further, it has been suggested that day services have become less inclusive and 'more narrowly focused on "care" than inclusiveness' (Harding 1999, p.46). This could be the case particularly for the most socially excluded groups such as older people with dementia who may be subject to 'enforced inclusion' in a specialised service which is exclusive and stigmatising (Cheetham and Fuller 1998, p.125).

On the other hand, the services may promote the social inclusion of older volunteers in the day units and, especially, of the older carers of day service users, at least in providing them an opportunity to carry out normal everyday activities. For carers of working age, however, day services are rarely flexible enough to allow full-time paid employment. Stevenson and Parsloe suggest that in the case of older users day centres put carers' interests first, whereas they did not do so for carers of adults with disabilities (1993, p.20). Barnes suggests that: 'In the language of social exclusion rather than citizenship, carers are to be included while those who are the recipients of their care are excluded' (1997, p.126). The balance of interests between users of day services and their carers is an area for further research.

Conclusion

This review shows that day services continue to be almost invisible in policy documents on caring for older people and that this is an under-researched area in social policy. The rhetoric of community care states aims of promoting independence, social integration, participation and empowerment, which are implicit in the provision of day services as part of community care. Yet there is little clear and explicit consideration of how these principles and values are to be put into practice by day services, the diverse aims of which include social care and company, rehabilitation and treatment, assessment and monitoring, and support for carers.

Since the implementation of the community care reforms of the early 1990s there has been some, but not much, increase in the provision of day services for older people, particularly for those with mental health problems. Day services are valued by those who use them and particularly by carers who would welcome more hours and greater flexibility of services. The introduction of new assessment and purchasing systems has led to a greater diversity of services and increased specialisation of services to meet the assessed needs of individuals. Areas of growth include day hospitals in psychiatry of old age, specialised day services for people with dementia, day care provided in community resource centres and residential and nursing homes, and innovative forms of day services such as day care in carers' own homes. Research evidence, however, shows overlaps between types of service and wide variation between geographical areas. Long-standing problems in relation to assessment and care management and the formal monitoring and evaluation of services persist and are to be addressed by new systems for assessment and new quality assurance systems.

Turning to the specific issue of social inclusion, examples of good practice show that it is possible to provide an inclusive service and to empower users in day services, even though this may not be widespread practice. A broader concept of inclusion, however, would involve participation in mainstream society. There are four levels at which the possible roles of day services in this respect could be explored. First, day services sited in community resource centres and other buildings used by the community could increase participation and would be welcomed by older people's groups who find traditional day centres unsatisfactory (Harding 1999, p.46). Second, day service users could be more involved in purposeful activities such as providing support for children; as suggested by Carter (1981, p.149): 'if the primary task in day services were to work on a project, rather than to offer company, day care might appeal to a wider group'. Third, a wider range of leisure, cultural and educational opportunities could be developed to meet the interests of older people to whom traditional day care does not appeal, including social contacts in their own home and social activities of their choice outside the home, with transport services if needed. Fourth, older people could enjoy fuller participation and citizenship through new roles in society and through political involvement to increase their own social inclusion. These stronger forms of participation, however, would require changes to broader societal systems than those offering community care (Barnes 1997, p.164; Walker 1999, pp.395–396). Programmes such as 'Better Government for Older People' have begun to address these issues.

This review of policy and research on day services suggests the following key areas for future research:

- The views of older people themselves, including users and non-users of day services.

- The implementation of the new assessment, care management, commissioning procedures and quality assurance systems to be introduced, specifically in relation to day services.

- A research review of day services 'to assess all available evidence…and synthesise key findings' as suggested in the *Quality Strategy* (Department of Health 2000a, p.14 para. 38).

- Issues concerning integrated or separate provision for older people with dementia and/or learning disabilities, those from minority ethnic groups, and in care homes.

- Effective ways of meeting the cultural needs of older people from minority ethnic groups within mainstream care services.

- The balance of interests of users and carers in relation to social inclusion and other aims of day services.

- The wider implementation of small localised innovative models.

For the future direction of policy, all the evidence points to a broader strategy for meeting the diverse needs of older people that current policy attempts to meet through the provision of day services, which remain the major form of community care offered to people with needs for company and social activity. This will need careful consideration before the introduction of new integrated health and social care systems and personal health and social care plans. These new systems could provide appropriate and flexible individualised care, including opportunities for following wider interests and developing greater participation in the wider society. The promotion of social inclusion of older people would not be advanced if the new systems merely perpetuated existing models of day services which appeal to a minority of older people and are mainly focused on care provision and support for carers rather than combating social exclusion.

References

Alber, J. (1993) 'Health and social services.' In A. Walker, J. Alber and A-M. Guillemard, *Older People in Europe: Social and Economic Policies.* Brussels: Commission of the European Communities.

Audit Commission (1997) *The Coming of Age: Improving Care Services for Older People.* London: Audit Commission.

Audit Commission (2000) *Charging with Care: How Councils Charge for Home Care.* London: Audit Commission.

Bacon, V. and Lambkin, C. (1997) 'The relationship between the delivery of day care services for older people and the design of day unit premises.' *Ageing and Society 17,* 41–64.

Barnes, M. (1997) *Care, Communities and Citizens.* Harlow: Longman.

Barry, M. (1998) 'Social exclusion and social work: An introduction.' In M. Barry and C. Hallett (eds) *Social Exclusion and Social Work: Issues of Theory, Policy and Practice.* Lyme Regis: Russell House Publishing.

Bowes, A. and Dar, N. (2000) *Family Support and Community Care: A Study of South Asian Older People.* Edinburgh: Scottish Executive Central Research Unit.

Bowes, A. and MacDonald, C. (2000) *Support for Majority and Minority Ethnic Groups at Home – Older People's Perspectives.* Edinburgh: Scottish Executive Central Research Unit.

Brearley, P. and Mandelstam, M. (1992) *A Review of Literature 1986–1991 on Day Care Services for Adults.* London: HMSO.

Brocklehurst, J. and Tucker, J. (1980) *Progress in Geriatric Day Care.* London: King Edward's Hospital Fund for London.

Brown, D. (1999) *Care in the Country: Inspection of Community Care in Rural Communities.* London: DoH/SSI.

Bytheway, B. (1995) *Ageism.* Buckingham: Open University Press.

Carter, J. (1981) *Day Services for Adults: Somewhere to Go.* London: George Allen and Unwin.

Challis, D. (1999) 'Assessment and care management: Developments since the community care reforms.' In *Royal Commission on Long Term Care, With Respect to Old Age, Research Volume 3.* London: The Stationery Office.

Cheetham, J. and Fuller, R. (1998) 'Social exclusion and social work: Policy, practice and research.' In M. Barry and C. Hallett (eds) *Social Exclusion and Social Work: Issues of Theory, Policy and Practice.* Lyme Regis: Russell House Publishing.

Cm 849 (1989) *Caring for People: Community Care in the Next Decade and Beyond.* Presented to Parliament by the secretaries of state for health, social security, Wales and Scotland by command of Her Majesty November 1989. London: HMSO.

Cm 4169 (1998) *Modernising Social Services: Promoting Independence, Improving Protection, Raising Standards.* London: The Stationery Office.

Cm 4192-I (1999) *Royal Commission on Long Term Care with Respect to Old Age: Long Term Care – Rights and Responsibilities.* London: The Stationery Office.

Cm 4288 (1999) *Aiming for Excellence: Modernising Social Work Services in Scotland.* Edinburgh: The Stationery Office.

Cm 4818-I (2000) *The NHS Plan: A Plan for Investment, a Plan for Reform.* London: The Stationery Office.

Cm 4818-II (2000) *The NHS Plan: The Government's Response to the Royal Commission on Long Term Care.* London: The Stationery Office.

Collier, E.H. and Baldwin, R.C. (1999) 'The day hospital debate – a contribution.' *International Journal of Geriatric Psychiatry 14,* 587–591.

Culbert, E. (1993) *Inspection of Day Care Services for Dementia Sufferers and their Carers in Northern Ireland: A Literature Review.* Belfast: SSI Department of Health and Social Services.

Curran, J. (1996a) 'The evolution of daycare services for people with dementia.' In R. Bland (ed) *Developing Services for Older People and their Families.* London: Jessica Kingsley Publishers.

Curran, J. (1996b) 'The impact of day care on people with dementia.' *International Journal of Geriatric Psychiatry 11,* 813–817.

Department of Health (1998) *Partnership in Action: New Opportunities for Joint Working between Health and Social Services.* London: Department of Health.

Department of Health (1999a) *Better Care, Higher Standards: A Charter for Long Term Care*. London: Department of Health.

Department of Health (1999b) *Health and Personal Social Services Statistics*. London: Department of Health.

Department of Health (2000a) *A Quality Strategy for Social Care*. London: Department of Health.

Department of Health (2000b) *NHS Day Care Facilities, England*. London: Department of Health.

Department of Health (2001) *National Service Framework for Older People*. London: Department of Health.

Department of Health and Social Services Inspectorate (1992) *Caring for Quality in Day Services*. London: HMSO.

Doyal, L. and Gough, I. (1991) *A Theory of Human Need*. Basingstoke: Macmillan.

Farrow, G. (1992) 'The role of day centres in caring for people in the final year of their lives.' *Ageing and Society 12*, 313–327.

Fasey, C. (1994) 'The day hospital in old age psychiatry: The case against.' *International Journal of Geriatric Psychiatry 9*, 519–523.

Harding, T. (1999) 'Enabling older people to live in their own homes.' In *Royal Commission on Long Term Care, With Respect to Old Age, Research Volume 3*. London: The Stationery Office.

Henwood, M. and Wistow, G. (1999) 'Clarifying responsibilities and improving accountability.' In *Royal Commission on Long Term Care, With Respect to Old Age, Research Volume 3*. London: The Stationery Office.

Horobin, G. (ed) (1987) *Why Day Care?* Research Highlights in Social Work 14. London: Jessica Kingsley Publishers.

Hughes, B. (1995) *Older People and Community Care: Critical Theory and Practice*. Buckingham: Open University Press.

ISD Scotland (1999) *Scottish Health Statistics 1998*. Edinburgh: Information and Statistics Division, National Health Services in Scotland.

Levin, E., Moriarty, J. and Gorbach, P. (1994) *Better for the Break*. London: HMSO.

Mitchell, R. (1999) 'Home from home: A model of day care for people with dementia.' *Generations, Quarterly Journal of the American Society on Aging XXIII*, 3, 78–81.

Moriarty, J. and Webb, S. (2000) *Part of their Lives: Community Care for Older People with Dementia*. Bristol: The Policy Press.

National Audit Office (1994) *National Health Service Day Hospitals for Elderly People in England*. London: HMSO.

National Consumer Council (1995) *Charging Consumers for Social Services: Local Authority Policy and Practice*. London: National Consumer Council.

Nies, H., Tester, S. and Nuijens, J.M. (1991) 'Day care in the United Kingdom and the Netherlands: A comparative study.' *Ageing and Society 11*, 245–273.

Perkins, E. and Allen, I. (1997) *Creating Partnerships in Social Care: An Evaluation of the Caring for People who Live at Home Initiative*. London: Policy Studies Institute.

Phillipson, C. (1998) *Reconstructing Old Age: New Agendas in Social Theory and Practice*. London: Sage.

Philp, I., McKee, K., Meldrum, P., Ballinger, B., Gilhooly, M., Gordon, D., Mutch, W and Whittick, J. (1995) 'Community care for demented and non-demented elderly people: A comparison study of financial burden, service use, and unmet needs in family supporters.' *British Medical Journal 310*, 11503–11506.

Pickard, L. (1999) 'Policy options for informal carers of elderly people.' In *Royal Commission on Long Term Care, With Respect to Old Age, Research Volume 3*. London: The Stationery Office.

Scottish Executive (2000) *Draft National Care Standards: First Tranche: A Consultation Paper*. Edinburgh: Scottish Executive.

Scottish Office (1998a) *Modernising Community Care: An Action Plan*. Edinburgh: The Scottish Office.

Scottish Office (1998b) *Statistical Bulletin: Community Care Scotland 1997*. Edinburgh: The Scottish Office.

Scottish Office (1999) *Non-residential Community Care, Scotland 1998: Statistical Information Note*. Edinburgh: The Scottish Office.

Stevenson, O. and Parsloe, P. (1993) *Community Care and Empowerment*. York: Joseph Rowntree Foundation.

Tester, S. (1989) *Caring by Day: A Study of Day Care Services for Older People*. London: Centre for Policy on Ageing.

Tester, S. (1996) *Community Care for Older People: A Comparative Perspective*. Basingstoke: Macmillan.

Tester, S. (1999) *The Quality Challenge: Caring for People with Dementia in Residential Institutions in Europe, a Transnational Study*. Edinburgh: Alzheimer Scotland – Action on Dementia (with Alzheimer Stichting Nederland, NZi Institute for Health Care Management, Federazione Alzheimer Italia and Fundacion Alzheimer España).

Tibbitt, J. and Tombs, J. (1981) *Day Services for the Elderly and Elderly with Mental Disability in Scotland*. Edinburgh: Central Research Unit, The Scottish Office.

Tinker, A., Wright, F., McCreadie, C., Askham, J., Hancock, R. and Holmans, A. (1999) 'Alternative models of care for older people: The main report.' In *Royal Commission on Long Term Care, With Respect to Old Age, Research Volume 2*. London: The Stationery Office.

Walker, A. (1997) 'Introduction: The strategy of inequality.' In A. Walker and C. Walker (eds) *Britain Divided: The Growth of Social Exclusion in the 1980s and 1990s*. London: Child Poverty Action Group.

Walker, A. (1999) 'Ageing in Europe: Challenges and consequences.' *Zeitschrift für Gerontologie und Geriatrie 32*, 6, 390–397.

Warburton, R. and McCracken, J. (1999) 'An evidence-based perspective from the Department of Health on the impact of the 1993 reforms on the care of frail elderly people.' In *Royal Commission on Long Term Care, With Respect to Old Age, Research Volume 3*. London: The Stationery Office.

Warrington, J. and Eagles, J. (1995) 'Day care for the elderly mentally ill: Diurnal confusion.' *Health Bulletin 53*, 2, 99–104.

Warrington, J. and Eagles, J. (1996) 'A comparison of cognitively impaired attenders and their coresident carers at day hospitals and day centres in Aberdeen.' *International Journal of Geriatric Psychiatry 11*, 3, 251–256.

Wimo, A., Mattsson, B., Adolfsson, R., Eriksson, T. and Nelvig, A. (1993) 'Dementia day care and its effects on symptoms and institutionalization: A controlled Swedish study.' *Scandinavian Journal of Primary Health Care 11*, 117–123.

Wright, F. (1995) *Opening Doors: A Case Study of Multi-purpose Residential Homes*. London: HMSO.

Zarit, S.H., Gaugler, J.E. and Jarrott, S.E. (1999) 'Useful services for families: Research findings and directions.' *International Journal of Geriatric Psychiatry 14*, 165–177.

CHAPTER 3

Inclusive Daytime Opportunities for People with Learning Disabilities

Kirsten Stalker

Introduction

In Britain, support for people with learning disabilities has changed dramatically since the early 1980s. Most of those who were confined to long-stay hospitals have now moved on; some institutions have closed and others have plans to do so. The majority of people are living in the community, many with their families, some in various forms of group home, a few alone or with a friend or partner. There is evidence that public attitudes towards people with learning disabilities are improving: 80 per cent of those questioned in a recent poll expressed the view that learning disabled children should attend ordinary schools, while 87 per cent thought people with learning disabilities could make good employees (System 3, 1999). A recent inspection of services to people with learning disabilities by the Social Services Inspectorate (1998) in England reported that day services were becoming more diverse and small-scale employment schemes increasingly available. Nevertheless:

> Services still need to improve and increase their range to meet the needs of users and the aspirations of users, carers and staff for better access to the mainstream of ordinary life. (Social Services Inspectorate 1998, 1.31)

Similarly, research conducted as part of a major Scottish Executive review of services to people with learning disabilities concluded that:

> Most people are still confined to segregated settings for many of their domestic, occupational and leisure activities. Scotland has a long way to go before people with learning disabilities are truly part of the mainstream. (Stalker *et al.* 1999, p.62)

This chapter begins with a brief history of policies relating to services for people with learning disabilities and then outlines the current situation regarding daytime supports. It examines the range and type of services and opportunities available. The associated benefits and limitations, particularly in relation to promoting social inclusion, are discussed.

Historical perspective

In order to understand why people with learning disabilities spend so much of their time with each other and apart from non-disabled people, giving rise to the idea that they are intrinsically 'different', it is necessary to look back at the way people have been treated historically. The Victorian institutions, which came to be regarded as dehumanising, were originally set up with philanthropic, if paternalistic, ideals in mind. Pioneering educationalists such as Seguin argued for the essential humanity of people with learning disabilities and sought to educate and 'improve' them (see Ayers 1971, p.44). The aim of these early institutions was to rescue people from poverty and homelessness, train them to have some useful occupation and enable them to return to the community able to make a living.

In the early part of the twentieth century, however, with the rise of the eugenics movement, perceptions of people with learning disabilities began to change. They came to be seen as 'moral degenerates' posing a threat to society (Ryan and Thomas 1987). People were increasingly consigned to institutions where, reflecting fears that intellectual impairment was genetically inherited, men were separated from women. This period also saw the development of intelligence testing. Although now largely discredited, IQ tests gave rise to the idea that individuals had fixed levels of intelligence that could not be improved. Thus there was little point in trying to educate those with learning disabilities, and the importance previously accorded to education diminished.

With the introduction of the National Health Service in 1946, the 'colonies' in which many people lived became 'hospitals' overnight. Learning disability was now a medical condition requiring treatment. Conditions in these huge and often isolated institutions deteriorated greatly, with a series of scandals breaking out in England and Wales during the 1960s and 1970s. This fuelled the impetus for community care and heralded the demise of the long-stay hospitals. It is important to remember that most people with learning disabilities have always lived in the community, very often with their families. It was not until the 1960s, however, that specific provision was made for them to do something during the day. The 1959 Mental Health Act (1960 in Scotland) gave local authorities powers to provide day care services within the community. Adult training centres (ATCs) with an industrial training focus were established in most local authorities by the 1970s, serving upwards of 100 people (Williams 1995).

In 1971, the Government published a White Paper *Better Services for the Mentally Handicapped* (Department of Health and Welsh Office 1971), followed by its Scottish counterpart (Scottish Home and Health Department 1972). These documents set targets for the development of services within the community. The English and Welsh paper, for example, recommended expansion of day care places from the 26,400 available in 1970 to 75,000 over the next twenty years, mostly to accommodate those who would be leaving hospital. That target was never achieved, however, partly due to the considerable difficulties involved in releasing money tied up in hospitals, but also because of changing ideas about the role and rights of people with learning disabilities in society.

Theoretical developments

Developments had been taking place beyond Britain that were to have a far-reaching impact on service provision for people with learning disabilities. The ethos of normalisation, originating in Scandinavia (Banks-Mikkelşon 1980; Nirje 1969), advocated that services be developed to enable people with learning disabilities to have similar lifestyles to everyone else. In North America, Wolfensberger (1972) developed the theoretical basis of normalisation, drawing on deviancy theory to explain the stigma attached to people who are seen as different in some negative way. He proposed that the term 'normalisation' be replaced with 'social role valorisation' (Wolfensberger 1983) to stress that people should occupy socially valued roles within their communities. Wolfensberger's ideas are complex and not without their critics (for example, Brown and Smith 1994). However, they have been enormously influential in changing perceptions of people with learning disabilities and the kind of opportunities which should be available to them.

In the UK, work carried out by leading academics and policy makers in the field focused on the concept of 'an ordinary life' (King's Fund Centre 1980; King's Fund Centre 1984). While these initiatives had a considerable impact on residential services, paving the way for many people with learning disabilities to live in ordinary houses, they have had less effect on daytime provision (Allen 1994). However, the thinking of John O'Brien in the USA has had a huge impact on the development of community-based services internationally. O'Brien (1987) developed the notion of the Five Accomplishments, or targets at which community services should aim, if they are to enact the principles of normalisation. These are:

- *Community presence* – meaning that people with learning disabilities should make use of ordinary, mainstream facilities.

- *Choice* – whereby people should have support in making their own choices both at a day-to-day level and about major life events.

- *Competence* – creating opportunities for people to reach their full potential by developing a range of skills.

- *Respect* – refers to a person's right to occupy a valued role within a network of reciprocal roles.

- *Community participation* – the importance of being part of a growing network of friends.

Allied to the work of Wolfensberger and O'Brien, and to broader civil rights movements, came the growth of the self-advocacy movement, whereby people with learning disabilities were increasingly speaking up for themselves. While it would be wrong to imply that people with learning disabilities are an homogeneous group, a striking consistency emerges across a number of studies exploring people's aspirations. Many people want to have paid work, to have friends, to live in an ordinary house perhaps with family or friends, to marry or have a partner and, in some cases, to have children (Flynn and Hirst 1992; Leighton Project 1998; Simons 1995). However, the extent to which people can realise these ambitions within the care, welfare and protection model associated with the personal social services is open to question. Despite some pockets of progressive practice, current policies and much provision continue to throw up barriers to the social inclusion of people with learning disabilities. The social model of disability (Oliver 1990) which locates disability in material, cultural and attitudinal barriers, has been developed mainly in relation to people with physical or sensory impairment: its relevance to those with learning disabilities should be further explored.

Day centre provision

During the 1970s, concerns about exploitation led to the value of ATCs being questioned (Allen 1994). People were paid very little for repetitive, subcontracted work: packing boxes or putting the lids on bottles of washing-up liquid were fairly typical pastimes. A call for day centres to broaden their activities, with particular emphasis on developing people's educational, social and daily living skills, was made by the National Development Group (1977), a body set up by the Government to advise on policy issues in the field of learning disability. Many ATCs were renamed 'social education centres' with four distinct functions – admission and assessment, development and activities, special care, and advanced work (Williams 1995). Most local authorities had various 'tiers' of centre, each one designed to offer more demanding work. Individuals were supposed to progress through these levels until they were able to look for open employment outside. This 'readiness model' proved largely unsuccessful however, with very few people moving 'upwards' or 'outwards'. People with high support needs (sometimes called profound learning disabilities) were generally consigned to 'special' centres and were not expected to progress (Sanderson 1995).

A study by Seed *et al.* (1984) found that while most centres had a general educational aim to develop people's potential, there were widely differing interpretations of that policy. He identified seven models of day care centre for people with learning disabilities in Scotland:

- Work
- Social care
- Further education
- Assessment and throughput
- Recreational
- Shared living
- Resource centre.

Seed adds that these models were not neatly divided between centres but that many services showed aspects of several types. This may have been a symptom of what Williams (1995) calls 'great confusion' about the aims of day services for people with learning disabilities in the 1980s, part of a wider policy vacuum in this field. The main emphasis was on moving people out of hospitals: the complexity of problems in that arena distracted much attention from day services.

By 1998, the Social Services Inspectorate was able to report that local authorities in England and Wales had identified 'sound principles' for their services to people with learning disabilities, namely promoting independence, respect and community presence. These are clearly derived from O'Brien's work and reflect the policies set out in the NHS and Community Care Act 1990. However, some problems remained: these principles were not always documented in ways which could best help front-line providers (Social Services Inspectorate 1998, 1.10). The SSI found that most day centres were now 'diversifying' to offer people a range of activities. Resource and recreational models were common, whereby the centre is used as a base from which to use community facilities and also to encourage other members of the local community to use the building, for example, by running a café or hosting community education classes. People attending such centres are likely to be called 'members' rather than 'trainees'. Activities may include attendance at further education colleges for anything from a half day to several days a week; forays into 'the community' to make use of mainstream facilities, such as the local swimming pool or library (although this is very often on a group basis (Stalker *et al.* 1999)); and some kind of work. The latter may take various forms, including voluntary work, work experience, or a few hours' paid employment per week.

With increasing realisation of the constraints imposed by buildings-based services, some authorities and voluntary organisations have dispensed with the bricks and mortar. 'Changeover' is a project run by SHS (Scottish Human Services) designed to support the process of user-led change in day centres. It has two linked elements: first, it offers distance learning courses for staff, users and their families, working together in particular centres; second, it provides a forum of local and national networks (Riddell *et al.* 1997). In 1994, the King's Fund and the National Development Team launched a similar project entitled 'Changing Days', designed to help people access leisure and employment opportunities in their local communities and to support local authorities in finding ways to work 'without walls' (Jackson 1998). 'Alternative' day services have been a feature of the All Wales Strategy for people with learning disabilities, including community-focused schemes and employment-development schemes (Felce *et al.* 1998). The former, averaging 12 places each, cater either for a small geographical area or for a specific 'group', such as older people. Although they have a local base, in some cases this is for administrative purposes only, local community facilities being used for other activities. I will say more about work and work-related opportunities shortly.

Perceived benefits and drawbacks of day centres

A number of studies have suggested that the main beneficiaries of day centres are family carers and professionals (Gattercole 1987; Seed 1996). The former often appreciate day centres because they provide respite care by another name. In addition, some parents value the perceived security and re-liability of a buildings-based service. Families may have concerns about al-ternative daytime activities, either because they think their relative would not be able to cope (for example, with paid work) or that another service would be less reliable.

From agencies' point of view, day centres are relatively predictable and easy to run (Simons 1998). For example, if staff shortages arise, two activity groups can be merged and coordinated by one member of staff. This is more difficult in the context of individualised day services.

From a user's perspective, however, day centres may have little to offer. People with learning disabilities consistently report that, while many enjoy the social aspects of day centres, the activities on offer are boring (see, for example, Beyer and Kilsby 1995; Flynn and Hirst 1992). This coincides with concerns identified in a number of studies about a lack of engagement and purposeful activity in day centres (Felce *et al.* 1998; Social Services Inspector-ate 1998). Recent research in Scotland found that users saw day centres as widely failing to recognise and meet their needs (Stalker *et al.* 1999). Some people felt they were denied choice about how they spent their day and in choosing their key worker, and that complaints procedures were ineffective. In addition, there were several reports of 'bossy' staff who shouted at people. While most members enjoyed the range of work or quasi-work opportunities available through day centres, people with learning disabilities have repeat-edly stated their preference to have a real job (Flynn and Hirst 1992; Leighton Project 1998). Flynn and Hirst found that those whose daily routine was closest to that enjoyed by non-disabled young people, involving full-time education, job training or employment, expressed the most satisfac-tion.

Research has also found that day centres are poor at meeting the needs of particular interest groups. Older people may find day centres too noisy and feel the activities on offer are of little interest (Felce *et al.* 1998). Those with labels of challenging behaviour are frequently refused day centre places (Allen 1994). People with high support needs have recently been supported in segregated units in day centres, with a focus on developing sensory awareness. Critics have suggested that any benefits arising from this work are related to one-to-one interactions with staff rather than the stimulation programme itself (Sanderson 1995). The Social Services Inspectorate (1998) found that individuals with high support needs are increasingly being integrated into main activity groups within day centres. However, some agencies have developed services that 'almost exclusively' enable people with multiple impairments to use community facilities on an individual basis (Sanderson 1995).

Supported employment

Supported employment was developed in the USA during the 1970s and 1980s to help people with a range of high support needs find work. It is based on the conviction that all citizens are entitled to full inclusion in society, including the workplace – participation in paid employment being central to Western industrial societies (Riddell and Wilson 1999). Corden (1997) describes supported employment as follows:

> The idea is that the disabled person who wants to work receives help from a supported employment agency to find a job that matches their skills, abilities and interests. The agency then provides a staff member, called a job trainer or job coach, to go to the workplace with the new employee, and help the employee learn what is required. This includes the responsibilities and tasks of the job itself, and other important aspects such as the journey to work and social integration in the workplace. The job trainer aims to gradually withdraw the intensive support as the employee learns the job, but keeps in touch with both the employee and the employer. (p.1)

This 'place, train and maintain' approach differs from the 'readiness model' used in tiered day centres. 'Systematic instruction' (Gold 1980), gradually 'fading' support over time, is favoured for two reasons. First, some people with learning disabilities have problems transferring skills learnt in one setting to another; second, by placing people in work from the outset, systematic instruction dispenses with 'hoop-jumping'. More recently, attention has been paid to the role of 'natural supports', be it work colleagues, family or friends, in supporting people with learning disabilities to get or keep a job. This again is seen as a more ordinary approach and more likely to result in the person being truly included in the workplace (Nisbet and Hagner 1998).

The first supported employment schemes in Britain were set up in the mid-1980s. Schemes may be run by local authority social work departments or voluntary organisations and funding comes from a variety of sources, such as local and central government and European funding. Beyer and Kilsby (1996) estimate that by 1996, 210 such agencies were supporting 5084 people in open employment. Ninety per cent of these people had learning disabilities (although this represents a very small proportion of the population with learning disabilities). Although supported employment was originally developed as a means of helping people with high support needs to secure work, it is those with lower support needs who form the bulk of employees (Beyer and Kilsby 1996). This is partly because it is easier to find jobs for them, and partly because they need less support over time, making it easier for agencies to meet their target numbers and thus maintain funding. However, a small number of services have emerged in the UK specifically aimed at people with high support needs (Jones 1994): these have had some success in securing jobs for individuals previously seen as 'unemployable'. At the same time, Bass and Drewett (1996) in a two-year study of six supported employment agencies in Merseyside, England, found that where people with 'severe and multiple' disabilities were employed, both the quality of jobs and the wages on offer were lower than those available to more able individuals.

Benefits and limitations of supported employment

There is now a significant literature from the USA about supported employment; less research has been carried out in the UK, although Beyer and colleagues have conducted several studies, as part of the evaluation of the All Wales Strategy for people with learning disabilities. Overall, the research provides strong evidence of the success of the model, both in the sense that people with learning disabilities have shown themselves to be reliable, hard-working and effective employees (Petty and Fussell 1997) and that they have gained from the experience. Bass and Drewett (1996) report that supported employees enjoy a better quality of life, increased leisure opportunities and more choice. The attitudes of other people are crucial and can act as facilitators or barriers to success (Barnes, Thornton and Campbell 1998). Bass and Drewett (1996), Eaton (1994), Petty and Fusell (1997), and Reid and Bray (1997) found that individuals were generally well integrated in the workplace. The last of these studies concluded that individuals who kept their jobs for some time had at least one important source of support, whether it was their line manager or their job coach. Beyer, Goodere and Kilsby (1996) report more mixed results: in a survey of all supported employment agencies in Britain, 40 per cent of managers rated the 'level of integration' experienced by supported employees as 'excellent', while 19 per cent reported that placements were segregated, affording little opportunity for supported workers to mix with non-disabled employees.

Despite the well-established evidence about its benefits, a number of policy constraints and structural barriers militate against people with learning disabilities taking up supported employment. Simons (1998) provides an excellent analysis of these, arguing that policy has been developed in one arena with little reference to that developed in another. Frequently the result, albeit unintended, is to perpetuate exclusion rather than promote inclusion.

The current system hinges on the concept of incapacity. An individual's capacity to work is determined either historically – that is, when the person has been seen to have a significant impairment, has attended learning disability services and so on – or through the All Work Test, which purports to measure functional capacity (Simons 1998). Those who are deemed fit to work can then claim Jobseekers' Allowance but are subject to the accompanying regulations without receiving any extra support. Like all unemployed people, they are required to prove they are actively seeking work, a process that demands some level of literacy and competence and which some people, despite having passed the All Work Test, may not possess (Simons 1998). In addition, current rates of unemployment mean that their chances of securing work are fairly slim, while the low-wage economy means that those who do find a job are likely to receive very modest earnings (Corden 1997).

While people on incapacity benefit are not required to seek work, they are in fact *allowed* to do so – but face a plethora of complex and perverse regulations. These will not be discussed in detail here: readers wishing to find out more should turn to Simons (1998). However, two main points will be highlighted. First, at the time of writing, people on incapacity benefit (most of those with learning disabilities) must restrict themselves to working no more than 16 hours per week or risk losing all their incapacity benefits. People working less than 16 hours must also beware they do not earn more than £15 per week, the 'earnings disregard' level, or they risk losing benefit on a pound for pound basis. The only exception applies to 'therapeutic earnings', for which the disregard is set at a higher rate, but the type of job which can be undertaken is restricted (Corden 1997) and this option seldom favours people with learning disabilities (Simons 1998).

The inter-related nature of various income-related benefits, and the financial aspects of some registered housing and support arrangements, mean that it is very difficult for most people with learning disabilities to achieve a higher net income through work than through not working (Corden 1997). This could be overcome by an individual moving directly from benefits to a well-paid full-time job, but for most people with learning disabilities, that is an unrealistic aim. At worst, the interaction of these different regulations means that a person taking on a new job which pays less than the cost of her housing and support arrangements, currently met through benefits, could be at risk of losing her home. Thus, to enable people to get into work, they may first need to come out of registered accommodation.

Other work-related opportunities

The supported employment schemes described above should be distinguished from the Department of Education and Employment's 'Supported Employment Programme'. Through this, individuals have traditionally been placed in a local authority, voluntary or Remploy workshop. Sheltered workshops, now in decline, have generally catered for people with physical and sensory impairment rather than learning disabilities. Lunt and Thornton (1994) argue that, at best, these enclaves offer people the chance to learn new skills and make the transition to open employment; at worst, they are a form of containment characterised by low wages, few benefits and under-employment.

Another part of the Supported Employment Programme is the 'Supported Placement Scheme' (SPS), which involves a 'sponsoring agency' carrying out an assessment of the extent to which a disabled individual can perform the tasks of a job: the sponsoring organisation pays the individual, and the employer pays the agency for the value of the work done (Simons 1998). SPS provides a financial incentive for employers to take on disabled people: it does not offer either side any additional support (Simons 1998). As Beyer and Kilsby (1996) note, there has been fierce debate about the value of the SPS, with critics arguing that the subsidy paid to employers would be better spent on on-the-job support for the individual.

There has been a succession of Government initiatives over recent years to create work, or quasi-work, opportunities for people facing long-term unemployment. These have not generally focused on disabled people. The New Deal, launched in 1998 for four years, was initially targeted at 18–24-year-olds who had been unemployed for over six months and was later extended to older people who had been out of work for two years. The New Deal offers four options – employment training, education, environmental work or training in the voluntary sector. As part of the New Deal, pilot schemes testing out different ways of helping disabled people move into, and maintain, work are being set up (Scottish Office 1999), such as the deployment of specially trained personal advisors.

Riddell *et al.* (1997) argue that most training and work opportunities for people with learning disabilities have a hidden barrier – the current ideological commitment to 'human capital', that is, the idea that investment in education and training must relate to an individual's likely future contribution to wealth creation. This ethos militates against the inclusion of those with learning disabilities in mainstream training programmes aimed at unemployed people. For example, these authors found that people with learning disabilities attending Skillseekers training schemes run by local enterprise companies were seen as 'marginal workers'.

A small but growing number of social firms, cooperatives and community businesses aim to promote inclusive job opportunities for people with learning disabilities, working alongside non-disabled people (Pannell, Simons and Macadam 1999). However, such initiatives are much better developed in other EU countries, notably Germany and Italy, than in Britain, where provision focuses more on users, or ex–users, of mental health services (Simons 1998).

Continuing education

Current policy initiatives in favour of lifelong learning aim to open up opportunities for wider participation in continuing education by under–represented groups. People with learning disabilities should be encouraged to participate in inclusive learning opportunities alongside the rest of the population (Sutcliffe and Jacobsen 1998). Baron *et al.* (1998) argue that many of the themes inherent in the notion of a 'learning society' – participation, human dignity and inclusion – are familiar terrain in current learning disability discourse, although the authors do not claim that these themes have been realised in practice.

The Further and Higher Education Act 1992, and its Scottish equivalent of the same year, required further education (FE) colleges to have regard to the needs of disabled students and made extra funding available for those with 'special needs' (learning disabilities). FE colleges offer a range of support, including learning support centres, individual tuition, support in class and access to specialist services (Harrison 1996). Many students attend FE colleges on a full–time basis for one or two years after leaving school, or as part of a Skillseekers course, or attend one or more classes as part of their weekly day centre programme (Riddell *et al.* 1997). While some are offered the training and education necessary for employment, for many the focus is on improving life skills with a view to leading a more independent life (Pattison 1998).

A study by Harrison (1996) explored the views of 46 students with learning disabilities and other impairments about FE. Forty were glad they had gone to college, felt they were making progress in their studies and enjoyed making new friends. However, some felt that the support needed to access their chosen courses was not always available, a finding echoed by Pearson (1996). FE provision for people with learning disabilities, who are usually expected to attend separate courses, has been criticised for its failure to be inclusive. Although social integration is intended to be a feature of most colleges, for example at mealtimes, in practice disabled and non-disabled students often remain socially isolated from one another. The 26 young people interviewed by Pearson (1996) thought more should be done to promote inclusion in FE colleges. They stressed that this would only be effective if people were brought together on equal terms and on the basis of shared interest.

Because of concerns about the quality of provision, the Tomlinson Committee was set up to examine FE in England and Wales. It recommended that colleges should develop *inclusive learning* in order to avoid 'a viewpoint which locates the difficulty or deficit with the student and focuses instead on the capacity of the educational institution to understand and respond to individual learner's requirement' (Further Education Funding Council 1996, p.4). However, concerns persist about the 'segregated' nature of FE provision (Riddell *et al.* 1997).

Local authorities are obliged to provide some form of education for those whose needs are not met by FE. Community education (CE), available to people over the age of 16, has a more open-ended definition of its target population (Riddell *et al.* 1997). Importance is placed on personal growth and community development rather than individual achievement. While FE provision for people with learning disabilities has increased over recent years, CE has seen some decline (Riddell *et al.* 1997).

Sutcliffe and Jacobsen (1998) found that certain sections of the population of people with learning disabilities were missing out on opportunities for continuing education. In a survey of all colleges and local education authorities in England and Wales, the authors found little provision for older people, those with high support needs and individuals from black and minority ethnic communities. What classes did exist were often fragile and vulnerable to cuts. However there were some exceptions, where colleges or authorities had developed appropriate and imaginative courses, such as Asian studies or classes that included people with profound or multiple learning disabilities.

Leisure and recreation

As Brown (1994) points out, leisure is a contested concept. For those who are unemployed, on low incomes, or who spend much of their time in services waiting for something to happen, too much 'leisure' can become very stressful. Russell (1995) points out that leisure and recreation have been largely neglected in community care policy. Where leisure does feature in policy documents, it is as part of a planned programme, with a therapeutic or rehabilitative function. Cavett (1998) defines leisure as 'freetime activity which is chosen to provide enjoyment' (p.97). Traditionally, and still today, many adults with learning disabilities spend much of their free time with their parents, sometimes doing relatively little, sometimes engaged in activities that are not age-appropriate (Sanderson 1995; Stalker *et al.* 1999). Successive studies have shown that many people with learning disabilities have few friends, tend to be socially isolated but would like a richer social life (Amado

1993; Emerson and Hatton 1994). Myers *et al.* (1998), in a review of the literature on 'community inclusion', found that many leisure activities still take place in segregated settings, or in public settings at 'special' times, while even 'integrated' activities may provide only fleeting contact with non-disabled people.

However, a number of recent initiatives have sought to tackle these issues, based on the premises, first, that people may require support to use ordinary leisure facilities and, second, that it is relationships with others which give most meaning to leisure (Sanderson 1995). Early attempts to promote social opportunities through domiciliary support schemes, which matched individual and worker on service-led rather than needs-led grounds, and in which the supporters were not necessarily part of the local community themselves, proved ineffectual (Felce *et al.* 1998). Many local authority schemes and voluntary organisations run befriending schemes, whereby the individual is linked up on a one-to-one basis with a person who has similar interests. Citizen advocacy schemes, although not primarily about friendship, may have the same effect. Both types of schemes are greatly valued by many people with learning disabilities (Myers *et al.* 1998; Simons 1995).

Another recent development, originating in the USA, has been 'community building', described by Bartholomew-Lorimer (1993) as aiming to 'create personalised space for individuals within the community and to build relationships' (p. 170). Amado (1993) identifies three ways that day services can help relationships develop – by supporting relationships on job sites; by seeking places to make community connections during the day, for example by assisting an individual to become a 'regular' in a local café and, third, by supporting the person in her social networks, using her interests as a way to link into community activities at weekends and in the evenings. An important difference between community building and befriending or advocacy is that the former does not involve the provision of long-term support by one person. Rather, the formal support fades away over time, once the person has established her own niche in the community. In addition, community building often has the aim of helping people move into socially valued roles.

Summary and conclusions

One of the many unfortunate legacies of long-stay institutions is an implicit perception of people with learning disabilities as somehow different from others, not needing or able to benefit from the same opportunities but preferring to be 'with their own'. The ethos of normalisation and, to a lesser extent, the social model of disability have challenged such views. Most individuals who have a learning disability now live in the community but tend to remain socially isolated. Despite much rhetoric about inclusion, and the very real achievements that have been made in some areas, the overall pattern, in social work services, in further and continuing education and in social and recreational activities, is that people with learning disabilities remain confined to segregated, congregate activities. The exception is the small but growing number of supported employment schemes which offer people the chance of a real job for the going rate, and all the benefits associated with paid work, which can act as passports to social inclusion. Unfortunately, however, most people with learning disabilities will not realise these benefits until the complex and perverse regulations surrounding benefits are reformed.

Social inclusion is a central plank of current Government policies. A social exclusion unit has been set up in the Cabinet Office; the Scottish Executive has its own social inclusion 'team'. However, the documents produced by these units to date have included little mention of disabled people; with many other disadvantaged sections of society competing for resources, some of whom may be seen as potentially more of a 'threat', those with learning disabilities are likely to remain on the margins. They will not become part of mainstream society until it is fully accepted by politicians, policy makers, practitioners, parents and the public at large that people with learning disabilities are first, individuals with a range of ordinary aspirations similar to that of the general population and, second, citizens with the same rights as any others. The limitations of the social welfare system – indeed, its propensity to exclude people from ordinary opportunities – must be addressed. Instead of 'caring' for people, we need to find ways to offer support which enable.each person, as far as she is able, to lead an ordinary life. As Simons (1998) argues, this means designing services around people's existing and developing relationships, enabling individuals 'to live and work in the places that matter to them, alongside the people that matter to them' (p.61).

Acknowledgement

Many thanks to Chris Jones of SHS for her helpful comments on this chapter.

References

Allen, D. (1994) 'Towards meaningful day activity.' In E. Emerson, P. McGill and J. Mansell (eds) *Severe Learning Disabilities and Challenging Behaviour.* London: Chapman and Hall.

Amado, A.N. (1993) 'Working on friendships.' In A.N. Amado (ed) *Friendships and Community Connections between People with and without Developmental Disabilities.* Baltimore: Paul H. Brookes.

Ayers, G. (1971) *England's First State Hospitals 1867–1930.* London: Wellcome Institute of the History of Madness.

Banks-Mikkelson, N. (1980) 'Denmark.' In R.J. Flynn and K.E. Nitsch (eds) *Normalisation, Social Integration and Community Services.* Austin, Texas: Pro-Ed.

Barnes, H., Thornton, P. and Campbell, S.M. (1998) *Disabled People and Employment: A Review of Research and Development Work.* Bristol: The Policy Press.

Baron, S., Stalker, K., Wilkinson, H. and Riddell, S. (1998) 'The Learning Society: The highest stage of human capitalism?' In F. Coffield (ed) *Learning at Work.* Bristol: The Policy Press.

Bartholomew-Lorimer, K. (1993) 'Community building: Valued roles for supporting connections.' In A.N. Amado (ed) *Friendships and Community Connections between People with and without Developmental Disabilities.* Baltimore: Paul H. Brookes.

Bass, M. and Drewett, R. (1996) *Supported Employment for People with Learning Difficulties.* Social Care Research Findings, 86. York: Joseph Rowntree Foundation.

Beyer, S., Goodere, L. and Kilsby, M. (1996) *The Costs and Benefits of Supported Employment Agencies.* London: The Stationery Office.

Beyer, S. and Kilsby, M. (1995) *Day Service Comparisons.* Highlight No. 6. Cardiff: Welsh Centre for Learning Disabilities Applied Research Unit.

Beyer, S. and Kilsby, M. (1996) 'The future of employment for people with learning disabilities: A keynote review.' *British Journal of Learning Disabilities 24,* 134–137.

Brown, H. (1994) 'What price theory if you cannot afford the bus fare: Normalisation and leisure services for people with learning disabilities.' *Health and Social Care in the Community 2,* 153–159.

Brown, H. and Smith, H. (1994) *Normalisation: A Reader for the Nineties.* London: Routledge.

Cavett, J. (1998) 'Leisure and friendship.' In C. Robinson and K. Stalker (eds) *Growing up with Disability.* London: Jessica Kingsley Publishers.

Corden, A. (1997) *Supported Employment, People and Money.* Social Policy Reports No. 7. York: Social Policy Research Unit, University of York.

Department of Health and The Welsh Office (1971) *Better Services for the Mentally Handicapped.* London: HMSO.

Eaton, L. (1994) 'Nice work if you can get it.' *Search*, Spring, 14–17.

Emerson, E. and Hatton, C. (1994) *Moving Out: Relocation from Hospital to Community*. London: HMSO.

Felce, D., Grant, G., Todd, S., Ramcharan, P., Beyer, S., McGrath, M., Perry, J., Shearn, J., Kilsby, M. and Lowe, K. (1998) *Towards a Full Life: Researching Policy Innovation for People with Learning Disabilities*. Oxford: Butterworth Heinemann.

Flynn, M. and Hirst, M. (1992) *This Year, Next Year, Sometime...? Learning Disability and Adulthood*. York: National Development Team/Social Policy Research Unit, University of York.

Further Education Funding Council (1996) *Inclusive Learning: Report of the Learning Difficulties and/or Disabilities Committee (The Tomlinson Report)*. London: HMSO.

Gattercole, C. (1987) 'Employment services for people with learning impairments.' In G. Horobin (ed) *Why Day Care?* London: Jessica Kingsley Publishers.

Gold, M. (1980) *Try Another Way*. Training manual. Champaign IL: Research Press.

Harrison, J. (1996) 'Accessing further education: Views and experiences of FE students with learning difficulties and/or disabilities.' *British Journal of Special Education 23*, 4, 187–196.

Jackson, C. (1998) 'Without walls.' *Mental Health Care 1*, 11, July, 362–363. ·

Jones, C. (1994) 'Innovative practice: Employment for people with multiple disability.' In S. French (ed) *On Equal Terms: Working with Disabled People*. Oxford: Butterworth Heinemann.

King's Fund Centre (1980) *An Ordinary Life: Comprehensive Locally-based Residential Services for Mentally Handicapped People*. London: King's Fund Centre.

King's Fund Centre (1984) *An Ordinary Working Life*. London: King's Fund Centre.

Leighton Project, The, with Grant, S. and Cole, D. (1998) 'Young People's Aspirations.' In C. Robinson and K. Stalker (eds) *Growing up with Disability*. London: Jessica Kingsley Publishers.

Lunt, N. and Thornton, P. (1994) 'Discourse and employment: Towards an understanding of discourse and policy.' *Disability and Society 9*, 2, 223–238.

Myers, F., Ager, A., Kerr, P. and Myles, S. (1998) 'Outside looking in? Studies of the community inclusion of people with learning disabilities.' *Disability and Society 13*, 3, 389–414.

National Development Group (1977) *Day Services for Mentally Handicapped People*. Pamphlet No. 5. London: HMSO.

Nirje, B. (1969) 'The Normalisation Principle and its human management implications.' In R.B. Krugel and W. Wolfensberger (eds) *Changing Patterns in Residential Services for the Mentally Retarded*. Washington DC: Residential Committee on Mental Retardation.

Nisbet, J. and Hagner, D. (1998) 'Natural supports in the workplace: A re-examination of supported employment.' *Journal of The Association of Persons with Severe Handicaps 13*, 260–267.

O'Brien, J. (1987) 'A guide to lifestyle planning: Using the activities catalogue to integrate services and natural support systems.' In B. Wilcox and G.T. Bellamy (eds) *A Comprehensive Guide to the Activities Catalogue for Youth and Adults with Severe Disabilities*. Baltimore: Paul H. Brookes.

Oliver, M. (1990) *The Politics of Disablement*. Basingstoke: Macmillan.

Pannell, J, Simons, K. and Macadam, M. (1999) *Baguettes and Bicycles: The Impact of Work Opportunities on the Lives of People with Learning Difficulties in France and the UK*. Bristol: Norah Fry Research Centre, University of Bristol.

Pattison, S. (1998) *Living Life to the Full: The Role of Further Education*. Paper presented at the British Institute of Learning Disability Annual Conference, Eastbourne, September 1998.

Pearson, S. (1996) *Baking Cakes at 50: Young Disabled People in Transition*. Edinburgh: Access Ability Lothian.

Petty, D.M. and Fussell, E.M. (1997) 'Employer attitudes and satisfaction with supported employment.' *Focus on Autism and Other Developmental Disabilities 12*, 1, Spring, 15–22.

Reid, P.M. and Bray, A. (1997) 'Paid work and intellectual disability.' *Journal of Intellectual and Developmental Disability 22*, 2, 87–96.

Riddell, S., Stalker, K., Wilkinson, H. and Baron, S. (1997) *The Meaning of the Learning Society for People with Learning Difficulties: Report of Phase 1 of the Study*. Glasgow: Department of Social Policy, University of Glasgow.

Riddell, S. and Wilson, A. (1999) 'Supported employment in Scotland: Theory and practice.' *Journal of Vocational Rehabilitation 5*, 57–70.

Russell, J. (1995) 'Leisure and recreation services.' In N. Malin (ed) *Services for People with Learning Disabilities*. London: Routledge.

Ryan, J. and Thomas, F. (1987) *The Politics of Mental Handicap*. London: Free Association Books.

Sanderson, H. (1995) 'Self-advocacy and inclusion: Supporting people with profound and multiple disabilities.' In T. Philpot and L. Ward (eds) *Values and Visions: Changing Ideas in Services for People with Learning Difficulties*. Oxford: Butterworth Heinemann.

Scottish Home and Health Department (1972) *Services for the Mentally Handicapped* (The Blue Book). Edinburgh: HMSO.

Scottish Office, The (1999) *Social Inclusion: Opening the Door to a Better Scotland*. Edinburgh: The Scottish Office.

Seed, P. (1996) *Is Day Care Still at the Crossroads?* London: Jessica Kingsley Publishers.

Seed, P., Thomson, M., Pilkington, F. and Britten, J. (1984) *Which 'Best Way'? A Preliminary Study of Day Services for People with a Mental Handicap in Scotland*. Tunbridge Wells: Costello.

Simons, K. (1995) *My Home, My Life: Innovative Approaches to Housing and Support for People with Learning Difficulties*. London: Values into Action.

Simons, K. (1998) *Home, Work and Inclusion; The Social Policy Implications of Supported Living and Employment for People with Learning Disabilities*. York: The Joseph Rowntree Foundation.

Social Services Inspectorate (1998) *Moving into the Mainstream: The Report of a National Inspection of Services for Adults with Learning Disabilities*. London: Department of Health.

Stalker, K., Cadogan, L., Petrie, M., Jones, C. and Murray, J. (1999) *If You Don't Ask, You Don't Get – Review of Services to People with Learning Disabilities: The Views of People who Use Services and their Carers*. Edinburgh: The Scottish Executive Central Research Unit.

Sutcliffe, J. and Jacobsen, Y. (1998) *All Things Being Equal? A Practical Guide to Widening Participation for Adults with Learning Difficulties in Continuing Education*. Leicester: National Institute of Adult and Continuing Education.

System 3 (1999) *Attitudes to Learning Disability*. Unpublished report prepared for SHS. Edinburgh: System 3.

Williams, P. (1995) 'Residential and day services.' In N. Malin (ed) *Services for People with Learning Disabilities*. London: Routledge.

Wolfensberger, W. (1972) *The Principle of Normalisation in Human Services*. Toronto: National Institute on Mental Retardation.

Wolfensberger, W. (1983) 'Social role valorisation: A proposed new term for the principle of normalisation.' *Mental Retardation 21*, 6, 234–239.

CHAPTER 4

Supported Employment in the Context of Day Care

Anne Connor

This chapter considers the features and underlying aims of supported employment services, and the extent to which supported employment can be thought of as a form of day care. It focuses on services used by people with mental health problems, although the findings and issues raised are also relevant to employment services for people in other circumstances; many of the research studies and policy documents referred to in the chapter address the circumstances of people with other disabilities and/or other types of additional needs. Some aspects of the circumstances and experiences of people with mental health problems are different from the other groups of people who use supported employment services, however. These include the fluctuating pattern of mental illness for many people, the 'hidden' nature of the disabilities, the disabling effects for many people of long experience of mental health services when there has been little emphasis on recovery or taking risks, and the attitudes and perceptions of other people.

The chapter examines in detail the findings from evaluations of one service used by people with mental health problems as a case study to explore some of the issues involved. It then considers the implications for the development of supported employment services and related policy issues, and the implications for research in this area.

The nature of supported employment services

Many accounts of day care opportunities for people with disabilities, including people with a mental health problem, place supported employment in the context of other day activities that provide meaningful occupation and support in daily living. For example, a review of day activities funded under the Mental Illness Specific Grant included supported employment services in the range of activities (SWSIS 1995). *The Framework for Mental Health Services in Scotland* notes several specific supported employment responses as part of the range of possible responses to people needing occupational activity, in high and low support settings, assessment and preparation for work, and training, education and the structured day (Scottish Office 1997). Many local community care plans take a similar approach in looking at the range of opportunities and services for people with mental health problems and for those with other disabilities. For example, supported employment services have been included in some local day services reviews.

Some services and individuals – including users, commissioners, those providing services and commentators – share this view. Others are uncomfortable with seeing supported employment as a form of day care, feeling that this reflects an outdated view of people's needs and aspirations, the way we regard disability in our society, and the way in which we regard employment and the other ways any person spends their time (see, for example, Barnes, Thornton and Campbell 1998; Beyer and Kilsby 1998).

Key elements of supported employment services

The term 'supported employment' is used as shorthand to apply to a wide range of services and activities that respond to a wide range of needs. Typically, these activities will focus on people with disabilities or illnesses who face additional barriers in accessing the open employment market and mainstream education and training opportunities. Services will aim to place clients in one or more of a range of settings, including paid work on a full- or part-time basis, work paid at therapeutic earnings or reduced rates, voluntary or unpaid work, and training and education places where there is a strong vocational element.

The accounts by services of what they do, and the exchanges within the professional networks, both in this country and internationally, show general agreement that the central aspects of a supported employment response will include:

- assessment of each person's abilities, needs and preferences
- support and/or training for the individuals, which is then organised on a group or individual basis
- identifying potential opportunities in employment or training settings, or negotiating access into mainstream settings on behalf of the users. (Hyde 1998; Lutfiyya, Rogan and Shoultz 1988; Sylvestre and Gottlieb 1992)

On this definition supported employment services are distinct from:

- services that primarily aim to provide social care, or daytime activity that does not have an employment, training or education focus
- therapeutic or rehabilitative care which takes place in an employment-like setting
- sheltered employment, where the project provides paid employment, or an employment-type activity, in a separate setting that does not involve participants working alongside people who do not have disabilities.

Seen in this way, supported employment is no longer part of a continuum, but rather provides a resource that complements other support services and social contacts that people might use. The distinctions between the different types of service may not be clear to people outside – potential users, referrers, policy makers, researchers. They also may not be understood by people who work in services, who can assume that everyone does it their particular way.

The range and variety of supported employment services
NEEDS OF INDIVIDUALS

Some services focus on people with a particular type of disability while others are generic. Some will work with people with a particular need, usually linked to skills or experience related to employment settings, such as communication skills. Some services will focus on supporting people who have a higher or lower level of need within the spectrum.

The circumstances of people who benefit from the service can vary widely; this covers those with any illness or disability as well as particular groups – people with mental health problems, learning disabilities, physical disabilities, behavioural and other problems stemming from brain injury. The age range is usually from 16 to retirement age, although some services have found ways to fudge the upper age when this suits participants' needs and choices. Some services focus on people who are entering employment or training; others include people who have had absences from work; some include people who are already in work but who need additional support because of their disability.

TYPES OF SUPPORT AND PLACEMENT

The length of time support is provided ranges from a few weeks to several years; many services linked to the national employment services in the UK and other countries are designed to offer time-limited support. The type and level of on-going support varies considerably. Most services provide a level of support to the individual after the placement or post has started. But whereas some follow up for a period of up to two to three months, and see this as part of the assessment process, other services have a longer or more flexible follow-up period, and see ongoing support in the medium-term as an integral part of the support tasks.

Projects take very different approaches as to how far the support and training is focused on employment-related skills and practical needs and how far it is also about social and interpersonal skills. The places at which the support and training is provided also vary: in the employment setting, at a project base, or through other agencies and services.

Services vary in whether they are individual- or group-based. Some are oriented to individual needs, with each person being offered a distinct, tailored response. In others, some or all of the training and opportunities are offered on a group basis. From anecdotal comment, it may be that the most frequent approach taken is when there is an individual package but within a limited range of options.

RANGE OF OPPORTUNITIES

Services take very different approaches to the way they go about identifying potential opportunities for participants. Some services aim to place all or most people in open employment settings. Others offer a range of settings including voluntary work, sheltered work placements, mainstream and distance learning, etc. Some services put as much, or their main, emphasis on training and learning opportunities as being ends in themselves as well as stepping stones to eventual employment.

The terms of the employment are one of the more noticeable differences between services. Some aim to have all or most places paid at the market rate for the job. This is a central feature of many services in the USA, for example. In the UK, however, the benefits system often provides disincentives, particularly for people who need higher levels of social care or some forms of community health service support.

Identifying places within the community takes a greater or lesser profile. Some projects put considerable effort into raising awareness among employers and other organisations (e.g. voluntary organisations when this is part of their remit). Other services work with a set range or number of placements with which the project has a long-term relationship. The support available to the employer or other setting also varies. Some projects do give advice and support to the employers. Some services aim to develop natural support systems within the placement setting, with a view to encouraging more robust and more flexible longer-term supports for the individual. Other services work only, or mainly, with the individuals who are their clients.

Models of supported employment

To be effective, employment support services need to link into other services and to link into employment opportunities in their local community. Services can take different approaches to these issues.

When working with services that provided employment-related support to people with mental health problems, I was struck by the way both staff and participants drew distinctions between their own and other local services, commenting on differences that seemed minor to someone coming from another perspective. The importance of links with other services, and how a service relates to the wider community, is probably of greater significance than many funders or care managers have appreciated.

With this in mind, I looked again at the way evaluations and service reports describe these aspects of their activities. From the policy documents and descriptions of approaches in the material by and about individual services, there seem to be six main models of supported employment initiatives. The central and shared element in each model is support for people with a disability to enable them to get (back) into employment. The main differences lie in the underlying philosophy and aims of the approach. However, this makes a crucial difference in the way apparently similar services' responses operate: for example, how they interact with the people who use the service, how they link with other activities and the outcomes for the individuals.

Although the models are listed separately here, there is considerable potential for several models to exist in a local area as part of a combined approach.

- *Model 1: Supported employment is part of the network of services for each identified client group.* Here, employment is seen as part of the therapeutic or rehabilitative process. Links are with, for example, other learning disability or mental health services, including those providing treatment and support.

- *Model 2: Services are part of a network of supported employment services for people with disabilities.* In this model the links are with projects and services providing support for other categories of people who have difficulties getting into employment because of illness or disability.

- *Model 3: Supported employment services are part of a general employment support network.* Here links are with training and support organisations for people who have difficulties getting back into the workplace because of time away, because they have no recent experience, lack job-related skills, and so forth.

- *Model 4: The supported employment service builds on a good employer approach.* Support for people with learning disabilities, mental health problems or other disabilities getting into employment is tackled alongside wider initiatives such as mental health in the workplace, health and safety awareness and training, and equal opportunities. The context is a culture of encouraging good, sensitive employment practices, which happen to be more likely to provide the flexibility and support that people with disabilities find helpful.

- *Model 5: Supported employment is part of the development of alternative employment settings.* Here, services are based in sheltered settings within client group or social care service networks. The links are with other initiatives exploring alternatives to conventional employment outside the care network and based in the community, such as flexible working hours and shared tasks. The types of tasks and settings are usually focused on people with disabilities; for instance, as part of a mental health regeneration plan. Less commonly, they are focused on people who choose not to be part of conventional models for whatever reason, or for whom some conventional models are not available – in some rural areas, for example.

- *Model 6: Supported employment services are part of an economic regeneration model.* Here, the links are with expanding or creating new employment opportunities for people with any or a specific disability. The focus is on increasing employment opportunities, with a degree of targeting on employment needs of people with disabilities rather than leaving this to trickle down from the general employment pool. The wider context includes local economic regeneration.

Notes and issues around these models

The central differences between the models turn on core values and philosophy: whether the person needs to adapt to the world, or whether the world can – and should – adapt to the person.

Models 1, 2, 3 and some examples of 5 start from the premise that the person has some deficiencies because of his or her disability, and that the person has to be helped to fit in with the current employment opportunities.

Models 4, 6 and some examples of 5 start from the premise that the reason the gap between people with disabilities and employment opportunities is so large is because the nature or levels of employment are flawed. If these flaws can be reduced, employment will become more accessible for everyone, including people with disabilities.

Model 1 is the traditional approach, and is reflected in the national (Scottish) Mental Health Framework, for example.

Advantages often attributed to model 1, and to a lesser extent model 2, are that the approach targets people with higher needs, and it can be easier to link the supported employment element into care plans. The approach encourages, and is encouraged by, links between services that individuals will be using: the staff are usually talking to each other about several clients. There are benefits for coordination of care for individuals and sharing ideas and perspectives across services working with that group of people.

Model 2 in particular has raised concerns among user groups as reinforcing stigma and labelling.

Model 5 was the original underlying philosophy of many workshops; for example, within the NHS. A common concern among people who use services is that these traditional services now often have limited contact with the community and offer limited employment opportunities. More recent examples tend to have a clearer philosophy, and one that is more often not centred on disability or dependency.

Project example: The National Schizophrenia Fellowship Scotland Ladder Initiative

NSF (National Schizophrenia Fellowship) Scotland provides an Employment Training Service in Dumfries and Galloway. This service aims to assist people who have, or are recovering from, mental health difficulties who wish to explore the opportunities of re-entering employment, education or training.

The current project – the Ladder Initiative – was funded by the European Community Social Fund and has run since January 1998. The services were developed by NSF Scotland in the context of the local Mental Health Strategy. The project provides a range of support according to the needs and preferences of participants. The project also gives information to employers and agencies in Dumfries and Galloway on employment, education and training needs and opportunities for people with mental health problems. This includes advice to employers on how to make their workplaces better suited to the well-being of people with mental health problems. By October 1999, around 150 people had been in contact with the initiative. The outcomes for the participants are listed in Figure 4.1.

- 17 people had moved on to full-time or part-time work

- 21 people were undertaking Information Technology training as a main subject or as back-up to another course, such as Open University or Higher National Certificate

- 23 people had gone onto other types of training

- 39 people had been supported by the employment advisers for individual packages of volunteer placements and help with job searches

---

Figure 4.1 Outcomes for participants of the Ladder Initiative – 154 people over 19 months

The evaluations of the Ladder Initiative

An independent evaluation of the early stages of the project was carried out in 1998 (Connor 1998). A core element of that evaluation was that the criteria used to assess the project reflected the priorities of the people who used the service – the User Participation in Quality Assessment model, developed by a consultant to the partner project in Denmark (Krogstrup 1997).

The evaluation centred on users' perceptions of:

- the criteria against which the projects should be assessed
- what helped people with mental health problems to live successfully in the community
- the ways in which the projects could help participants to live in the community
- the benefits they gained from the projects.

The study also gathered feedback from carers, staff in the project and staff in other organisations who work with the project (Connor 1998).

NSF Scotland commissioned a further evaluation in 1999 (Bonthron *et al.* 1999). This time the focus was on assessing how the project had progressed since the previous review and following up aspects of the service that the first evaluation had identified as gaps. The evaluation was carried out by an independent team, Alpha–Omega Evaluation. The core team comprised people who had used the service and Anne Connor, whose role was to ensure the evaluation was carried out to a good professional standard and provide a link with the previous evaluation. A member of staff was assigned to work with the team, to provide practical support and to be a source of information about the project. A finding from the second report was that this evaluation model was an effective way of assessing the impact of the project and contributing to future planning. There was also a separate review of the process, to assess the impact of the user-led evaluation model (White 2000).

Participants' assessment of the project

The criteria proposed by participants as the basis for any assessment of the service's achievements largely focused on the impact for individuals. These criteria are shown in Figure 4.2.

- Gaining self-esteem

- Gaining in confidence: general, covering most aspects of life, rather than limited to mental health needs

- Having a sense of achievement

- Providing an activity, something meaningful to do

- Offering friendships and support from other people

- Learning specific skills

- Learning how to work (again): e.g. coping in a working environment

- Having more choices about future activities, training and work-related

- Having more choices about the future in other aspects of life

- Gaining confidence to move on to do other things, or to try for other things, including work and training-related activities

- Becoming better able to cope with the barriers associated with mental health problems

Figure 4.2 Participants' criteria for assessment of project

Participants were clear that moving on to employment or another training place was not the most important outcome for them, particularly if that place did not properly value them and what they could contribute.

In the first year, participants found the projects were helping them to live more successfully in the community and to have more choices about training and support. They considered that their criteria had been met at least to some extent for everyone, and for most people to a substantial level.

These assessments were confirmed by the positive feedback from professionals in other agencies and by family carers. In general, the carers and the professionals from care services tended to have lower hopes and expectations about possible future opportunities for the project participants than did the participants themselves.

Professionals were asked to assess the project against the criteria identified by the participants. Most people replying agreed with these factors as useful ways of assessing the project. If a criterion was not met in their view, it was usually noted that this was because of inherent difficulties rather than any failure of the project. The feedback from participants and professionals in other services raised questions of the expectations of supported employment services, of appropriate timescales over which changes can be expected to happen for individuals, and what the appropriate targets or outcome indicators ought to be.

In the second evaluation, similar benefits were noted in detailed feedback from participants. Again, employment was seen as less important than other benefits. Typical comments were:

Social contact and something to do is more important than work.

All the people in Genesis are friendly and encouraging, and I feel as if I am getting somewhere and doing something useful for the first time in years.

As in the earlier evaluation, these assessments were confirmed by the positive feedback from the staff who often suggested to clients that they come to the projects. The evaluation team carried out a series of interviews with social work and nursing staff in the Community Mental Health Teams (CMHTs) and in some NHS settings. All the teams interviewed by the evaluation team identified benefits for clients in terms of confidence building, personal development and increased independence. Some staff were aware of clients who had taken on some voluntary work or open employment. However, this was seen as an additional benefit rather than the main reason for the referral or the most important outcome:

The Ladder Initiative increases participants' self esteem and confidence, and expects them to take some personal responsibility for their own future personal development. This is in contrast with some general employment services.

It's a good way of bringing people into the community through the use of open learning or voluntary placements. It treats our clients as 'normal'.

There are good mental health outcomes. We can identify a clear drop in dependency levels of people on the Ladder Initiative.

The project in relation to other services

An issue that was raised by participants in the first evaluation was the relatively low expectations that other people had of them. Most people had found the staff in the mental health services, and especially those based in hospitals who had contact mostly with people when they were most ill, to have limited ambitions for their clients. Frequent comments were:

- staff see the illness or the disability before they look for the person and their abilities
- staff wish to protect people from disappointment or failure, but are too protective or protective for too long
- staff have less knowledge of the range of possible opportunities and of supports that are available
- staff see 'employment' just as another form of day care.

Some project participants had very good experiences of the main mental health services and were pleased their CPN or social worker had encouraged them to come to the project, which was well suited to their needs. Others had been directed to the project for the 'wrong' reasons, but the response they had received from the project had after all been right for them. There was, however, considerable concern about the lack of awareness about the supported employment project among some staff in the mental health services.

There was also a strong view that the project should, if possible, raise the horizons and expectations among staff in other settings. There was agreement that this could be done through raising the general issue and providing general feedback on what participants can achieve, for example as feedback following the evaluation. A minority of participants wanted more feedback to other services on the benefits for them personally, and were looking for ways of achieving this.

In the second year, the evaluation team decided to interview staff in the mental health and social work services, to find out how they made their decisions about who to refer or encourage to use the supported employment services. We also wanted to check how far the increased information from the Ladder Initiative – following the first evaluation – had made an impact.

Figure 4.3 notes the factors mentioned by staff in the decision whether to suggest someone comes to the Ladder Initiative. These factors seem to stem partly from staff's perceptions of the project, and partly from their expectations around employment.

- There is a need to build up self-confidence and self-esteem

- Employment will give structure to the day

- Project provides a route into 'normal' community activities

- The client will be enabled to become part of the wider community

- Can the person cope with the routine, challenge and being with other people?

- The interests of the individual, what will stimulate and engage them

- The project provides preparation for employment at some point in the future, especially for younger people

---

Figure 4.3 Factors influencing other agencies' staffs' decisions to refer clients to the project

In terms of the models discussed above, the staff's expectations would put the supported employment service within the context of other services for people with mental health problems – model 1. The participants' concerns are more about general support. They are looking to the project to reflect aspects of model 3 – part of a general employment support – and would like to see more emphasis within society on model 4 – building on a good employer approach.

Barriers to moving on

Project participants identified three main barriers to people with mental health problems moving on to employment in the local area. The first barrier was the attitudes of employers and the community generally towards people with disabilities, and particularly towards people with mental health problems. A related barrier was the low availability of employment and training opportunities appropriate to the needs and preferences of people with disabilities. The third barrier is a national one: the incentives to work, and particularly the interaction with the benefits system. The carers and professionals were in strong agreement with the participants about the barriers facing people with mental health problems living in the community. They particularly emphasised the stigma associated with mental health problems.

Figure 4.4 on p.82 lists the main reasons identified by the participants why people are unlikely to get mainstream jobs as a follow-on from the project. Linked to these are aspects of the wider social and economic environment that would need to change if the barriers experienced by the participants were to become easier to overcome.

Many participants described difficult experiences at Job Centres and of the benefits system, which they considered was not supportive of people with mental health problems. A distinction was drawn between individual members of staff and the assumptions about the nature of disability that underpinned the system. Particular issues identified were:

- the system sees disability and being able to work as cut and dried when it isn't like that

- too much focus is put on numbers and the employment advisers' targets, rather than on the needs of individuals

- the arrangements reinforce negative consequences of illness/ disability.

Figure 4.5 on the next page lists the changes to the environment that partici-pants thought would assist the aims of the project. The experience of the pro-fessionals echoed these points.

- Stigma associated with mental health

- Background of general prejudice in employment settings against people with disabilities; mental health worse within this

- Pressures associated with most jobs, such as timescales, deadlines, targets

- Similar pressures associated with conventional college courses

- Recruitment processes for most jobs: more attention to recent employment history and job titles than to the person's skills

- Attitudes of employers to gaps in employment and skills/experience for non-employment settings, e.g. domestic responsibilities

- Attitudes to retraining: it is not valued; it is not seen as inevitable and normal; and employers are not investing enough in retraining for their workforces

- Type of work available in the local area, such as little demand for people with computer skills

- The way employers and society reward the range of contributions and skills that people bring: types of employment with low wages; part-time and flexible work is less well regarded and rewarded; creativity and other skills are less valued than some types of contributions

- Employers generally do not understand about types of disability and the impact of mental illness: aspects include the impact on work tasks and the types of support that people need and to get around the impact/problem

Figure 4.4 Barriers to entering employment and training

An issue raised by these findings is the way in which supported employment services are assessed, and which outcomes are taken for criteria or targets. The project staff did feel they were being judged on the extent to which participants gained longer-term employment, for example, even though the opportunities were limited in that geographical area, and the jobs that were available often did not reflect the choices and abilities of the participants.

- Greater understanding among employers about mental illness, disability etc.

- Less pressure within jobs, better working environments

- Opportunities for flexible models of working, e.g. job-sharing, team working – alternatives to 100% input 100% of time

- Alternatives to conventional employment, such as working from home, cooperatives and supported settings

- A public-relations job on employers, persuading them to be (more) pro-active about the positive contribution people with mental health problems – and other disabilities – can make

- Benefits system: avoiding the benefits trap, and taking a longer-term view of people's abilities and disabilities

- Easy access to information and advice about benefits: most participants had this, but on-going information is essential as the benefits system changes so often

- Access to information and advice about other financial matters: in their experience this was not as easy to get as was the information on benefits

---

Figure 4.5 Changes that would help supported employment projects achieve their aims

Expectations of good employment and training settings

The evaluations confirmed that one of the main barriers to people moving on to employment settings from the project was the scarcity of suitable opportunities. It was noted that rather than expecting special allowances to be made, many people with mental health problems would be comfortable and able to cope in employment settings that aimed at being supportive and flexible towards the needs of all their employees. Ways of meeting the employment-related needs of people with mental health problems are easier for all involved when they complement the standards and practices of good employers, who value and encourage all employees to realise their full potential in a supportive environment.

Participants highlighted aspects of the support that people who have moved on to, or are considering, employment are looking for. The main need for support is in generally building up confidence. There is not a clean distinction between being out of employment and needing support, and being in employment: people value flexibility and being able to come back for support once they are in employment. An area of employment that causes anxiety for many people with mental health problems is job-related training: people can need extra help here when they are not well, and many people need more time than their colleagues to absorb new ideas and information.

Again, these findings challenge the way the processes and outcomes of many supported employment services are assessed.

Application of the wider research on supported employment services

The problems and issues identified in the Ladder Initiative studies are not new and are not restricted to that project, or to services that support people with mental health problems. Research from ten years ago highlights the same range of barriers to people with a range of disabilities gaining access to employment, and identifies similar frustrations with the limited range of opportunities (Floyd 1991).

A strong message from the research is that people with a range of disabilities want to work, and that they are looking to employment support, training and personal support services to help them gain access to and make use of a range of opportunities that suit their interests and skills (Barnes *et al.* 1998; Beyer and Kilsby 1998; Jones and Wilson 1998; Kestenbaum 1998).

Many research studies and writers have identified the inflexibility of the benefits system, which acts as a major disincentive especially for people with higher support needs and those with fluctuating health problems (see, for example, Barnes *et al.* 1998; Durie 1999; Floyd 1991; Hyde 1998; Jones and Wilson 1998). A related problem is the 'personal assistance trap' highlighted by Kestenbaum (1998) – the situation where someone with severe disabilities has to earn enough to pay for personal assistance.

There are also long-standing issues around how we assess the outcomes of services. In a review of training projects provided by a major voluntary organisation in the mid-1990s, Cunningham (1996) noted tensions between the targets set by funders, which focused on the numbers of trainees moving on to employment and further education, and the outcomes identified by users, staff and other people who referred clients or were interested in the overall mental health services, who focused on benefits to individuals such as self-esteem and confidence. This was also highlighted in the feedback from disabled people and by service providers in the review of research and development initiatives by Barnes *et al.* (1998), and in the views of people with disabilities reported by Hyde (1998).

Other consistent messages are:

- the limited range of training and employment opportunities (see, for example, Barnes *et al.* 1998; Jones and Wilson 1998)

- the barriers posed by stigma around mental health (Durie 1999; Jones and Wilson 1998) or learning disabilities (Beyer and Kilsby 1998)

- the importance of the local economic situation – for example in rural areas (Monk *et al.* 1999) and areas with a history of industrial decline

- the potential help – or barriers – from employers' general practices towards all their employees, such as flexible working arrangements and accessible buildings (Barnes *et al.* 1998; Kestenbaum 1998).

The research also confirms many of the ideas suggested by people in Dumfries and Galloway on possible ways forward. Restructuring the way we think of employment and day opportunities for people with disabilities is often regarded as an important starting point – see, for example, Ritchie, Jones and Broderick (1998).

Another approach is to extend the range of work opportunities for individuals, for example through a more person-centred approach (Jones and Wilson 1998; Ritchie *et al.* 1998). This may have helpful parallels with other developments in social work, social care and health care. The ideas and practice developed by the Center for Psychiatric Rehabilitation at Boston University and its partner organisations reflect this approach.

More recently, the national policies on social inclusion, or exclusion, have led some researchers and commentators to raise the possibility of developing more links and opportunities within people's own communities – see, for example, the Beattie Report (Beattie 1999). The hope is that this would help tackle several barriers – stigma, economic regeneration – and unpick general barriers facing many people who want to get back into employment settings.

Other identified potential solutions tackle other aspects of the links between disability and unemployment. Some studies suggest extending the range of employment opportunities through tackling the structural barriers facing people with disabilities who want to work (Hyde 1998; Jones and Wilson 1998; Monk *et al.* 1999). Other writers have highlighted the links with wider mental health – or learning disability or disability – awareness campaigning (Jones and Wilson 1998; Kestenbaum 1998), as a means of tackling stigma or unhelpful working practices in mainstream employment settings. Other reports have noted the impact on policies set by national or local government, and suggested reviews of local and national policies around charges for services and access to financial support: again, this would be in the context of a wider debate about work and the place it is given in our society (Hyde 1998; Meadows 1996).

The research studies also highlight lessons that can be bedded into the practice of individual services. Taken as a whole, the research suggests that all supported employment services would benefit from a more coordinated effort with other people, whether within the supported employment movement or across wider alliances.

Implications for programme structure and service evaluation

The issues raised in the Ladder Initiative and in the other studies also raise questions about the type of research that is done in this area, and how the research is used. In a very useful study, Barnes *et al.* (1998) looked at available research, including service evaluations and other grey literature, and gathered the views of people with an interest in using this research to inform and develop practice. Priorities identified in this study include:

- including potential services users or the wider users' movement, as well as the people in touch with services (also noted by Jones and Wilson 1998)

- inclusion of, and a focus on the circumstances of, people from the black and ethnic minority communities, older disabled workers and young people leaving school

- research that reflects the needs of employers and of staff delivering supported employment services, although Hyde (1998) highlights the risk of programmes concentrating too heavily on this aspect

- more systematic reviews of approaches, rather than the current concentration of evaluations of specific services against the requirements of particular funders

- more research on the experiences of disabled people in the workplace (also a conclusion of Hyde 1998).

A strong message from this review is that much research in the supported employment field would benefit from a more rounded understanding of the outcomes of the services and employment opportunities. At present, much of the focus is on activity targets – numbers of clients seen, numbers placed in employment or training settings. The views of the people involved as to the usefulness of the service, or whether they feel this is the right placement for them, and the benefits they have gained in other aspects of their lives, often appear to be interesting but of less importance. There appears to be a need for a set of indicators which bring together the employment-related outcomes for participants, social/personal outcomes for participants, outcomes for the employers of training settings, and the efficiency of the service. This could be developed for, or by, each project; but there would also be many benefits in a generally recognised set of core indicators, which would permit comparisons across projects.

Many projects have attributed the problems facing them concerning the way they are assessed to the nature of their funding programmes. Supported employment services are generally funded either as part of a programme focused on creating jobs – where the indicators for all parts of the programme are jobs created, numbers of people or places, etc. – or as part of a mental health (or other client-group specific) programme – where the indicators reflect long-term provision of treatment or social care. In each case, there is often a feeling that the programme does not accommodate the different focus of supported employment, and cannot or will not take account of such aspects as the different timescales and the importance of matching the placement to the circumstances of the participant. Where supported employment projects are facing the uncertainties of short-term funding, it can be difficult for them to take the initiative and put forward alternative, if more appropriate, ways of identifying their achievements.

As part of the follow-up to the user-led evaluation of the Ladder Initiative, NSF Scotland was awarded a short term of European Community funding to bring together a project team to develop an account of good practice in evaluating supported employment services and disseminating the findings of such evaluations. The guide shows how the various interests – including participants/service users, providers and commissioners/funders – can help develop and make use of user-led evaluations that reflect the range of perspectives and outcomes. This work is currently being completed (NSF Scotland 2000). The guide should contribute to the debate about how we assess supported employment services and whose questions the research should answer. It may also enable those who provide services, participants, funders/commissioners and other people, to be part of the debates about where supported employment fits into the range of day care and other social care services, and how it is part of the way we enable all members of our societies to make a valued contribution.

Issues for day services

The research on the Ladder Initiative and other supported employment work or issues also raises important questions about the range of day activities to which people with disabilities have access and their relationship with supported employment services.

How clear are providers of day services about the underlying philosophy and aims of their work? Where would the services fit within a range of models that included being an extension of care services, being part of the leisure opportunities for people living in that community, or being part of training and education resources? Are they starting from the basis that the clients need help in fitting in to society, or do they start from the premise that society needs help in valuing and including all members of the community?

Why does the way we structure financial and other supports to people with disabilities often undermine choice and limit opportunities to become more independent or to live in a different way? If people had the choice to do what they would like to do during the day, would they turn to these services? How can the services that people use during the day provide the support and encouragement for individuals to live the kinds of lives they want, and to develop self-confidence and other skills that are important and useful to them? Would some of the people who are part of other day services at the moment prefer to work if they had that choice and the support to make it possible?

Against whose expectations and standards are day services assessed? What part are the people who use those services, and their families and friends, having in setting the context for the service, as part of overall plans? What training and encouragement are the people who work in those services getting to enable them to work in ways that meet the expectations and ambitions of their clients? Are staff getting caught between conflicting criteria and targets that are no longer appropriate for the type of work they need to do?

It is to be hoped that this chapter and the other contributions to this volume will stimulate and lend stamina to those taking part in these debates.

References

Barnes, H., Thornton, P. and Campbell, S.M. (1998) *Disabled People and Employment: A Review of Research and Development Work.* Bristol: Policy Press.

Beattie, R. (1999) *Implementing Inclusiveness, Realising Potential: Report of the Advisory Committee on Post-School Education and Training for Young People with Special Needs* (The Beattie Report). Edinburgh: Scottish Executive.

Beyer, S. and Kilsby, M. (1998) 'Supported employment in Britain.' *Learning Disability Review 2*, 2, 6–14.

Bonthron, P., Connelly, M., Connor, A., Douglas, C. and Slavin, D. (1999) *The Second Year of the Ladder Initiative – Report by the User-led Evaluation Team.* Dumfries: National Schizophrenia Fellowship Scotland.

Connor, A. (1998) *The Ladder Initiative – An Evaluation of Employment Training and Support for People with Mental Health Problems.* Dumfries: National Schizophrenia Fellowship Scotland.

Cunningham, G. (1996) *Work at Your Own Pace – An Evaluation of SAMH Training Projects.* Edinburgh: Scottish Association for Mental Health.

Durie, S. (1999) *Pathways to Work: Towards an Action Agenda to Create Valued and Sustainable Employment Opportunities for People with Mental Health Problems in Scotland.* Edinburgh: Scottish Development Centre for Mental Health Services.

Floyd, M. (1991) 'Overcoming barriers to employment.' In G. Dalley (ed) *Disability and Social Policy.* London: Policy Studies Institute.

Hyde, M. (1998) 'Sheltered and supported employment in the 1990s: The experiences of disabled workers in the UK.' *Disability and Society 13*, 2, 199–215.

Jones, C. and Wilson, E. (1998) *Employment for People with Mental Health Problems: A Study of Needs and Priorities in Fife.* Edinburgh: Scottish Human Services.

Kestenbaum, A. (1998) *Work, Rest and Pay: The Deal for Personal Assistance Users.* York: York Publishing Services.

Krogstrup, H.K. (1997) 'User participation in quality assessment.' *Evaluation 3*, 2, 205–244.

Lutfiyya, Z.M., Rogan, P. and Shoultz, B. (1988) *Supported Employment: A Conceptual Overview.* Syracuse: Center on Human Policy, Syracuse University.

Meadows, P. (ed) (1996) *Work out – or Work in? Contributions to the Debate on the Future of Work.* York: York Publishing Services.

Monk, S., Dunn, J., Fitzgerald, M., and Hodge, I. (1999) *Finding Work in Rural Areas: Bridges and Barriers.* York: York Publishing Services.

NSF Scotland (2000) *The Next Step: The Guide to User-Led Evaluations of Supported Employment Services.* Edinburgh: NSF Scotland.

Ritchie, P., Jones, C., and Broderick, L. (1998) *Ways to Work.* Edinburgh: SHS.

Scottish Office (1997) *A Framework for Mental Health Services in Scotland.* Edinburgh: HMSO.

SWSIS (Social Work Services Inspectorate for Scotland) (1995) *Time Well Spent – A Report on Day Services for People With Mental Illness.* Edinburgh: HMSO.

Sylvestre, J.C. and Gottlieb, B.H.(1992) 'A critical appraisal of supported employment for persons with developmental disabilities.' *Developmental Disabilities Bulletin 20,* 2.

White, J. (2000) *Report on the User-Led Evaluation of the Second Year of the Ladder Initiative.* Dumfries: National Schizophrenia Fellowship Scotland.

Copies of the evaluation reports about the Ladder Initiative, and information about the project, can be obtained from: NSF Scotland, 130 East Claremont Street, Edinburgh EH7 4LB.

CHAPTER 5

Working with People who are Homeless, Vulnerable or Insecurely Housed

Abi Cooper

It is too easy to underestimate the value of day centres for single homeless people; they are a place to go, to be dry and warm, to have shelter, find food and washing facilities and to find acceptance and assistance. There are over 250 such day centres in the UK working with over 10,000 people each day (Cooper 1997, p.i). They offer a mixture of practical services and emotional support provided in a flexible way, under one roof. This has proved to be vital to the lives of many homeless, vulnerable or insecurely housed people around the country. However, because the focus on homelessness services has tended to be on housing, day centres and the valuable work they do are often forgotten or ignored. There is very little written information about this kind of day centre and very little analysis has been carried out to prove the value of the work they do. Day centres, largely the domain of the voluntary sector, are often described as the Cinderella services of the homelessness world.

This chapter will explain the work of 'day centres for single homeless people', the term by which they are commonly known. It will outline why, outside the sector, so little is known about this type of centre; who the client group is and the type and value of services the centres offer. It will then consider the work of day centres in light of the social inclusion debate, looking at its relevance to this sector, before investigating whether such centres are enabling clients to achieve greater social inclusion or exacerbating their exclusion. This question is one that was being asked of day centres long before the term 'social exclusion' was common parlance.

As will become clear, very little research data is available on day centres working with people who are homeless. Most of the literature published is recent and focuses on good practice issues, funding and networking. Consequently, the claims made here are based on the limited number of publications available; small-scale, unpublished surveys carried out by the National Day Centres Project (NDP) and anecdotal evidence I gathered over a four-year period of travelling around the country working for NDP.

The recent overview of research conducted by Glasgow University into homelessness over the last ten years confirms that 'There is...little other research or published material available on day centres' (Fitzpatrick, Kemp and Klinker 2000, p.42). Indeed, the reason that the National Day Centres Project was established was that day centre workers felt their work was being marginalised and little attention was given to the issues they were facing and the particularly challenging work they were carrying out.

What do day services for single homeless people do?

Day centres offer a massive range of services. The services are usually developed as a result of unmet needs identified from within the client group. At times services are also developed as a result of the available funding, which will be discussed later.

A recent survey carried out by the National Day Centres Project (NDP 2000), in keeping with previous surveys, shows that basic services are particularly important to the most vulnerable clients. They rely on day centres for a source of cheap food, a place to wash and keep clean, a place to shelter and somewhere to socialise with others. It is often the case that particularly vulnerable or suspicious clients will be using these services for a considerable amount of time before they feel able to access other available services such as housing advice, a health worker or alcohol advice. They have to feel comfortable with the centre before they can be ready to make changes in their lives.

Whilst the basic or 'primary care' type services are the backbone of the majority of centres, many offer a good deal more. It is at this point that the different approaches of particular services begin to show. For example, the majority of projects believe that attending to their clients' health needs should be a priority; whether they should be provided on site, or whether clients should be referred to external agencies will depend on the philosophy and the resources of particular organisations. Some see themselves as one-stop shops and others as agencies which signpost their clients to other services and support them in accessing these services effectively. However, day centres frequently point out that other agencies do not understand the needs of their client group and do not provide effective services. Day centres frequently find themselves having to provide the necessary service because no one else is doing it, or quite understands what providing the service will entail.

As a result of this there are day centres that offer unusual and quite specific services. For example, homeless people in Edinburgh are able to access the Cowgate Centre during the night. Other cities are looking at this model to see if it can help them address the needs of their more vulnerable and challenging clients, or could enable them to offer a useful service to those potential clients who currently refuse to engage with any services. Handel Street Day Centre in Nottingham has been providing a centre for heavy drinkers for the last few years and its success has led other cities to think about setting up a similar service. A day centre for drinkers was recently set up in Brighton. There was recognition amongst day centre workers that homeless women continued to be under-represented in day centre attendees. A number of day centres have responded to this by providing women-only sessions or women's workers. There are at least two women-only day centres in London: one, run by Barnado's, is specifically for young women, while the other, run by the Church Army, is on the same site as a women's hostel and works with a wider age range. (For contact information see Palframan 1998.)

There are a significant number of day centres working with the younger age group and specialising in the specific concerns they present. These centres are also growing and developing; there are thought to be links between homelessness and truancy. In response to this Base 51 in Nottingham works with young people who are not attending school; in conjunction with the school, family and young person they try and devise a schedule for that person that ensures that their school work gets done but that they receive the support and assistance they need.

Common elements

In many ways it is unhelpful to define day centres by the client group they see and the services they offer. What they have in common is, first, their commitment to working with people who have difficulty getting the help and support they need to find housing, or to prevent themselves from becoming homeless. The second common link is the principle of open access. This is what separates them from many other day centre services; their client group is self-selecting (with the few exceptions of centres for a particular age group or gender). Open access in this context of day centres for homeless people means:

- clients can use the service without having to be referred or having to disclose a great deal of personal information about themselves
- rules and regulations are kept to the minimum required to provide a safe and welcoming environment
- cases are rarely closed and clients can drop in as and when they need to.

This combination makes day centres attractive to people who feel alienated from or suspicious of more mainstream services. It also makes them attractive to people who are lonely or vulnerable, and to people who have alcohol and drug problems, but do not want to be defined by their substance misuse. The level of acceptance and anonymity also tends to attract people who have multiple needs and those whose behaviour is challenging to service providers. Day centres see themselves as a safety net, a way of ensuring that service users can, at very least, get their basic needs met without having to disclose information. Day centres try very hard to work with those people who have fallen through every other safety net. An example of this is the recent Day Centres Inclusion Project (DCIP), commissioned by Homeless Network (Ball and Griffin 2000). This recent research project was carried out to consider how the more vulnerable and challenging clients in the central London area could get out of the cycle of being banned and barred from day centres, and to identify good practice in working with people with challenging behaviour in order to reduce exclusions. It was a recognition that there is a group of people who have nowhere else to go.

Why are day centres so little understood?

The lack of knowledge and understanding about this type of day centre is in part due to the fact that historically such centres have tended to work in isolation. Their inward-looking approach reflects their origins. Many were set up by concerned individuals, to respond to immediate local need with very limited resources. It is only relatively recently that many day centres have started to recognise that sharing information, learning from each other and working together can improve the service received by their clients. The network of day centres was set up in 1994 and prior to that communication between services only existed if individual workers felt it to be important. Waters (1992) argues that fighting for the same funding further prevented cooperation within the sector and compounded the isolation:

> Individual projects have always had to compete for the same funding, and the current social welfare and housing crisis has sharpened this competition. This has resulted in a marked disparity between resources available to different services, which has impeded dialogue between them. (p.7)

One of the main reasons for day centres being 'sidelined' is that their work is so difficult to define. This is probably because many were set up to respond to perceived gaps in local services and unmet needs. The local nature of many services has meant that they have grown and expanded in different ways. Some day centres are well-staffed, employing professionals and specialists, while others exist with a minimal staff team directing the work of volunteers, and there are still a very few with no paid staff at all. Although there are similarities, no two day centres provide exactly the same service in an identical fashion; there is no blueprint outlining what day centres of this type should provide. They are expected to respond to their local environment.

The most accurate and useful definition has been drawn up by the NDP, the umbrella organisation for day centres. It incorporated the differences by defining the centres they work with as those which:

- provide an 'open access' building-based facility

- offer a variety of services usually involving a mix of support, advice, information, food and practical help

- are committed to equal opportunities, maintaining a safe and welcoming environment and empowering service users

- have a primary focus on working with homeless, vulnerable or insecurely housed people (Cooper 1997, p.i).

Understanding this type of day centre is made all the more difficult by the fact that the centres cannot be defined by the service user group they attract. This is because of the complex nature of 'homelessness' and the different ways in which it is manifested in different parts of the country. For example, day centres in certain cities may be working with more rough sleepers because of the lack of affordable, available housing; while day centres in other areas are working with people who are housed temporarily and insecurely. Some centres work exclusively with rough sleepers because they feel this to be a priority or because their facilities make it necessary for them to prioritise particular groups; others view themselves as working with any groups which, without support or assistance, might be in danger of becoming homeless. The majority of services work with single people or childless couples, as they are the groups that face the most difficulty in using existing legislation to find housing. However, a small number of centres believe they also need to provide for their service users who have children and whose needs are not being met by other mainstream services. This flexibility is an aspect of day centre provision that some other agencies and professionals find difficult to comprehend.

Issues

Funding

Day centres are frequently in the position of having identified a service that they would like to provide, but being unable to fund it. The issue of funding is particularly important to day centres because very few have a regular source of funds; unlike hostels, for example, they do not have rents. Their funding comes from applications to statutory and charitable funders for a particular piece of work that they undertake to do (Gordon 1997). This has proved to be problematic in recent years when funders have wanted to fund new and interesting projects but day centres have still needed money to maintain the ongoing basic services their clients require. Murdoch and Llewelin (1996) comment:

> Nearly everything in a day centre has to be done by people, not by machines or computers. Day centres are staff intensive. Frontline workers have to make numerous decisions every day, some of them crucial to the life or death of another person. (p.6)

Joint working

Working cooperatively with other services is a relatively new concept within the day centre sector. In some cities there have been organisations with close links and good working relationships but this has generally been due to individual efforts. While this has improved over the years and the existence of a network has been significant in improving links, it is still patchy. Often day centres work most closely together where there is an umbrella organisation that facilitates it, examples of this being the Scottish and Glasgow Councils for Single Homeless and the London Homeless Network.

One of the biggest changes within the sector in the last six or seven years has been the moves many day centres have made towards working more effectively with other agencies providing similar services, and statutory and mainstream providers of care who have traditionally ignored the needs of homeless people. It would be wrong to suggest that all day centres have this spirit of cooperation and for many, run on a shoestring, relying on volunteer staff and operating at capacity, time to build better working relationships seems like a luxury or an irrelevance. However, it is clear that providing effective, good quality services to vulnerable people who have housing problems, and often have a myriad of other difficulties, is going to require the cooperation and specialisms of many different professionals. Services that have invested time in building these relationships usually benefit and are able to provide a much more holistic service to their clients.

It is true that, historically, people who are homeless have proved a challenge to the working practices of statutory organisations. Chris Leigh (1993) sums this up in his work on the difficulties homeless people face in trying to get community care assessment:

> [Homeless people] have no secure accommodation in which to receive services, often lack clear case histories, tend to bypass statutory provision and move across Local Authority boundaries, they often have a range of problems and needs that do not easily segment into standard assessment.

Measuring value

The need for open access drop-in services providing crisis intervention and practical support is clear to anyone who has spent any time talking with people who use day centre services. However, proving this with statistical data remains very difficult. One reason for this is that the measurement of success and change will vary quite dramatically from service user to service user. For example, many centres might say that the month's biggest achievement was seeing a service user smile and say good morning for the first time after using the service for six months. Setting those difficulties to one side it is still true that monitoring and evaluating work is a relatively new concept within the day centre sector. There are some organisations, such as St Botolph's in London, which have, for the last few years, been focusing on measuring the outcomes of their work. However, on the whole, day centres have tended to adopt the approach of measuring their achievements by outputs; that is, if people are coming to use their services they must be doing something right. This is reasonable in that nobody has to use a day centre – users go there by choice – they can leave whenever they want and they never have to return. This is, though, too simplistic. People in difficult circumstances are likely to use whatever is available, whether or not they think is a good quality service. While being very helpful in engaging someone and ensuring they get access to the basic services they need to keep themselves alive and healthy; services which are not responsive to their clients' needs are unlikely to assist people in making helpful changes to their life circumstances.

Social exclusion and the Rough Sleepers Unit

The new Labour Government arrived with a new approach to social policy spearheaded by the Social Exclusion Unit and the New Deal. While it is too early to judge its success, the establishment of the Rough Sleepers Unit (RSU) has certainly been the most important and influential change in the homelessness sector since the introduction of the Rough Sleepers Initiative in the early 1990s. Day centres had grown used to new initiatives and opportunities for money being directed at the provision of accommodation. To generalise, other than money for resettlement work and health work, the majority of day centres felt they had to look outside of central Government grants for their money. Whether or not the RSU will dramatically change this remains to be seen; but for the first time day centres have received recognition for their work, and an acknowledgement of their central place in providing services for the most vulnerable and challenging homeless people. What the RSU seems to value is that many day centres work with a significant number of rough sleepers, and particularly that they continue to see them when their behaviour means that other services are no longer prepared to do so.

In many ways 'social exclusion' becoming a fashionable term has helped day centres. It is much easier for them to explain their work under that heading than under the heading of 'homelessness' because, as we have seen, homelessness has so many different definitions. In the Cabinet Office (1999) report explaining what the Social Exclusion Unit was, the following definition was used:

> Social Exclusion is the shorthand term for what can happen when people or areas suffer from a combination of linked problems such as unemployment, poor skills, low incomes, poor housing, high crime environments, bad health, poverty and family breakdown.

Day centre workers were immediately able to relate to this definition; it was the life experience of a significant proportion of their service users. This was supported by a brief survey undertaken by the National Day Centres Project in order to prepare a response for the Social Exclusion Unit (NDP 1998). The 16 day centres recorded as working with the highest number of rough sleepers were contacted. They reported that 75 per cent of their service users were or had been rough sleepers. Reasons for people having to sleep rough were given by staff and service users. In order of frequency the causes were given as:

- relationship breakdown
- result of family breakdown, poor skills and the tensions of low income and unemployment
- unable to cope with previous accommodation – which again relates to poor skills, trying to live in high-crime environments, being used to institutional living and having to cope with poor-quality housing
- financial problems and loss of job
- low incomes, unemployment, bad health and poor skills.

Although only anecdotal and from a small sample the responses confirmed that people using day centres were exactly the people the Government defined as being socially excluded. Interestingly, there are already established services to help with these types of problems but they do not seem to be able to work with people who are homeless; or at least, day centre service users do not feel able to access them. One of the major reasons that day centres are so important to this group is that they can either offer a range of services in one place, or continued support in accessing appropriate assistance. At their best, day centres provide an holistic approach to clients' needs.

The effect of recognition

This is an interesting time for day centres: they are now recognised as integral to helping rough sleepers, and those in danger of rough sleeping, back into mainstream society. While this recognition will be gratifying to many, for some it may prove to be a double-edged sword. Historically, day centres have gone unrecognised or ignored and while this has been frustrating it has meant that individual projects have been able to get on with working in their own ways. The RSU wants to see results; it wants the reduction of rough sleeping by two-thirds by the year 2002. If day centres are going to be part of that plan they are going to have to focus their work and be prepared to prioritise work with rough sleepers. This is likely to cause some concern to projects set up locally in order to respond as quickly and effectively as possible to the needs of *all* their clients. It may also prove to be divisive, as many day centres are working primarily with temporarily and inadequately housed people in order to prevent them from becoming street homeless; while prevention is important to the RSU plan, the current priority is working with existing rough sleepers.

It is likely too that greater recognition will lead to higher expectation. To date day centres have been making claims for the quality and cost effectiveness of their work, but very few have been measuring or even monitoring the outcomes of their involvement with clients. One of the reasons for this has been that day centres have encouraged clients to take the lead in requesting any long-term, in-depth or individual help they want. The new strategy clearly expects projects to take more of the initiative and to encourage rough sleepers to use the assistance offered to them.

Do day centres exacerbate social exclusion?

It is clear that day centres are working with exactly the people the Government defines as being socially excluded. However, as has been demonstrated, the problem facing day centres has been that, while they are working with people who are socially excluded, they too have traditionally been excluded services. There are, it seems, potential difficulties with day centre provision, not just practically, but with their 'open door' ethos and with their providing, for the most part, services that are open-ended. In her polemical and thought-provoking book Jackie Waters (1992) states that the role of day centres is not to create ghettos but to enable their users to have a place and say in the community of their choice. The book acknowledges the work day centres do in providing services to people we would now term as socially excluded – but it makes equally clear that day centres can themselves be marginalised services and that some of the practices they adopt can have a detrimental effect on those who use them. It has become increasingly important, in the light of the social exclusion debate in the homelessness sector, that day centres ask themselves not only 'how are we alleviating the social exclusion experienced by our services users', but also 'are there ways in which we exacerbate their exclusion?'

A way of explaining how this might happen is to consider how some of the strengths of day centres can have the unwelcome side effect of exacerbating clients' exclusion from mainstream society. That is to say, what day centres do which enables them to attract and work with clients whom other services reject or ignore can also have the effect of making those clients overly dependent on day centre services, and unable or unwilling to access other services.

Easy access to essential services is one of the main strengths of the day centre sector. There is no need for individuals to wait for a referral, or to undergo a lengthy interview process. Many of the people who use day centres would not be able to find the basic services they require anywhere else. For many this would mean that they would have an even more difficult life. Day centres, as a specialist service, have filled these gaps – but they too are often limited in what they can offer. In many ways they are a crisis intervention service that can also provide low-level, basic support to people who might become homeless if such support was not available. It must be recognised that day centres will always have a proportion of clients who will not 'move on'. However, that should not be the prognosis for all day centre clients. Day centre workers should constantly be encouraging their clients to access the services that everyone else uses. The day centre sector needs to inform mainstream services of the ways in which they can be more welcoming to people who are homeless. They need to facilitate their service users in accessing the activities available in their locality. If they do not, clients are limited to services for people who are homeless; which are, in the longer term, only ever going to be second best.

Day centres are able to offer a sense of community to many of their service users. For some clients the day centre is the only place they go to where they feel welcomed and comfortable. While this is a valuable aim, day centre staff have to raise their expectations for their clients. They have to work to give service users the confidence and skills they will need to access services and activities away from the day centre. They have to be encouraged to have higher, but realistic, aspirations for themselves. Although there will always be a proportion of clients who will need to use the day centre on a regular basis, and for whom it will always be central to their life, accumulating clients who never move on from the day centre cannot be a primary goal. Day centres have to start measuring their success with clients not by how many times a week they attend, but by how much they achieve.

Conclusion

The social exclusion debate is asking many of the questions that need to be asked of day centres. Services are having to think about what they define as success, what it is they want to provide for clients, and the ways in which they want clients to use their services. However, the social exclusion agenda within the homelessness sector is focusing on rough sleeping when the majority of day centres have a wider remit. Day centre workers know that there is not a sharp distinction between rough sleepers and other groups of homeless people. They are aware that if they do not continue to provide support for people in insecure accommodation they will see many presenting as rough sleepers at a later date. The time and skills required to achieve greater integration into society for this client group are considerable, requiring skilled staff and adequate resources.

Undoubtedly, then, there needs to be a greater understanding of the work carried out by day centres working with people who are homeless. They work with some of the most socially excluded people in our society. Consequently, day centres are at the cutting edge of the social exclusion debate, and their vital role must be recognised. However, they too are having to examine their own role critically, and to think through the ways in which their clients might be held back from realising their own potential by becoming too involved in a service which can serve to limit their horizons.

The real question that day centres should be asking themselves, and many are, is that first asked by Waters in 1992 – how can they equip people to live resourcefully in society?

References

Ball, L. and Griffin, S. (2000) *Breaking and Entering: Tackling the Cycle of Exclusion.* London: Homeless Network.

Cabinet Office (1999) *The Social Exclusion Unit.* www.cabinet-office.gov.uk/seu/index/whats_it_all_about.html

Cooper, A. (1997) *All in a Day's Work: A Guide to Good Practice in Day Centres Working with Homeless People.* London: Char.

Fitzpatrick, S., Kemp, P. and Klinker, S. (2000) *Single Homelessness: An Overview of Research in Britain.* Bristol: The Policy Press.

Gordon, A. (1997) *Pay-day or May-day: A Guide to Day Centre Funding in England and Wales.* London: National Homeless Alliance.

Leigh, C. (1993) *Right to Care – Good Practice in Community Care Planning for Single Homeless People.* London: Char.

Murdoch, A. and Llewelin, S. (1996) *Saving the Day.* London: Char.

NDP (National Day Centres Project) (1998) *Response to the Social Exclusion Report.* Unpublished.

NDP (National Day Centres Project) (2000) *Survey of Day Centres for Single Homeless People.* Unpublished.

Palframan, M. (1998) *The NDP Directory of Day Centres in the UK for Homeless People.* London: National Homeless Alliance.

Waters, J. (1992) *Community or Ghetto? An Analysis of Day Centres for Single Homeless People.* London: Char.

PART II

Innovations in Management, Provision and Practice

CHAPTER 6

Day Care for Older Adults

Developing Services for Diversity

Jo Moriarty

The first step in any evaluation of day care for older people is to consider some of the factors that have contributed to shaping the service as it currently stands. Of these, by far the most important is the increasing recognition that older people, carers, service providers or commissioners may all have differing perspectives about the purpose of day care and the extent to which it is achieving its objectives. Second, day care as a whole has been shaped by differing traditions; those of assessment and treatment in day hospitals and those of social and recreational activities in day centres (Tester 1989). Third, it is essential to be able to distinguish between different service components; for instance, to differentiate between issues relating to transport and those that concern the range of activities provided. Finally, while the prime focus of day care is to assist older people themselves, studies have clearly shown that one of the most frequent reasons for referring a person to day care is to provide respite or a break for his or her carer (Gilleard *et al.* 1984). In this sense, the service must equally be measured by its ability to meet carers' needs.

To some extent, evaluations of day care have perhaps been hampered by the very familiarity of the service. It is notable that, while the community care changes might have provided an ideal opportunity to re-evaluate the role of day care services, work replicating the major national studies completed in the 1970s (Carter 1981) and 1980s (Tester 1989) has yet to be undertaken.

Taken together, the effect has been to produce a very uneven picture. For example, within the literature, internal reports and studies of a single centre or unit would appear to outnumber evaluative studies examining how day care fits in with other community services, its impact upon entry rates to long-term care, and whether or not it is meeting the diverse and changing needs of older people and their families.

Scope of chapter

Only a minority of older people attend day care. However, as these users range from patients receiving treatment in day hospitals attached to large departments of geriatric medicine to people attending their local lunch club, it is clear that every form of service delivery cannot be covered in a single chapter. In considering the role of day care in combating social exclusion among older people, this chapter will argue that its potential benefits have been neglected through a failure to invest in developing services in ways which more clearly reflect wider developments in society.

Demographic and social changes have important implications for the development of day care services. The likelihood of disability increases strongly with age (Bennett *et al.* 1996; Bowling, Farquar and Grundy 1993). In the past, many older people attending day clubs or centres were able to travel there independently and may have chosen where they wanted to attend from a range of venues available locally. Now, the current trend in targeting day care services towards an increasingly frail client group is likely to continue with the rise in the proportion of people aged 85 and over in the population. This provides the context for a discussion on the current provision of day care and a description of some of the ways in which health and social care services in different parts of the country have responded to serving an increasingly old and frail client base in terms of funding, dealing with transport problems and finding new models of service delivery.

The increasing numbers of older people from minority ethnic groups necessitates the provision of more culturally diverse forms of care. Here, the chapter includes examples where day care has been used as part of a wider strategy to improve fair access to care across all sectors of the population.

Most older people lead independent lives in which they make their own choices about their social and leisure needs (Jerrome 1992). However, a minority have physical and mental health needs which make it harder for them to participate in the social and leisure facilities available to older people as a whole. The chapter will describe approaches to making the range of activities provided at day care more responsive to individual preferences, at the same time as taking account of those disabilities that might influence the way in which users are able to participate.

Across the European Union, two-thirds of the care given to older people comes from family members, with only 13 per cent coming from publicly provided services and 11 per cent from services arranged and paid for by older people themselves (Walker 1995). The effects of intensive family caregiving may mean that carers may also find themselves at risk of social exclusion. An important part of the chapter, therefore, will be to recognise some of the ways in which day care supports those caring for older people.

Provision of day care

Proportion of people attending day care

The General Household Survey, based on data collected from a nationally representative sample of all adults living in private households, reported that 11 per cent of adults aged 75 and over attended day care (Bennett *et al.* 1996). Figures collected from local authority purchased or provided day centres show that during one survey week an estimated 250,800 people attended day centres. However, less than half of these were clients aged 65 and over. This differs markedly from home care where older people comprise the majority of users (Department of Health 1999).

The availability of day care for older people is also extremely variable. Across local authorities in England, the number of older people attending day centres per 1000 of the population aged 65 and over ranges from 2 to 44.

By comparison, the comparable figures for the 16–64 age group are much more uniform (Department of Health 1999).

Since the community care changes, there has been a trend towards rationalising day care. This has led to health and social services departments (SSDs) placing more emphasis upon their role in supporting people with higher levels of need, with a corresponding reduction in funding provision for older people whose needs were primarily social.

Expenditure on day care

In contrast with other services for older people, such as home care, community nursing and residential and nursing care, comparatively little is spent on day care. At 1995/96 prices, out of a total expenditure of £11.1 billion on long-term care services, just £380 million was spent on day care. Of this, the Royal Commission on Long Term Care estimated that about a third was provided by the NHS (Cm 4192-I 1999). In contrast with home care, residential and nursing care, almost three-quarters of day centres are directly provided by local authorities (Department of Health 1999).

Costs of providing day care

At 1999/2000 prices, a single session at a local authority day centre for older people has been estimated to cost £19. This is similar to the figures for NHS trust day care. Costs in the voluntary sector are more variable, ranging from £15.91 to £34.47 per client per day. The capital costs of day care in the voluntary sector are currently kept lower by the widespread use of venues such as local church halls (Netten and Curtis 2000).

Charging for day care

Over the last ten years, it has become more common for local authorities to charge for community care services. The overall effect of means testing upon service uptake and its specific effects upon disabled people with low incomes has been debated strongly within the anti-poverty movement (National Consumer Council 1995). In terms of day care, clear charging anomalies do exist. For instance, people attending day care as part of a programme of after-care provided under Section 117 of the Mental Health Act 1983 must not be charged; but in some parts of the country, people with learning disabilities have been asked to pay the full costs of their day care. On the whole, older people attending day care are more frequently asked to pay a flat rate charge to cover some of the costs of transport and meals. However, the extent of the variation in charging policies between authorities was confirmed in a report by the Audit Commission (2000a). They pointed out that people with similar needs could be paying very different rates for a similar level of service. The Government's response has been to issue draft guidance on charging policies (Department of Health 2001). It recommends that councils must ensure that users' net incomes are not reduced below basic levels of Income Support. The question of charging for day care serves as a reminder that strategies for social inclusion in the context of community care services need to be considered in conjunction with wider policies aimed at reducing the impact of poverty.

Characteristics of day care users

Within the literature, much has been made of the distinction between different day care settings: between purpose-built dedicated venues and units attached to a community centre, residential home or sheltered housing complex; between day care for 'mixed' groups of clients and specialist day care for people with a specific illness or condition. However, a study comparing the characteristics of older people attending different venues showed that there was a spread of different types of disability across *all* types of day unit. In particular, almost every unit had at least one client with mobility problems, a sensory impairment or a mental health problem (Bacon and Lambkin 1997).

New approaches to funding

There has been a long-standing debate about the apparent similarities between people attending day hospitals and those attending day centres

(Audit Commission 2000b; Currie, McAllister-Williams and Jaques 1995; Pahl 1988a; Warrington and Eagles 1996). The separate patterns of day hospital and day centre provision can be shown to have had unfortunate consequences. These include both the duplication of services and under-provision. The impact of separate provision has also accentuated the problems for service users who have found themselves passed between day hospitals and day centres as a result of failures between the two services to reach agreement about their respective eligibility criteria.

More positively, there are also examples where health and social services have worked together to maximise the resources available for day care. These include the Petersfield Centre in Havering where health and social care professionals work alongside each other in a centre funded by health and social services and run by Age Concern (Audit Commission 2000b). An alternative approach taken in the South London and Maudsley NHS Trust has been to set up outreach services in which input from health care professionals can be offered on a sessional basis (Goss 2000).

Day care in rural areas

The extent to which models of day care designed for urban areas are suitable for translation to rural communities has been identified as a source of concern (Gibson and Whittington 1995). Issues especially applicable to rural areas include the extent to which the older population is geographically dispersed and problems in providing suitable transport services. This was part of the rationale behind the establishment of the first travelling day hospital in Hampshire in 1982. The service was provided in different locations each day, meaning that users and carers had reduced journey times and transport costs. They also felt that it created a more homely and comfortable atmosphere when compared with a conventional day hospital (Powell and Lovelock 1987).

Home-based day care

Another solution, and one which is also more often associated with rural settings, has been for a host carer to provide day care in his or her own home. In Ipswich, the Homeshare day care scheme was set up by Suffolk social services department in 1985. The aim was to provide a choice of day care venues for clients and to offer an alternative to people who might find it hard to integrate into a conventional day centre (Burningham 1991).

Providing day care in domestic settings

The success of Homeshare has been the stimulus behind a project entitled 'Home from Home', which is intended to extend home-based day care to other parts of Suffolk. Start-up funding for the scheme has been obtained through funding from the European Social Fund, the East of England Development Agency, and Age Concern Suffolk. Ongoing funding will come from contracts with the local social services department for providing day care for frail older people and people with dementia. Age Concern will recruit and train host carers. Unlike some similar schemes, host carers will be salaried Age Concern staff. The project will also have funding for additional care hours to support the host carers, thereby providing a higher ratio of care staff to clients when necessary.

One of the most comprehensive evaluations of this model of service delivery was undertaken in Finland. Here, hosts were primarily recruited among childminders, resulting in some mixed groups of children and older people. This was felt to promote inter-generational solidarity. The study also concluded that, while there were difficulties in establishing the service, it was more cost-effective than residential care and appeared to be able to delay entry into long-term care (Sepänem 1998).

Day care for older people from minority ethnic groups

Proportion of older people from minority ethnic groups

Policies to combat social exclusion among people from minority ethnic groups have often focused upon the younger population, such as improving educational support for children of school age or addressing differential rates of unemployment. However, the fastest-growing age group among minority ethnic communities in Britain is that of people aged 65 and over (Butt and Mirza 1996). Reflecting the varying patterns of migration among different ethnic groups, the proportion of people aged 65–74 is highest among the black Caribbean (13%) and Indian ethnic groups (7%) and lowest among the Bangladeshi and Pakistani communities (4%). As a point of comparison, 14 per cent of the white population are in this age group (Office for National Statistics 1998).

Double and triple jeopardy

In describing the position of older people from minority ethnic groups, some commentators have developed the concept of double jeopardy (the cumulative disadvantages of racial discrimination and old age) or triple jeopardy (the cumulative disadvantages of age, racial discrimination and the inaccessibility of services). However, while acknowledging the usefulness of these concepts, other commentators have suggested that they require further clarification. For example, black older people experience discrimination in ways that rarely differentiate between age or race (Butt and Mirza 1996). Furthermore, it is not clear whether the disadvantages of poorer health and lower income among older people from minority ethnic groups become relatively greater or relatively less with age compared to the process of ageing among white older people (Blakemore and Boneham 1994).

Under-representation of people from minority ethnic groups among service users

Studies of service utilisation have repeatedly shown that people from minority ethnic groups are under-represented across social and specialist health services. In some cases, it may be owing to lack of awareness about what is available. In others, it may be because the services offered are not culturally appropriate (Butt and Mirza 1996). It has also been suggested that some health and social care professionals have stereotyped images of the extent of family support available within different communities. This may deter staff from referring people from minority ethnic groups onto the appropriate specialist services (Social Services Inspectorate 1998). Importantly, black and minority ethnic older people are less likely to live in districts with a higher proportion of people aged 65 and over than is the case for white older people. This may mean that older people's services in their districts may be less well developed (Butt, Box and Cook 1999).

Developing day care services with local communities

In terms of day care, the evidence suggests that when black Caribbean and Asian people know what exists, there are very similar levels of demand for the service to those found among white people (Atkin and Rollings 1993). Experience in one London borough shows that with effective service planning and consultation with service users and their families, culturally acceptable day care can be offered as part of an integrated programme of care.

Providing day care to users from different ethnic backgrounds

Alzheimer's Concern Ealing is an independent voluntary organisation that aims to help people with dementia and their families. It offers an integrated programme of care in the home, day care, welfare rights and benefits advice. In 1988, the organisation was given funds from the then Mental Illness Specific Grant (MISG) to help identify hidden carers and to improve uptake of services from people from minority ethnic groups. Ealing is a very ethnically diverse borough whose largest minority ethnic group consists of Indians. This dates from the 1950s and 1960s when many people emigrated from the Punjab. When the project began, just one Asian man was attending a local authority day centre. However, consultation with local families showed that there was, in fact, a large unmet demand for day care. This resulted in the establishment of a special weekend day service, designed to supplement Alzheimer's Concern's own home-based care service and local authority day care. There are now 100 weekend day care places spread across three centres. This is to ensure that no person has a journey lasting longer than an hour. Even with this level of provision, there is still a waiting list.

The experience of Alzheimer's Concern shows the importance of ensuring that day care services are developed in ways that reflect the needs and preferences of the local community. Key lessons from their experience include the need to:

- *Monitor service uptake.* In each part of their service, Alzheimer's Concern has ensured that uptake reflects the wider distribution of each community within the borough.

- *Provide a range of activities.* Members from different ethnic groups do not attend specific centres or on specific days. (In fact, consultation showed that users did not want this.) However, by providing bilingual workers and a range of meals and social activities, Alzheimer's Concern has found that different cultural beliefs and practices can be respected in settings designed for users from many different ethnic communities.

- *Match care workers to clients.* This is not simply a question of language skills. Some users found it easier to relate to workers who had been brought up in the same cultural traditions as themselves.

- *Maintain good links with other services.* The borough provides two day centres for older Asian people and these have become important as a source of referrals to Alzheimer's Concern and in raising awareness of services for people with dementia within their local communities.

In some circumstances, older people from minority ethnic groups may especially value the opportunity to attend centres designed for people from a similar background to themselves. The Pepper Pot club in Ladbroke Grove in west London draws its membership from local older Caribbean people. One of the ways in which members can draw on their shared heritage is by visiting local schools and telling children about their experiences of growing up and living in the Caribbean (Butt *et al.* 1999).

Support for service providers

Studies have shown the vital role played by local communities in developing services for people from minority ethnic groups. However, newly develop-

ing service organisations may not necessarily have the experience and resources to provide specialist forms of care or to set up complex contractual
arrangements with funders and those commissioning services.

Helping voluntary organisations to develop

'El Portal' ('the gateway') began in Los Angeles in 1993 as a specific response to
concerns about the under-representation of Latinos among people who attended
day care. The project is coordinated by the Alzheimer's Association of Los Angeles
but receives federal and state funding. Its services include care management,
support groups, legal services, and adult day service centres. In developing
resource packs for day centres, the project staff found that most of the pre-existing
materials had been designed for organisations whose staff already had high levels
of knowledge of providing day care for people with dementia. They designed a 'day
care in a box' kit especially for community organisations that may not have staff
with specific education and training in dementia care. It includes all the items that
those starting a service might need, such as templates for client assessment forms.
(Trejo 1998)

Improving the range of activities at day care

The traditional image of the activities available at day care tends not to be encouraging. As one of the informants for this chapter explained: 'It seems to be
that if we stick them in front of a TV or give them a game of snakes and
ladders, then it's mental stimulation'.

The questionable validity of commonly held presumptions about what
older day care users would and would not like provides the context for the
following section, which shows how older people's preferences can be used
as the basis to expand the range and type of activities available at day care.

Lifelong learning at day care

Probably the best-known example of lifelong learning for older people is
that of the University of the Third Age (U3A) (Laslett 1989). It is based upon

the recognition that older people themselves have the skills to organise and teach in their own autonomous learning groups. Lifelong learning is an important part of current Government policy (Cm 4392 1999). Although much of its emphasis is directed towards helping people continue to learn in order to maintain and improve their employment prospects, the White Paper also recognises that some older people may lack either the confidence or the resources to participate in learning activities. It intends to establish a Learning and Skills Council, which will have a particular duty to address the needs of learners with disabilities.

This raises a potentially interesting difference between the priorities given to educational activities in models of day care for older people and those for adults with learning difficulties. In some centres for adults with learning difficulties, the educational component can comprise nearly 40 per cent of activities undertaken (Seed 1996).

It is possible that the lack of emphasis upon using day care as a means of enabling older people to undertake new activities and new learning may be the result of stereotyped beliefs about age and class (working-class older people tend to form a majority in many day centres). However, there may also be a legacy from adopting the assessment/treatment versus social/recreational models when developing day care for older people.

This was the conclusion drawn from a joint evaluation of a health promotion project and a community arts programme which were both undertaken in sheltered housing schemes, community centres, day centres and residential homes. The projects placed strong emphasis upon consultation with the older users themselves and it is striking that some of the activities they provided, such as abseiling, canoeing and compiling a book of songs with a local singer, are not among those to be found generally in mainstream provision. The evaluation suggested that the philosophical approaches underpinning 'traditional' day care for older people were less successful in developing critical and progressive practice than discourses concerned with education, learning and equality and with the kind of reciprocity involved in notions like friendship and conversation (Carter and Everitt 1998).

Access to the arts and creative expression at day care

The value of widening the professional base of people involved in day care is shown by the Baylis Programme, which provides an example of how day care can be used to extend access to the arts and the experience of creative expression.

The Westminster Opera Team

The Baylis Programme is an education, community and outreach team that has been working since 1985 to bring the English National Opera (ENO) into communities that traditionally tend not to have access to the arts. An example of its work with older people is the Westminster Opera Team, which was funded by the Arts Council and Westminster Council to work in day centres in Westminster. Many users could not read or write music, but with the assistance of a composer to help with notation they were able to create their own composition. This culminated in a concert in which a string quartet played the music they had written.

Experience in undertaking the programme showed how important it was for the artists themselves to adapt their approach to take account of users' disabilities. For instance, the pace of workshops for people with dementia had to be adjusted to allow for lapses in concentration. A man with mobility problems needed assistance to fulfil his aim of conducting the music that he had composed.

Developing the skills of day care staff

While the majority of staff working in day hospitals have professional qualifications, audits of staff in local authority or voluntary day centres for older people have shown that the proportion of staff with a professional qualification is low. Furthermore, it has been shown that very few staff currently have access to professional training or National Vocational Qualifications (NVQs) (Social and Health Care Workforce Group 1998). This highlights the current importance of on-the-job training as a way for staff to extend their repertoire of skills.

Developing skills in reminiscence work

There is now a considerable literature outlining the value of reminiscence in work with older people (Bornat 1993). In the UK, the pioneering Age Exchange Reminiscence Project provides an example of the way in which staff working in group settings can acquire techniques which they can incorporate into their day-to-day work. It involves workers who have been trained by Age Exchange working with staff and users over a six-week period. This is to help ensure that reminiscence becomes not simply a one-off experience but something that users can enjoy on a permanent basis (Arigho 1998).

In one case, Hammersmith and Fulham social services department paid for two Age Exchange reminiscence workers to work in a day centre for clients with dementia. The project showed staff how they needed to acknowledge that participants had very different histories. This meant that reminiscence topics could not be specific to one cultural group. Equally, when the clients' ages ranged from 70–95, even the popular songs that were important to them would be different.

The reminiscencing did not just involve visual or aural memories. It was especially noticeable that sensory triggers, such as mothballs or the feel of different fabrics elicited responses from people with severe dementia. In this case, additional continuity was obtained by the day centre's continuing to employ one of the reminiscence workers on a freelance basis.

User views about day care x

It was noted above that, since the changes in community care, local authorities have sharpened their policies towards the type of day care they are likely to fund. This will probably accentuate the distinctions between venues which are primarily social clubs and those which provide day care. However, for many older people, the most valued aspect of day care is the social contact it engenders (Pahl 1988b).

If increasing levels of frailty are to be found among those attending day centres, then one of the major skills required by day care staff will be to provide care which takes account of the impact of users' disabilities without losing the social aspects and companionship which are most valued by older people themselves. Here, the experience of people with dementia at day care provides an example of the expertise required in integrating the two.

In some cases, users' reaction to day care will be influenced by their own personalities. As one carer pointed out, her husband's reluctance to attend day care reflected his personality traits over a lifetime: 'My husband's never been a clubby sort of man' (Levin, Moriarty and Gorbach 1994).

In other instances, dementia leads to a loss of confidence in social situations. One woman with dementia explained: 'It seemed a long time and I was glad to get home. My memory is not as good as it was and I would rather not go than say the wrong thing or upset someone' (Moriarty and Webb 2000, p.62).

This last quotation came from a study which included interviews with 45 people with dementia attending day care, of whom 34 were able to talk about the service. In the context of the increasing interest in how the fulfilment of occupational need relates to well-being (Perrin 1997; Perrin and May 2000), it was striking that comments from the people with dementia themselves suggested that undertaking activities they enjoyed was an important component of whether or not they enjoyed the service. Women have traditionally predominated at day care and one of the issues raised by some of the male participants was the impact of this gender imbalance: 'We keep away from the ladies because they are noisy. I lie down and keep quiet'.

The importance of responding to user preferences will be discussed later when the question of what should happen when people refuse to attend day care is considered further.

Not every day care venue will be able to have access to innovative arts and activity programmes or specially-trained reminiscence workers. The example of Poplar Farm on the next page shows that it is still possible to draw on users' preferences as the framework for the activities offered at day care.

Matching activities to users' preferences

Poplar Farm is a local authority day centre in the London Borough of Hillingdon that has places for 12 people with dementia each day. Service times are standard, with clients generally arriving at 10.00 a.m. and leaving at 3.00 p.m. The small size of the unit is felt to make it easier for clients to feel more relaxed. Activities include weaving, reminiscencing, and discussion groups. Staff experience suggests that the activities which men attending the centre seem to prefer include talking to each other, playing dominoes and some of the more physical activities such as carpet bowls, skittles and indoor gardening.

Supporting carers

There are four major reasons why day care needs to be included as a major part of any strategy to support carers.

First, a high proportion of older people who attend day care are supported by carers (Twigg and Atkin 1994; Twigg, Atkin and Perring 1990).

Second, day care is able to operate in combination with other more direct forms of carer support. For example, carers can attend support groups held in day hospitals and day centres without having to make separate arrangements to look after the person for whom they care. In the same way, providing day care and short stays (respite) in the same venue is an option favoured by many carers. It means that the person for whom they care will be in familiar surroundings and, depending upon the staff rota system in operation, there may also be improved continuity of care if staff are able to work in both the day care and short stay sections.

Third, day care tends to be more acceptable to many carers than other forms of service, such as short stays, because they perceive it as more beneficial to the person for whom they care (Curran 1996; Levin *et al.* 1994).

Finally, the literature on caring shows that many carers use services in the absence of support from other family members or friends (Lewis and Meredith 1988; Qureshi and Walker 1989; Wenger 1997). In this context, day care often provides their only regular source of a break.

These advantages should not imply that areas of dissatisfaction with the service do not exist. Although there are examples of extended day care for older people, the majority of day care for older people still generally takes place between 10.00 a.m. and 4.00 p.m. This may not accord with the preferences of older people and their carers. For example, in the morning, there are often inconvenient delays between visits from home care and the arrival time of transport to day care. Equally, many carers find it hard to maintain hobbies and leisure interests because of the lack of availability of care in the evening.

The hours are also often unsuited to supporting carers who wish to remain in paid employment (Levin *et al.* 1994). This is a disappointing situation as many studies have suggested that there are clear advantages when people are able to combine caring responsibilities with paid employment. These benefits include:

- having time away from caring (Levin, Sinclair and Gorbach 1989; Levin *et al.* 1994)

- mitigating the effect of caring upon current income (Caring Costs 1996)

- mitigating the effect of caring upon pension rights and income in old age (Ginn and Arber 1996)

- for employers, avoiding re-training and recruitment costs caused when carers leave paid employment (Carers in Employment Group 1995).

The relative unavailability of extended day care for older people contrasts with developments in home care and day care for adults with mental health problems over the last few years. Since the community care changes, it is now far more usual to provide home care in the evenings and over the weekend. In one study, twenty-two of the forty nine home care users received the service over the weekend. By contrast, just six of the forty-six people receiving day care at the weekend (Moriarty and Webb 2000). A similar contrast can be drawn with the number of resource centres for adults with mental health problems which operate from 9.00 a.m. to 9.00 p.m. These have increased steadily and are seen as according with the preferences of service users and also of reducing the likelihood of admission to in-patient units because of the lack of an-out-of hours service.

An increase in the availability of extended day care for older people also raises the question of whether day care might help with the changes arising from women's increased participation in the labour force. Although there is now more interest in developing family-friendly employment policies, this has tended to be couched in terms of supporting parents with children. Such practices may be predicated upon an under-estimate of the number of people in paid employment who also care for a disabled or older adult. In fact, one survey of staff working in social services departments concluded that, at 27 per cent, the proportion of people caring for an older adult or disabled person was as high as that caring for a child aged 0–12 (McFarlane 2000). Overall, Government estimates suggest that around 11 per cent of all employees are carers of disabled or older adults (Her Majesty's Government 1999).

Discussion

Day care in the context of other services

There is some evidence that day care does have benefits in comparison with other services. Macdonald *et al.* (1982) compared four groups of older people matched by dependency and probability of dementia across hospital wards, residential homes, day hospitals and day centres. Over a nine-month period, the greatest improvements were seen in those attending day centres. Among people with dementia living in the community, day care users have consistently been shown to have more severe dementia than non-users (Levin *et al.* 1989; Levin *et al.* 1994; O'Connor *et al.* 1989). The receipt of day care has been shown to be associated with a reduced likelihood of entry into long-term care among a group of older people with dementia who had received a local authority community care assessment (Andrew *et al.* 2000).

Limitations of existing research on day care

The next question is whether these benefits are better met, or might be better met, in the future, by any other service? This is where the limitations of existing research on day care become most apparent. In writing this chapter, it quickly became clear that there was a shortage of studies with an evaluative design which enable proper comparisons to be made within and between different day care services. This means that decisions about the amount and type of day care available within a given locality are often made on the basis of historical spending and in the absence of reliable evidence to underpin them. Even where useful accounts describing the setting up and day-to-day running of specific services do exist, they are often only published in the grey literature and may not appear when databases are searched.

Given the limited resources for service evaluation, an equally important issue is what type of funded research might best lead to real improvements in the service. For example, high levels of depression have been found among older people living at home (Banerjee *et al.* 1996; Crawford *et al.* 1998) and in long-term care (Schneider, Mann and Netten 1997). Many referrals for day care give 'social isolation' as the reason for requesting the service. Reports from day care users certainly suggest that they rate day care as having had a positive impact upon their social contacts. However, because studies have tended to concentrate upon users of a single day care service or have compared different types of day care user, very little information exists on comparing people attending day care with those who do not. If one of the purposes of day care is to reduce social isolation and improve opportunities for companionship, it seems clear that there is a real need for information on whether and in what ways the experiences of day care users differ from those who do not attend.

In the same way, there has been very little attention to using information from people who are reluctant to attend day care as a way of making alterations and improvements to the service. Although the most frequent reason for stopping day care is entry into long-term care, a high proportion of new referrals leave after one or two visits (Salter 1992). It is also not uncommon for people to be asked to leave day care, either because the level of assistance they require is too high or because of behavioural problems (Levin *et al.* 1994). In this context, an examination of the interaction between personal preferences, dissatisfaction with the activities available, and the atmosphere and eligibility criteria which operate in individual centres would be a very useful source of inquiry.

Lessons for the future

Day care with other client groups may provide some useful pointers for developing services for older people. These include extending the resource centre model to offer a 24-hour service in which overnight care, advice and information, and appointments with health and social care professionals could all be provided. Greater emphasis upon using day care as a way to extend opportunities for learning and new activities would help improve the range and quality of its operation.

There have always been problems in mainstreaming innovative developments. This is demonstrated by the examples of some of the schemes described in this chapter which actually began some years ago. Staff working in day care need access both to information which could help them in adapting their own service and to training which could help them extend their own skills as workers.

In describing day care for older people, the chapter has included many references to the experiences of older people with dementia. This reflects the high proportion of people with dementia to be found in many day care settings. It also shows where dementia care can provide a lead in innovative practices in working with older people. In considering the future role of day care, there is another lesson to be learned from the experience of many older people with dementia.

The importance of helping users retain their capacity to enjoy the company of others and to offer and receive friendship should not be under-estimated.

The experience of people with dementia is also apt in that it reinforces how it is possible to obtain views from service users. In developing models of day care for older people, the most important point to acknowledge is that:

> 'Old people' are not, and never have been, a single, simple category. They are divided by gender, class, income, race, by multiple individual characteristics, and also by age; people in their sixties may – or may not – be very different from those in their nineties. (Thane 2000, p.459)

This chapter has aimed to show how, by adapting itself to the changing preferences of different types of user, day care can renew itself in ways which ultimately strengthen its place within the range of community and long-term care services.

Acknowledgements

I should like to acknowledge the expertise of the following people in providing specific information for this chapter: Lesley Curtis, Cassandra Fleming, Kulbir Gill, Robert Hawes, Deborah Haworth, Olive McManus, Ann Netten, Wendy Pugh and Gordon Slack.

References

Andrew, T., Moriarty, J., Levin, E. and Webb, S. (2000) 'Outcome of referral to social services departments for people with cognitive impairment.' *International Journal of Geriatric Psychiatry 15*, 5, 401–405.

Arigho, B. (1998) 'The Age Exchange Reminiscence Project at White Gables Day Care Centre.' In P. Schweitzer (ed) *Reminiscence in Dementia Care.* London: Age Exchange Theatre Trust.

Atkin, K. and Rollings, J. (1993) *Community Care in a Multi-Racial Britain.* London: HMSO.

Audit Commission (2000a) *Charging with Care: How Councils Charge for Home Care* (National Report). Abingdon: Audit Commission Publications.

Audit Commission (2000b) *Forget Me Not: Mental Health Services for Older People.* Abingdon: Audit Commission Publications.

Bacon, V. and Lambkin, C. (1997) 'The relationship between delivery of day care services for older people and the design of day unit premises.' *Ageing and Society 17*, 1, 41–64.

Banerjee, S., Shamash, K., Macdonald, A.J.D. and Mann, A.H. (1996) 'Randomised trial of effect of intervention by psychogeriatric team on depression in frail elderly people at home.' *British Medical Journal 313*, 1058–1061.

Bennett, N., Jarvis, L., Rowlands, O., Singleton, N. and Hasleden, L. (1996) *Living in Britain: Results from the 1994 General Household Survey.* London: HMSO.

Blakemore, K. and Boneham, M. (1994) *Age, Race and Ethnicity: A Comparative Approach.* Buckingham: Open University Press.

Bornat, J. (1993) *Reminiscence Reviewed.* Buckingham: Open University Press.

Bowling, A., Farquar, M. and Grundy, E. (1993) 'Who are the consistently high users of health and social services? A follow up study two and a half years later of people aged 85+ at baseline.' *Health and Social Care in the Community 1,* 277–287.

Burningham, S. (1991) 'Good practice: Homeshare daycare Ipswich.' *Alzheimer's Disease Society Newsletter* (October), 8.

Butt, J., Box, L. and Cook, S.L. (1999) *Respect: Learning Materials for Social Care Staff Working with Black and Minority Ethnic Older People.* London: Race Equality Unit.

Butt, J. and Mirza, K. (1996) *Social Care and Black Communities.* London: HMSO.

Carers in Employment Group (1995) *Carers in Employment: A Report on the Development of Policies to Support Carers at Work.* London: The Princess Royal Trust for Carers.

Caring Costs (1996) *The True Cost of Caring: A Survey of Carers' Lost Income.* London: Caring Costs Alliance.

Carter, J. (1981) *Day Services for Adults.* London: George Allen and Unwin.

Carter, P. and Everitt, A. (1998) 'Conceptualising practice with older people: Friendship and conversation.' *Ageing and Society 18,* 1, 79–99.

Cm 4192-I (1999) Royal Commission on Long Term Care *With Respect to Old Age: Long Term Care – Rights and Responsibilities.* London: Stationery Office.

Cm 4392 (1999) *Learning to Succeed: A New Framework for Post-16 Learning.* London: Stationery Office.

Crawford, M.J., Prince, M., Menezes, P. and Mann, A.H. (1998) 'The recognition and treatment of depression in older people in primary care.' *International Journal of Geriatric Psychiatry 13,* 3, 172–176.

Curran, J. (1996) 'The impact of day care on people with dementia.' *International Journal of Geriatric Psychiatry 11,* 813–817.

Currie, A., McAllister-Williams, R. H. and Jacques, A. (1995) 'A comparison study of day hospital and day centre attenders.' *Health Bulletin 53,* 6, 365–372.

Department of Health (1999) *Community Care Statistics: Day and Domiciliary Personal Social Services for Adults.* London: Department of Health.

Department of Health (2001) *Fairer Charging Policies for Home Care and Other Non-Residential Services.* London: Department of Health.

Gibson, F. and Whittington, D. (1995) *Day Care in Rural Areas.* York: Joseph Rowntree Foundation.

Gilleard, C.J., Belford, H., Gilleard, E., Whittick, J.E. and Gledhill, K. (1984) 'Emotional distress amongst the supporters of the elderly mentally infirm.' *British Journal of Psychiatry 145,* 172–177.

Ginn, J. and Arber, S. (1996) 'Patterns of employment, gender, and pensions: The effect of work history on older women's non-state pensions.' *Work, Employment and Society 10,* 3, 469–490.

Goss, T. (2000) 'Caring for the Carers – Improving Care Management.' Paper presented at the conference A New Agenda for Dementia Care – Raising Service Standards, London.

Her Majesty's Government (1999) *Caring about Carers: A National Strategy for Carers.* London: Department of Health. http://www.doh.gov.uk/pub/docs/doh/care/pdf

Jerrome, D. (1992) *Good Company: An Anthropological Study of Old People in Groups.* Edinburgh: Edinburgh University Press.

Laslett, P. (1989) *A Fresh Map of Life: The Emergence of the Third Age.* London: Weidenfeld & Nicholson.

Levin, E., Moriarty, J. and Gorbach, P. (1994) *Better for the Break.* London: HMSO.

Levin, E., Sinclair, I. and Gorbach, P. (1989) *Families, Services and Confusion in Old Age.* Aldershot: Avebury.

Lewis, J. and Meredith, B. (1988) *Daughters Who Care: Daughters Caring for Mothers at Home.* London: Routledge.

Macdonald, A.J.D., Mann, A.H., Jenkins, R., Richard, L., Godlove, C. and Rodwell, G. (1982) 'An attempt to determine the impact of four types of care upon the elderly in London by the study of matched groups.' *Psychological Medicine 12*, 193–200.

McFarlane, L. (2000) 'Managing a Dual Role: Working Carers in Social Services.' Paper presented at the conference Evaluation for Practice, Huddersfield.

Moriarty, J. and Webb, S. (2000) *Part of Their Lives: Community Care for People with Dementia.* Bristol: The Policy Press.

National Consumer Council (1995) *Charging Consumers for Social Services: Local Authority Policy and Practice.* London: National Consumer Council.

Netten, A. and Curtis, L. (2000) *Unit Costs of Health and Social Care.* Canterbury: Personal Social Services Research Unit, University of Kent.

O'Connor, D.W., Pollitt, P.A., Brook, C.P.B. and Reiss, B.B. (1989) 'The distribution of services to demented elderly people living in the community.' *International Journal of Geriatric Psychiatry 4*, 339–344.

Office for National Statistics (1998) *Social Trends 28.* London: Stationery Office.

Pahl, J. (1988a) 'Day services for elderly people: Misunderstandings and mixed metaphors.' In J. Morton (ed) *New Approaches to Day Care for Elderly People: Proceedings of an Ageing Update Conference.* London: Age Concern Institute of Gerontolgy.

Pahl, J. (1988b) *Day Services for Elderly People in the Medway Health District.* Canterbury: Health Services Research Unit, University of Kent.

Perrin, T. (1997) 'Occupational need in dementia care: A literature review and implications for practice.' *Health Care in Later Life 2*, 3, 166–176.

Perrin, T. and May, H. (2000) *Wellbeing in Dementia.* Edinburgh: Churchill Livingstone.

Powell, J. and Lovelock, R. (1987) 'The role of consumers' views in the evaluation of services: A case study – the travelling day hospital.' *Social Services Research 1*, 1, 16–29.

Qureshi, H. and Walker, A. (1989) *The Caring Relationship: Elderly People and their Families.* Basingstoke: MacMillan.

Salter, C. (1992) 'The day centre: A way of avoiding society's risk.' *Critical Social Policy 3*, 2, 17–23.

Schneider, J., Mann, A. and Netten, A. (1997) 'Residential care for elderly people: An exploratory study of quality measurement.' *Mental Health Research Review 4*, 12–15.

Seed, P. (1996) *Is Day Care Still at the Crossroads?* London: Jessica Kingsley Publishers.

Sepänem, R. (1998) 'Day care: Young and old together.' *Journal of Dementia Care 6*, 2, 18–19.

Social and Health Care Workforce Group (1998) *Social Services Workforce Analysis Main Report.* London: Employers' Organisation.

Social Services Inspectorate (1998) *They Look After their Own, Don't They? Inspection of Community Care Services for Black and Ethnic Minority Older People.* London: Department of Health.

Tester, S. (1989) *Caring by Day: A Study of Day Care Centres for Older People.* London: Centre for Policy on Ageing.

Thane, P. (2000) *Old Age in English History: Past Experiences, Present Issues.* Oxford: Oxford University Press.

Trejo, L. (1998) Workshop presentation at the American Society on Aging 4th International Conference on Long Term Care Case Management, 'Case/Care Management at the Crossroads: Which Way to Quality?' San Diego.

Twigg, J. and Atkin, K. (1994) *Carers Perceived: Policy and Practice in Informal Care.* Buckingham: Open University Press.

Twigg, J., Atkin, K. and Perring, C. (1990) *Carers and Services: A Review of Research.* London: HMSO.

Walker, A. (1995) 'Integrating the family into the mixed economy of care.' In I. Allen and E. Perkins (eds) *The Future of Family Care for Older People.* London: HMSO.

Warrington, J. and Eagles, J.M. (1996) 'A comparison of cognitively impaired attenders and their co-resident carers at day hospitals and day centres in Aberdeen.' *International Journal of Geriatric Psychiatry 11,* 251–256.

Wenger, G.C. (1997). 'Social networks and the prediction of elderly people at risk.' *Aging and Mental Health 1,* 4, 311–320.

CHAPTER 7

Trends and Aspirations in Day Services for Older People

Susan Hunter and Glenda Watt

The quality of social work practice with older people has been much criticised for its service-led approach, for its focus on narrowly practical solutions
and for its reliance on unqualified staff to undertake the bulk of the work
even though services for older people consume the lion's share of local authority expenditure on social services (CIPFA 1998/9). The NHS and Community Care Act 1990, many of the provisions of which had been triggered
by political and professional concerns about services to older people, represented an opportunity to reshape services in a number of ways. These
included the development of needs-led assessment and care management,
the promotion of packages of care and service development, which gave
priority and emphasis to maintaining older people in their own homes.

Ten years on and reinforced by the publication of *Modernising Community
Care* in 1998 (Scottish Office 1998), one might have expected day services
for older people to feature prominently in the practice and research literature
as a key component in care packages, especially for frail older people. With
the possible exception of the field of dementia practice, and in strong
contrast to other domains of practice such as learning disabilities, there is sur-
prisingly little detailed practice writing about day services for older people.
Indeed, as we shall argue later, the deep changes in service aspirations and development which reflect considerations of inclusion as well as welfare and
which characterise services for most other vulnerable groups, are only just

beginning to take root in services for older people. Initiatives such as 'Better Government for Older People' (All Our Futures 2000), which promote partnership between older people, local policy makers and service providers, are a reflection of this trend.

While the reasons for this probably include pervasive ageism within society as a whole and a lack of professional champions (Marshall 1990), the comparatively under-developed baseline from which services for older people are developing is all too plain. Furthermore, research and evaluation of practice developments in the area have been minimal and such writing as exists is primarily descriptive.

We have therefore taken as our focus for this chapter a number of initiatives that reflect changing trends in service development, in user aspirations, and in policy expectations. After setting the background against which these developments are taking place and providing an account of them, we reflect on their strengths and weaknesses and consider the implications for future developments.

Scene setting

The use of the term 'day services' rather than 'day care' in this volume signals the increasing attention being given to individual support as opposed to building-based care. However, it makes sense to start with the classic definition by Tester (1989) from more than a decade ago:

> A day care service offers communal care, with paid or voluntary carers, in a setting outside the user's home. Individuals come or are brought to use the services, which are available for at least four hours during the day, and return home on the same day. (p.37)

The historical roots of day care for older people are multiple and diverse. Much of the policy literature is characterised by debate and definitional refinements which attempt to clarify the distinctions between day care, day services, day hospitals, lunch clubs and social clubs (Carter 1981; Tester 1989). The post World War II era saw rapid developments, especially in psychiatric day hospitals, geriatric day hospitals and day centres, culminating in the rapid expansion of local authority services at the end of the 1960s. However, this growth has been described as 'unplanned' and 'untrammelled' (Tester 1989) resulting in the diversity described in more detail below.

Under the terms of the above definition of day care for older people it is possible to find all permutations of location (from purpose-built centres to hospitals to residential homes to church halls); of service provider (from the statutory social work sector to health to voluntary organisations); of intensity of access (from a few hours to several days a week); and, most critically, of purpose (from social stimulation to care and assessment to rehabilitation and therapy, and frequently to respite for carers).

Since their heyday of expansion in the early 1970s, day hospitals have now revised their role and reduced the number of people who attend. The service is now conceptualised as a therapeutic one offering assessment and treatment rather than social support, followed by transfer of people on to day centres or other community services as soon as possible.

Up to the present, day care provided by social services has tended to reflect Tester's definition quite closely with large stand-alone units catering for about 30 people between 10.00 a.m. and 3.00 p.m. once or twice a week or, to a lesser extent, similar provision within residential units. There are often links between social work department day care units and local voluntary groups and day hospitals. The closeness of the day care staff to social work assessment colleagues and to primary health care varies but, with the possible exception of services catering for people with dementia, tends to be under-developed.

A common pattern in the voluntary sector is for local organisations to identify a need for a service, sometimes linked with the availability of a building; for example, an upgraded church hall. They begin in a small way, perhaps without any paid staff at all, and then may move on to employing a paid coordinator to recruit, train and support the volunteers. The next step is to apply for additional funding to pay for one or more care staff and to look for premises and transport of their own. The size of the development varies, as does the access to facilities for personal care. Most organisations raise funds. In some instances these are used to meet core expenditure and in others the benefits bought are more likely to be special outings or events for members. The reliance of some local authorities on volunteers to establish and run day services for older people, in a way which is not found in services for other vulnerable groups, is a reflection of the ageism referred to above.

Private sector day care is rather an unknown quantity and there is a gap in the market. Some residential or nursing homes will take limited numbers of people at any time from 7.30 a.m to 9.00 p.m. at an approximate cost of £25 per day.

From this plethora of services has emerged the idea of specialist provision and resource centres. Although specialist provision has drawn attention to specific needs, allowed models of good practice to develop and been able to access particular development funds, it carries with it the risk of marginalisation and offers an excuse for not developing mainstream services properly.

A prime example of this is in the field of dementia. While many dementia sufferers or people with functional mental health problems attend non-specialist day care centres and may find themselves well integrated and involved in the daily activities, those with more advanced dementia are more likely to require specialist provision. This seems to work particularly well where small groups are matched with high ratios of voluntary helpers who in turn are well trained and have good professional support. It is also clear that in the main, minority ethnic elders have wanted to have their own centres which meet their specific social, cultural, recreational and language needs and provide services such as information, advice, befriending and social contact that mainstream services have failed to provide (Bowes and Dar 2000). The increasing longevity of older people with learning difficulties has generated debate about where primary service responsibility should rest – with services for older people or with services for people with disabilities (Walker and Walker 1998).

Ideas of what constitutes a resource centre vary. In the main they offer a one-door access to advice and information about a range of matters likely to affect older people and their carers. It was not until the early 1980s that it was recognised that carers required relief and support from their caring role, and since then day care programmes have increasingly included the needs of carers. There is now legislation and dedicated funding to develop specific services for carers including the provision of respite (Carers Services and Recognition Act 1995; Department of Health 1999). Resource centres can also be places where local staff meet and exchange information about vulnerable people; a centre from which domiciliary staff are managed; a place which provides day care and sometimes overnight stays; somewhere to do the laundry and have a bath, to see the chiropodist, get a hot meal at a reasonable price and meet friends as well as providing the base for a dispersed alarm service. More recently, resource centres have been developed which encompass both residential and day care provision, operating seven days per week with local groups also using the premises.

Current issues in the delivery of day services

As already suggested, conventional day care assumed service outwith the older person's home by paid or voluntary carers for at least four hours a day. As the primacy of service-led approaches has given way to more person-centred orientations, so has the definition of day care softened to the broader contemporary notion of day services. In response to community care and these more holistic approaches, contemporary service aims have been recast in the ways described below.

From a service-led to a person-centred approach

Traditional assessment of older people has been criticised for being overly functionally oriented, deficit-focused and service-led to the exclusion of the individuality of the person. There have been attempts, predating community care, to re-orientate assessments of older people away from purely functional concerns and towards quality of life. The biographical approach to assessment is an example (Key 1989). Interestingly, this approach was found to work well except in crisis situations where rapid decisions were required.

These 'crisis' decisions typically involve social workers, who have been found to be notable by their absence in the lives of older people requiring community support (Samuel *et al.* 1991).

One innovative way of working is person-centred planning. It is emerging in all community care groups, though it is probably most developed in the field of learning disability and it is only just beginning to be applied within services and assessments for older people. Person-centred planning (PCP) is an umbrella term encompassing a number of assessment and planning tools that share certain features:

- the individual and his/her aspirations as the starting point

- the attempt to match resources to individuals

- an understanding that only some of these resources will be services in the traditional sense

- a realisation these will only be delivered in part by professionals – the expertise and greater knowledge of community members may be more relevant and potent.

Sanderson, Kennedy and Ritchie (1997) describe an evolution in approaches from key-working, familiar in many social care settings, which was originally about 'fixing' the individual; to approaches based on training and rehabilitation; to a subsequent emphasis on coordination of professional activity; to the recent person-centred approach, which emphasises the centrality of the individual aspirations and options for individuals to transform their lifestyles. There is a philosophical similarity with the social model of disability here in so far as the aspiration is that, 'The job of services is not to fix the individual but to reduce the restrictions they face and to support them in leading their own life' (Sanderson *et al.* 1997, p.34).

The reasons the approach has been slower to take root in services for older people are at least twofold: an absence of champions and activists compared with other fields such as disability (Marshall 1990), and the impact of ageism in terms of attitudes and expectations both of older people themselves and many, though not all, professionals. This has led to the dominance of ideas around disengagement at worst and protection at best, as opposed to the developmental assumptions that characterise person-centred planning. It therefore comes as no surprise that those who have attempted to use this approach report considerable resistance and scepticism from professional carers and reticence from users who do not wish to 'upset' people. Nonetheless it represents both a challenge and a way forward for not only meeting the dependency needs of older people but also for recognising that older people still have lifestyle aspirations and remain citizens and members of their communities despite their frailty.

Although we could find no examples of PCP being used in day services for older people, some initiatives are developing in the wider field of services for older people. What is being reported at the moment is an influence of PCP approaches on existing ways of working rather than outright adoption of the methods. One example is a residential unit where the individuals did not wish to undertake PCP but the techniques were used to help these individuals spend their time better, such as the former shepherd who was helped to go to the Highland Show and the lady who was linked up with a children's community group (Wilson 2000). The tools of PCP have also been used to collect information in the context of community care assessments and to 'problem solve' in situations of impasse between staff and users of service (Welsh 2000).

From building to person focus

The last major review of day care, which took place towards the end of the 1980s, brought into focus the extent to which services should be centre-based or not (Tester 1989). More recently, Brearley and Mandelstam (1992) have argued that two dimensions to service development can be discerned: one concerned with the extent to which services are building-based – in other words, the extent to which people go to buildings or services go to people wherever they happen to be – and the other concerned with the balance between provision of care and promotion of empowerment through self-development.

Though clearly related to Tester's conception, Brearley and Mandelstam take the distinction a stage further by couching the contrast between care and stimulating activity in the language of empowerment, and by introducing the concept of services going out to people rather than vice versa. Although outreach models – for example, day care buses in rural areas – are not entirely new in day services, such developments are now driven by considerations of flexibility, user-responsiveness and person-centred planning rather than essentially pragmatic and logistical considerations.

In other client sectors this debate has progressed considerably; indeed the argument has been won. This is particularly true in the field of learning disabilities where activists, parents and professionals have campaigned so effectively for access to mainstream, community-based resources that most authorities now have policies which effectively reverse the trend that used to favour building-based, segregated service development.

From care to empowerment

A long-standing and familiar debate relates to whether services should be oriented towards care and rehabilitation or towards education, leisure and empowerment. One organising principle for service development was the distinction between 'day care services' and 'day facilities' (Morton 1989). Day care meant the provision of social and medical care, assessment and rehabilitation together with long-term relief and support of carers. The provision of day facilities, however, offers a greater emphasis on education, community activities, social contact and stimulation. Brearley and Mandelstam (1992, p.1) suggest that these distinctions are not purely a matter of semantics but reflect the 'fundamental philosophical and operational dilemmas' described above. We would argue that these tensions have persisted into the era of legislated community care and been reinforced by it. However, the aspirations of the community care legislation associated with maximising user choice and control, together with efficiency and effectiveness, have transformed the discourse around these tensions into one of 'welfare' versus 'rights' and 'targeting' versus 'citizenship'.

These are, however, competing discourses that cannot ultimately be reconciled in a single day care service or model. The way forward for service development is to be found in the creation of strategic alliances with health on the one hand, to provide a continuum of services to targeted vulnerable individuals, and with education and leisure services on the other, to develop and provide support for older people to access local amenities, community centre activities and adult education classes. Such developments will be facilitated, and possibly required, by recent guidance to health and social work on creating inter-agency links, and by recent changes in local government that promote inter-departmental planning and corporate responsibilities (Scottish Office 1998).

The Community Care (Direct Payments) Act 1996 aimed to promote choice, empowerment and the meeting of individual need. Although initially a contentious issue, older people have been eligible to apply for direct payments since June 2000. This mechanism should provide an additional pathway to individual needs-led, rather than service-led, support. However, a recent study (Witcher *et al.* 2000) of direct payments in Scotland found low levels of implementation in general, lack of representativeness across user groups and confusion about the provision amongst local authority staff. If this is indicative the road to widespread advantage to older people will not be straightforward.

From low intensity services to packages of care

There were 82 day centres in Scotland providing 4753 places in 1983. By 1997 the number of day centres had increased by three-and-a-half times to 301 with a total of 7309 places. Around 15,000 older people were attending, 70 per cent of them on one or two days per week and only 8 per cent on five or more days. In 1997, 40 per cent of local authority day centres provided one day of attendance per week, 38 per cent offered two days, 13 per cent were giving three days, 5 per cent had four days and 8 per cent had access to five or more days (Scottish Office 1997). This low intensity of use seems more suited to recreational or educational service aims. If this is a service targeted at very frail people the intensity of use is clearly unlikely to meet the levels of need unless it is part of a more extensive package of care.

We also have evidence, typified by local authority service reviews (Brace 1990; Goldberg and Connelly 1982), that suggests that although the other services most commonly used by day care users were home care and district nurses, the majority of users were not using a wide range of other community-based services. Where day care was offered alongside other services, there was a lack of integration into an overall package of managed care (Tibbitt 1987). Such ad hoc service delivery, combined with reported low levels of contact with field social workers, is no longer appropriate in the world of community care targeted on the most vulnerable people. Despite the aspirations to target services, there seems to be a mismatch here.

Assuring quality and good practice

Notwithstanding the inspection and regulation requirements in residential care that were strengthened by the community care legislation of 1990, the first document to give a high profile to service standards for older people which were driven by social values rather than buildings' health and safety requirements was *Homes are for Living In* (Department of Health/Social Services Inspectorate 1998). This report drew attention to the significance of choice, dignity, fulfilment and a caring, homely environment in achieving quality of life for older people in residential care. These values are reflected in subsequent guidance on day care (Social Services Inspectorate 1992), which endorses and quotes the values and principles developed in relation to day services for people with long-term mental health problems (Swallow 1989). It proposes that day services should be:

- comprehensive and coordinated with the rest of the network
- accessible
- friendly and informal
- flexible
- non-stigmatising

- providing opportunities to foster social contacts
- subject to monitoring and evaluation.

It also concludes that despite some differences between user groups many similarities emerge, which makes it possible to apply a generic framework posing questions such as: why are services being provided? by whom? for whom and with what aims and objectives?

Recent proposals for the regulation of care have set standards for staff training and qualification that will be applicable to day services and home care (Scottish Executive 1999, 2000). This reinforces the trend for quality assurance in day services.

The introduction of 'Best Value' (Scottish Office Development Department 1997) will further require that older people with community care needs and their carers are:

- supported in their own homes through an equitable provision of day care and allied services
- offered services in homely, local settings
- charged for the service in a fair way which does not disadvantage those on low incomes
- offered services that promote social inclusion.

In summary, good user-centred practice is likely to include support in people's own homes or local communities for more people than was true in the past. This will mean services that are local, accessible and informal in character, that pay attention to coordination and targeting and are sensitive to carer issues.

It follows that if 'there is no single entity "day care" or "day service", there is no one way forward for development' (Brearley and Mandelstam 1992, p.19). We believe that good practice will be achieved by reference to a set of aspirations and values that are applicable across a range of service designs and settings and staff groupings.

Examples from practice

In the absence of evaluative studies, we have selected several practice accounts that illustrate some of the issues described above. We reflect on whether these examples meet the challenges posed by recent thinking in policy and practice.

Aiming to be local and inclusive

There are few accounts giving examples of the kind of one-to-one individual support that is beginning to feature in services for people with learning disabilities (Hunter and Lewin 2000; Simons 1998). However, the projects described below in Falkirk, Sutton and Ipswich do begin to show how support can be provided outwith traditional building-based centres in ways that are more person-centred and practical.

'Home from Home' in Falkirk is described as an 'attempt by a small development team to push back the boundaries of community care, listen to what people with dementia are trying to tell us, and provide services that are as inclusive and ordinary as possible' (Mitchell 1998, p.17). It is a scheme for people with dementia in which four older people spend their day at the house of someone in their neighbourhood and a helper. It is described as the 'difference between going out to day care and going to a friend's for lunch' (p.16). Such a scheme has self-evident advantages of being local, familiar, small, domestic in scale and with the capacity for choice and flexibility. The 'hostesses' are described as mostly volunteers who undertake this once or twice a week on average. Over a three-year period some amazing stories of holidays together are recounted. There are also two groups for five people running five days a week, which provide self-employed status for the scheme's carers.

'Homeshare' in Sutton, though not focused on people with dementia, is comparable to Home from Home and is described as 'a form of day care for older people which offers them weekly visits to the homes of volunteers' (Dalley, Peretz-Brown and Seal 1995, p.4). The scheme serves vulnerable older people for whom the standard day centre is 'inappropriate'; it offers companionship with two or three other people in a domestic environment;

and it depends on volunteers both as 'home-sharers' and as drivers who are paid expenses.

Feedback from users and carers was generally enthusiastic. The homeliness, good meals, companionship and contact with the home-sharer's family and friends were positively viewed. The small number of negative comments related to group dynamics, which were resolved by seeking alternative arrangements. Carers saw the scheme as almost a treat rather than a service, so positive was its impact on the morale of their relatives; this contrasted with the experience of some whose relatives were reluctant to attend traditional day centres. Of particular importance to the carers was the perceived commitment of the home-sharers and the scheme's friendliness.

A similar scheme in Ipswich (Dalley *et al.* 1995), which has been running for longer and more explicitly within the authority's community care arrangements, has developed a pattern of two to three days' a week care for people at risk of institutionalisation. The home carers assume self-employed rather than volunteer status. Contrary to the fears that professionals express about continuity of care, this scheme has only lost two home carers in ten years. However, in common with the Sutton experience, women over 50 years old are the main source of recruitment as home carers, which is likely to have implications for their own fitness and availability over the years.

Some on-going issues appear to be the balance between informality and planned support; training and support issues around volunteers and staff; and costs, which are not necessarily cheaper. These accounts exemplify attempts at supporting individuals in their own communities, if not their own homes, which offer the advantage of maintaining links with other local people. The flexibility, informality and personalised attention successfully addressed some carers' concerns about traditional day centres.

This model, as suggested by the Falkirk project, may well suit homogeneous groupings of individuals based on gender or locality, whether rural or urban. It also has some versatility in so far as it is being used both for individuals who are still coping in the community but require support, as well as part of a care package for individuals with a degree of frailty and on the brink of institutional care. Interestingly, evaluation of the Sutton project revealed a vulnerable user group: 80 per cent over 80 years; 50 per cent with sensory disabilities; almost 66 per cent with restricted mobility; 40 per cent with mental health issues; and 73 per cent living alone. Care managers, however, indicated the scheme was for people with low to medium needs, some of whom did not see themselves as requiring services. In terms of eligibility and targeting, workers need to be alert to such discrepancies. Concerns raised by professionals related to how home-sharers communicated with case managers; whether 'volunteers' were being asked to take on too much; and how to ensure continuity.

The home-sharers themselves were happy with the level of dependence of their 'visitors', including 'confusion', but incontinence did seem to be a de-marcation line. Continuity had not been an issue but due to the typical age and life stage of the home-sharers, the Ispwich scheme was facing the loss of up to two-thirds of its very stable home carers group over a two-year period. So, planned replenishment of formal carers is an issue. Selection, training and induction processes typical of social work departments, and some support ar-rangements, were in place but may need to reflect an informality not charac-teristic of these services to date.

One tension raised in the Ipswich evaluation is the extent to which the very essence of the success and value of such schemes, namely their informal-ity and their friendliness, is jeopardised by expansion and incorporation into care planning processes. As community care and, in particular, the contract culture start to bite, tensions have begun to emerge between the 'informal' style of such schemes – which is one of their strengths – and the demands of care management, developing care packages, targeting and 'best value', all of which introduce formality and procedures into a previously informal arena.

It seems to us that one way round this would be replication within natural communities rather than expansion within service catchment areas. This would be a form of community building (O'Connell 1990). It would be im-portant to avoid a false assumption that services are for the truly frail while community support is for the less frail and has a preventive focus.

Aspiring to provide a continuum of care through collaboration

Despite an historical lack of coordination of day services with other services, there are some encouraging examples of how this can begin to be achieved including using building-based services as the starting point. Kay Park (within the Rosebank complex) in the west of Scotland and the Wade Centre in the Highlands demonstrate this.

Rosebank, a residential home for 40 people comprising four self-contained units, is described as providing 'a comprehensive and flexible package of care linking residential, daycare and community care with local resources' (Archibald and Carr 1995). Of particular interest is the unit within Rosebank for people with dementia. The initiative, called Kay Park, supports people at home as well as through day care and respite, and offers advice, support and counselling to carers as well as older people. Day care is offered in units of two hours, available flexibly throughout the day from 5.00 a.m. to 11 p.m., the most popular blocks being 8.00–12.00, 12.00–4.00 and 4.00–11.00 p.m. Some users attend once, others two or three times a week; occasionally the unit has accommodated full-time care in a crisis to enable a carer to continue caring.

The unit seemed to be able to respond to such varying demands. However as demand increases the pressure to adopt the more regimented patterns typical of day care intensifies. Although it is not joint funded by health and social work authorities, health services have provided support funding in specified ways on a tapering basis.

The Wade Centre (Cook 2000) is an innovative initiative that predates the community care legislation. It is a community unit funded by social work in a rural area of Scotland covering 1000 square miles. Its services are delivered from a small town though its resources are accessed by people living within 15 miles of the centre. Noteworthy features included the planned continuum of care offered: from residential care through sheltered and very sheltered housing, with the flexibility to provide extra personal care when required, to respite, day care, home care, meals on wheels, domiciliary alarms and some care management and assessment.

Because of the nature of the first group of day care users, a group of men very physically impaired as a result of strokes, the service developed in response to their needs rather than offering an existing programme. The service therefore had to address how to accommodate carers too anxious to leave their spouses; physical access; male-appropriate activities; the development of condition specific activities as in the case of stroke victims; and collaboration with other specialist services such as nursing, GPs and physiotherapists.

Involvement of the community in the centre grew through social events in which carers and users invited guests, through the use of the premises for community events and the holding of a benefits advice surgery in the centre once a week which was well used by the community. Some carer-specific groups were run, such as the support group for carers of relatives with dementia, which was run jointly with the charge nurse from the local hospital.

Obstacles included 'institutionalisation' of staff, which was described as a 'constant hazard'. One effect of the pressure on staff to meet diverse demands was a temptation to 'tidy up' individualised activities such as baths, to maximise staff time for communal activities rather than to reflect user choice and preference (Cook 2000). Training, exposure to other good services, proactive supervision, flexible and changing working patterns, as well as individual user reviews, were seen as the antidotes to this kind of institutionalisation.

These two projects demonstrate how a range of services can be developed in a way which provides a continuum of care to the older person and which addresses the carer agenda. Certainly the Wade Centre has begun also to develop collaborative initiatives with other professionals and gained experience of making the resource more community-friendly and thereby sustaining social inclusion.

It is interesting to note that both in these services and the home-based ones described earlier, their flexibility and informality, which is a central characteristic of their design and much valued by users, are threatened both by increasingly bureaucratic demands of the community care system and by staff attempts to manage workload pressures as the service expands. In this regard constant vigilance is clearly required. For existing services attempting to re-orientate their approach to become more person-centred, the persistence of institutionalised thinking among staff is a constant pitfall.

SADSA (South Ayrshire Dementia Support Association) is an organisation that epitomises many of the new developments in practice (Clarke 2000). It is a voluntary organisation that supports people with moderate and severe dementia. It was developed by a local professional in conjunction with carers, funded latterly through Mental Illness Specific Grant and Resource Transfer moneys. It provides individually tailored support (day centre attendance, home support, out and about in the community); it provides an intensive service (365 days of the year, users averaging four days a week); it promotes collaboration and partnership through its funding mix, by having seconded workers as well as project workers and the involvement of carers in project development; it provides continuity by adjusting support in line with changing circumstances, and reports that users are much more likely to be admitted to hospital or nursing home for medical reasons rather than a deterioration in their dementia. While there are some volunteers, support is provided primarily by paid workers with good conditions of service and appropriate training. It is not difficult to imagine how the next steps in relation to inclusion and community-building might be tackled through, for example, the recruitment of neighbourhood-based home supporters and the solid foundation of carer involvement might be extended to give users more of a voice also after the manner described below.

Aiming for empowerment and community involvement

In addition to reflecting certain of the aspirations of community care legislation, social inclusion and the empowerment of citizens have become something of a political mantra for the Blair Government. Initiatives such as 'Better Government for Older People' have provided funding to find ways of involving older people in decisions that affect their lives through the development of 28 pilot projects (All our Futures 2000). For frail older people who may have limited access to information, limited energy to spare and a habit of deference to expert opinion, the ambition for empowerment and participation through such means is difficult to realise but not impossible to achieve, as demonstrated by the examples from Edinburgh described below.

The Pentland Project (City of Edinburgh Council, undated) is a generic community care resource developed within and for a local neighbourhood over a ten-year period. Originally developed to work with people with dementia, it has now become an umbrella organisation for a wide range of groups including some children with special needs. Seven of the 15 groups which meet regularly serve older people specifically and encompass resources for older people with dementia, learning disabilities or mental health problems, or who are frail and housebound. There is also a lunch club and users may indeed attend other groups such as a smokers' group and the food cooperative. Funding is shared by the health service (paid via the social work department) and the community development worker is managed by community education. The project uses volunteers and has been very successful in raising funds, although its core funding position is unsatisfactory because of the impossibility of getting funding projections for the impending year. A particular feature of this project is the systematic way in which user views are sought through questionnaires and involvement in committees; the way it has developed from its early days reflects user wishes and recognised community needs.

The Springwell Project (Shand 2000) is not a generic resource but targets older people with functional mental illness. This tiny project, which is a collaborative partnership between health and social work, offers a resource for two hours a week to 12 people whose needs are not met by existing psychiatric services. The operational model is more social than medical with an emphasis on leisure, information and advice activities 'to support any existing medical interventions' (Shand 2000). Members (not 'patients', 'users' or 'clients') are involved in planning group activities. It is dependent on support from volunteers, voluntary transport through WRVS and other voluntary organisations and goodwill, for example rent-free premises such as the local library for the development of its second group which brings the project activity to four hours a week. Its aims are to link people into community resources where possible; inevitably, however, given the age and frailty of the group, some individuals have moved into nursing homes.

These projects show how older people, some of them quite frail, can be drawn into and be involved in mainstream resources, albeit in specialist groups. They provide evidence that user involvement can be achieved with dedicated worker time, and that community education may be a much under-used and perhaps under-appreciated resource in relation to older people. They also show that innovative initiatives, even those with a successful track record, continue to be at the mercy of 'soft' funding arrangements and find it difficult to secure their futures.

The projects also demonstrate that one way forward for social work could be to adopt a dual focus: on the one hand seeking collaboration with health services for very frail people who need care and therapy, and on the other working with education and community services on behalf of individuals wanting social participation and civic involvement. Notwithstanding the logic of this functional division, the use of the social model of disability and the adoption of a developmental assumption in relation to older people in the Springwell project, even if some individuals are eventually institutionalised, show how a person-centred philosophy and values can permeate both service orientations.

Meeting special needs

As suggested earlier, the debate about specialist as opposed to mainstream provision of services has been a vexed one, both ideologically and professionally. Historically specialist, expert services emerged in response to the inadequacies of existing services and were developed by 'champions' of the vulnerable group in question. Over time there seemed to be a tendency for such services to stagnate and become marginalised, with a consequent decline in service outcomes and morale. This process is particularly well demonstrated by the history of services for people with learning disabilities (Atkinson, Jackson and Walmsley 1997) and has generated a counter-ideology in the form of normalisation, namely the right of vulnerable citizens to access society's resources in ways valued by the mainstream community. Normalisation provides the precursor to the philosophy of inclusion to which most services now aspire. This poses an interesting dilemma for practitioners working with older people who have learning disabilities in so far as accessing mainstream services for older people may produce a less desirable experience for their clients (Walker and Walker 1998).

St. Helen's is a day centre in Edinburgh for people with learning difficulties which has developed a self-contained project to meet the requirements of its ageing population, a relatively new phenomenon amongst people with learning difficulties (Hogg 1997). The service comprises three outreach teams which support individuals in a variety of settings appropriate to each individual's circumstances – for example, at home or in local community resources – for up to three days a week. It aims to provide flexible support in familiar surroundings to maintain and support individual interests, skills and relationships. Central to its success has been the tailoring of support to individual need, an understanding that staff need to enter the users' world view rather than vice versa, a recognition that individuals will deteriorate and support will need to accommodate that and that eventually the service may become inappropriate or inadequate to the needs of some individuals.

Unlike the St. Helen's project, which developed organically out of an existing service, the MILAN organisation (MILAN 1998–99) is a free-standing resource in the same city. It was set up in 1991 in response to the perceived cultural inappropriateness of mainstream day care in meeting the befriending, information and advice needs of older Asian people in Edinburgh and the Lothians. Its objectives include providing a place for relaxation and reminiscence, sharing a meal and providing educational and recreational opportunities, and aimed to involve users in the development of the project.

The development of MILAN has been rather typical of those voluntary initiatives, described by Naina Patel (1990), that respond to insensitive or inaccessible mainstream services and remain under-resourced but ambitious. Due to limited resources it operates two days a week, only having access to transport for two days. It has 310 members ranging in age upwards from 50 years. There is one full-time development worker; all the other workers, who provide support, befriending, care assistance, information, advice and book-keeping and administration, are part-time. It is now seeking support to finance a purpose-built day centre, expanded to cater specifically for people with dementia and other disabilities and respite needs. Where the project is unusual is in bringing together Christian, Muslim and Hindu elders within the same service. It is not clear yet to what extent, if at all, subsequent generations from the ethnic communities will continue to seek separate provision and how successful current resources will be in developing multi-cultural services.

Both these projects are good examples of how services can respond to particular circumstances in flexible and individualised ways and can acknowledge the contribution of solidarity and mutual support as well as inclusion. The St. Helen's project seems a particularly good example of this. It is less clear how either project has been able to impinge on mainstream services to make them more accessible to a broader constituency. As the social movement for inclusion gains momentum throughout age ranges and life stages, services will increasingly be expected to meet this aspiration.

Conclusions and the challenge ahead

Prompted originally by the emergence of the welfare state and by the identification of groups of people as vulnerable and in need of support, day service provision has not been driven by an articulated philosophy but rather by the availability of existing institutional resources or newly developed ones, the goodwill of practitioners and voluntary endeavour. The result has been provision not only lacking in uniformity of application but also inadequately focused on the individual needs of recipients.

Professionals hoped that with the introduction of community care policies, a window of opportunity would open to develop both services and practice. However, as Harding remarks, the decade since the introduction of community care has seen an emphasis on targeting resources towards the most frail individuals at the expense of those services with preventive and inclusive capacities: 'Most day centres are places that provide "care" for the "frailest" and most "needy" rather than opportunities for a fuller, more productive and more interesting life' (Harding 1997, p.29). If this is true, it sets up an immediate tension between service aspirations and service delivery and militates against the development of initiatives such as the Pentland Project except within the broader context of community, as opposed to social work, activity.

Nonetheless, it is clear from the above descriptions of new initiatives in the field of day services for older people that there has been a move away from day care within Tester's definition and the search for unitary service characteristics. There is now a welcome diversification of day services. In the absence of an explicit national strategy for day care and well developed research activity, professionals have to fall back on such service aspirations and values as are available. Such guidance as exists points to the development of local, informal services, designed to maintain people in their own homes, delivered in collaboration with other services in ways which take into account individual need and degrees of frailty. Furthermore, there is an expectation that outcomes such as the exercise of choice and social inclusion will thereby be enhanced. As an increasing number of frail older people stay at home or in sheltered care, some services report beginning to favour home carers and supporters to enable individuals to access everyday activities in their own communities. Ultimately this will take away the necessity for building large day centres.

Examples of support for people in their own homes and communities do exist. These services are valued for their informality, but increasing requirements for monitoring threaten to intrude in ways that undermine that informality. Creating an environment which values community and voluntary effort while supporting professional service delivery is a delicate balance. The challenge for 'best value' and professional workers will be to find a balance between accountability and line management concerns on the one hand, and supporting responsiveness and innovation on the other.

While the search for a single model and all-encompassing definition of day care no longer makes any sense, recurring features of these new initiatives are their flexibility, their person-centred orientation and their intention to provide continuity and support community presence and involvement wherever possible.

In the wake of the raft of initiatives known as community care, best value and social inclusion, we now have a set of ambitious expectations in services and possibly in the public imagination. Though there is some way to travel, the emergence of innovative practice developments and the adoption of person-centred approaches, albeit on a limited scale, suggest that a change of climate in the way frail older people and their carers are supported not only in their own homes but in their communities is under way. We now need to be ready to evaluate the nature and impact of that change in a systematic fashion.

References

All Our Futures (2000) *Report of the Steering Committee of the Better Government for Older People Programme.* London. http://www.bettergovernmentforolderpeople.gov.uk/reference/pub161.htm

Archibald, C. and Carr, J. (1995) *Rosebank.* Stirling: Dementia Services Development Centre, University of Stirling and Age Concern.

Atkinson, D., Jackson, M., and Walmsley, J. (1997) *Forgotten Lives: Exploring the History of Learning Disability.* Kidderminster: BILD.

Bowes, A.M and Dar, N.S. (2000) 'Researching social care for minority ethnic older people: Implications of some Scottish research.' *British Journal of Social Work 30*, 305–321.

Brace, S. (1990) *Day Care for Older People in Lothian.* Available from West Lothian Social Work HQ, Cheviot House, Owen Square, Livingston EH54 6PW.

Brearley, P. and Mandelstam, P. (1992) *A Review of Literature 1986–1991 on Day Care Services for Adults.* London: HMSO.

Carter, J. (1981) *Day Services for Adults: Somewhere to Go.* London: George Allen and Unwin.

CIPFA (Chartered Institute of Public Finance and Accountancy) (1998/9) *Personal Social Services Statistics.* London: CIPFA.

City of Edinburgh Council (undated) Pentland Community Care Project: Interagency Evaluation. Second Draft. (unpublished).

Clarke, E. (2000) Personal communication. Project Manager, Ayr.

Cook, H. (2000) Personal communication. Community Care Coordinator, Highland Region.

Dalley, G., Peretz-Brown, F. and Seal, H. (1995) *Homeshare in Sutton: A Report of an Evaluation Study.* London: Centre for Policy on Ageing.

Department of Health (1999) *Caring about Carers: National Carers Strategy.* London: HMSO.

Department of Health/Social Services Inspectorate (1998) *Homes are for Living In.* London: HMSO.

Goldberg, M. and Connelly, N. (1982) *Effectiveness of Social Care for the Elderly.* London: Policy Studies Institute.

Harding, T. (1997) *A Life Worth Living: The Independence and Inclusion of Older People.* London: Help the Aged.

Hogg, J. (1997) 'Intellectual disability and ageing: Ecological perspectives from recent research.' *Journal of Intellectual Disability Research 41,* 136–143.

Hunter, S. and Lewin, M. (2000) *Stepping Out: A Report on the One Step Further Project.* Edinburgh: Edinburgh University and City of Edinburgh, Department of Social Work.

Key, M. (1989) 'The practice of assessing elders.' In O. Stevenson (ed) *Age and Vulnerability.* London: Edward Arnold/Age Concern.

Marshall, M. (1990) 'Proud to be old.' In E. McEwen (ed) *Age: The Unrecognised Discrimination.* London: Age Concern.

MILAN (Senior Welfare Council) (1998–99) *Annual Report 1998–99.* Edinburgh: MILAN (Senior Welfare Council).

Mitchell, R. (1998) 'Home from home by the fireside.' *Journal of Dementia Care 6,* 2, 16–17.

Morton, J. (ed) (1989) *New Approaches to Day Care for Elderly People.* Proceedings of an Ageing Update Conference, University of London 7 December 1988. London: King's College.

O'Connell, M (1990) *Community Building in Logan Square.* Evanston, Il: Center for Urban Affairs and Policy Research, Northwestern University.

Patel, N. (1990) *A Race Against Time: Social Service Provision to Black Elders.* London: Runymede Trust.

Samuel, E., Brace, S., Buckley, G. and Hunter, S. (1991) *Process and Preference: Assessment of Older People for Long-Stay Institutional Care.* Edinburgh: Central Research Unit, Scottish Office.

Sanderson, H., Kennedy, J., Ritchie, P. (1997) *People, Plans and Possibilities: Exploring Person-centred Planning.* Edinburgh: SHS.

Scottish Executive (1999) *Regulating Care and the Social Services Workforce: Consultative Paper.* Edinburgh: Scottish Executive.

Scottish Executive (2000) *The Way Forward for Care: A Policy Paper.* Edinburgh: Scottish Executive.

Scottish Office, The (1997) *Statistical Bulletin,* 9 November. Edinburgh: The Scottish Office.

Scottish Office, The (1998) *Modernising Community Care.* Edinburgh: The Scottish Office.

Scottish Office Development Department (Local Government Division) (1997) *Best Value Task Force Report No. 1.* Edinburgh: The Scottish Office.

Shand, F. (2000) *Springwell Project for Older People with Functional Mental Illness.* Edinburgh: Springwell House Social Work Centre.

Simons, K. (1998) *Home, Work and Inclusion: Social Policy Implications of Supported Living and Employment for People with Learning Difficulties.* York: Joseph Rowntree Foundation.

Social Services Inspectorate (1992) *Caring for Quality in Day Services.* London: HMSO.

Swallow, B. (1989) 'Day Services for People with Long-term Mental Health Problems.' MSW dissertation. Hull: University of Hull. Quoted in Brearley and Mandelstam (1992).

Tester, S. (1989) *Caring by Day: A Study of Day Care Services for Older People.* London: Centre for Policy on Ageing.

Tibbitt, J. (1987) 'Day Care – a "Good Thing"?' In G. Horobin (ed) *Why Day Care?* London: Jessica Kingsley Publishers.

Walker, A. and Walker, C. (1998) 'Normalisation and "normal" ageing: The social construction of ageing among older people with learning difficulties.' *Disability and Society 13*, 1, 125–142.

Welsh, B. (2000) Personal communication. Birmingham Social Services.

Wilson, H. (2000) Personal communication. Edinburgh Development Group.

Witcher, S., Stalker, K., Roadberg, M. and Jones, C. (2000) *Direct Payments: The Impact on Control and Choice for Disabled People.* Edinburgh: SHS and Central Research Unit, Scottish Executive.

CHAPTER 8

Supported Employment and Learning Disability[1]

A Life-Changing Experience?

Julie Ridley

Emergence of supported employment

During the 1990s, supported employment became a significant alternative to traditional day services for people with learning disabilities in the UK. It challenged the notion that individuals need to be 'ready' for work and the fundamental assumption that people with learning disabilities need to receive a service in a segregated setting. Supported employment claimed to provide valuable opportunities for social integration in ordinary workplaces. Facility-based services such as day centres, and developmental approaches, were failing to achieve community integration in ways demanded by people with disabilities and their families (Bradley 1994). Even though segregated centres still dominated the service landscape, the number of supported employment agencies, and therefore the number of people with learning disabilities in local employment, grew substantially from around 200 in 1985 to over 5000 in 1995 (Beyer, Goodere and Kilsby 1996).

In the same way that community care philosophy and legislation have meant that it is no longer considered best practice to deliver residential services in large segregated institutions, it is increasingly accepted that during the day individuals should be able to access ordinary community resources, including employment, alongside other members of the community.

This requires radical change from conventional 'job readiness' rehabilitation approaches, emphasising transferable skills developed in work training settings, to a support-orientated approach.

Supported employment developed out of dissatisfaction with the outcomes of sheltered workshops, and undeniable reports about the learning capacity of people with severe disabilities to learn skills once considered too difficult or complex (Gold 1980). Gold's ground-breaking research during the 1960s pioneered a practical hands-on programme of task analysis known by its slogan as 'Try Another Way', later to become 'Training in Systematic Instruction' or TSI, making employment a realisable goal for thousands of people with disabilities. His work was founded on a fundamental belief that the more competent a person becomes, the more tolerant society will be of any differences, a theory resonating with one of the core themes of personal competence in Wolfensberger's (1972) principle of normalisation. In the UK, supported employment grew out of a parallel dissatisfaction with poor integration employment outcomes of traditional day centres and a concurrent desire to move from segregated provision to ways of promoting community presence and participation.

Originally, supported employment was intended to facilitate competitive work in integrated settings for people for whom employment had not traditionally occurred and who, because of the nature and severity of their disability, needed on-going support to keep their jobs. It is a highly structured approach to placing people in jobs, providing individual training and support which emphasises a 'place and train' approach rather than one which emphasises getting ready for work or 'train and place'. As Noonan-Walsh, Rafferty and Lynch (1991) emphasise, the importance of the model lies in its promotion of social integration by offering real jobs in ordinary work settings.

The drive towards integrated employment has in large part come about because people with learning disabilities have expressed a preference for paid jobs (Racino and Whittico 1998). For example, over 80 per cent of respondents in a survey of people attending day centres during 1990 stated that having a paid job was either their first or second most important desire in life (Steele 1991). More recently, the Leighton Project (1998) and other studies exploring the aspirations of people with learning disabilities have consistently identified the wish for paid jobs. Dowson (1998), in a discussion paper on day services, remarks:

> Employment has more potential than any other occupation to help people with learning difficulties to realise the Five Accomplishments (O'Brien 1986): It places them within the community; offers a basis for the development of relationships with community members; demonstrates their ability to make a useful contribution; enhances their social status; and by the income it provides and in other ways gives them greater choice and control over their lives. (pp. 15–16)

An increasing body of research has, however, drawn attention to the poor social integration outcomes of supported employment. In a UK-wide survey of supported employment agencies, managers indicated that around a fifth of supported employment jobs offered no opportunity for the development of relationships (Beyer *et al.* 1996). Most of the research has examined opportunities for 'vocational integration' or mixing with non-disabled people at work, rather than the wider implications of the relationships and social support networks of people with learning disabilities. Bass and Drewett (1997) found that although supported employment is likely to offer opportunities for interaction with non-disabled people, for most people with learning disabilities this does not result in a broadening of relationships and social networks beyond the workplace.

This chapter uses the findings from a recent qualitative study of subjective experiences of supported employment in Scotland (Ridley 2000) and other research, to discuss key issues around the social integration potential of supported employment and its impact on community participation. A major issue to emerge from both the literature review and findings was the apparent failure of supported employment to achieve the social integration outcomes expected of it. Furthermore, there is disagreement about what is meant by 'social integration' as well as a glaring gap in the research knowledge about the nature of acceptance and quality aspects of relationships at work. In conclusion, it is suggested that supported employment may need to use more intentional strategies to promote social integration and become truly user-led.

Role of traditional day centres in providing employment opportunities

Two significant studies of day centres illustrate differential development of day services in different parts of Britain. Seed (1988) studied 15 day centres in Scotland and Beyer, Kilsby and Lowe (1994) surveyed day centres in Wales. Both found a variety of different models in existence. Seed found that with little policy guidance, adult resource centres in Scotland had pursued a range of different and sometimes conflicting objectives (Seed 1988; Seed *et al.* 1984). Past research had similarly found a variety of different and, at times, conflicting models (Stalker in Chapter 3).

Ordinary work has been a goal, albeit not the major one, of the adult resource/training centre programme. The centres of the 1960s and 1970s provided industrial contract work experience as it was assumed that 'trainees' would progress to real jobs with community employers. The assumption proved to be flawed. Several studies found few people who actually moved on from centres (Independent Development Council 1984; Seed *et al.* 1984). In fact, Seed (1988) found less than 1 per cent of those attending day centres moved from adult resource centres into jobs, or onto anything else for that matter. The general lack of throughput from the adult resource centre system has since galvanised national and local reviews of day services.

Seed's overall conclusion was that day services were segregated services with an extremely wide remit and commitment to personal support and social integration that they found difficult to sustain. The provision of services within day centres was failing to meet individual needs. The main recommendation of the research was for centres to develop as resource centres for work, further education and community integration, a direction reminiscent of the 1984 proposals of the Independent Development Council.

For many years, policy makers have been grappling with the notion that centres should provide employment opportunities and thus ensure a regular throughput of 'trainees'. The problem was not perceived to be with the system itself however, but with its capacity to achieve throughput. This assumption is gradually being eroded by programmes such as 'Changeover' and 'Changing Days', mentioned by Stalker in Chapter 3. Since the 1980s, renewed calls for greater emphasis to be placed on employment have sprung from this concern to free places in the centres, principally to make way for people leaving long-stay hospitals to live in the community. In contrast, supported employment emerged as a revolutionary approach developed in the USA, principally through advances in training technologies and with research evidence to show its successful outcomes. Consequently, the supported employment model migrated to this country, and was to radically influence thinking about the pursuit of employment from the 1980s on.

Supported employment and social integration

> Integration must be a central part of supported employment in all aspects of marketing, job matching, training, and supporting individuals in employment; not an afterthought, not an add-on, but the centrepiece of supported employment. (Mank 1988, p.143)

The development of supported employment was built upon an assumption that physical presence in ordinary workplaces would lead to social participation and interactions with non-disabled people. The findings of Ridley (2000) described below, and other researchers, challenge this assumption. The professional literature is awash with claims about the benefits of integrated employment, especially in terms of the positive effects on social inclusion and acceptance of people with disabilities as valued productive members of the community (Wolfensberger 1972). It offers both proximity and connection through shared experience with non-disabled people, both of which are pre-requisites to the development of friendship (Wehman and Kregel 1998).

However, social integration or inclusion is a difficult concept to define: 'integration is easier said than done' (Storey and Langyel 1992, p.46). Parents, professionals and self-advocates have all expressed concern about the quality of integration experienced by supported employees (Parent *et al.* 1991). Research has generally found wide variations, and although strategies have been proposed to promote social integration – including social skills instruction, role-play and problem-solving, self-management and natural supports – few researchers have measured social networks, friendship patterns or used global measures of integration (Storey and Langyel 1992). Biklen and Knoll (1987) reported that people with severe disabilities may be placed in a setting without becoming part of it, and Rusch, Chadsey-Rusch and Johnson (1991) found that co-workers associated during the day and assumed evaluation and training roles with supported employees, but rarely invited them to share activities outwith the worksite. Little is known about how supported employees feel about these situations.

Early reports about reasons for losing jobs identified social reasons as the most significant, and concerns about finding ways to improve work performance fuelled a research interest in studying social interactions (Calkins and Walker 1990; Greenspan and Shoultz 1981; Martin *et al.* 1986; Salzberg, Lignugaris Kraft and McCuller 1988). Supported employment researchers have tended to examine the level and quality of social interactions at work and to assume that this is synonymous with social integration (Hughes, Kim and Hwang 1998).

Different work settings have been found to afford different opportunities for social integration. Storey and Horner (1991) suggested that features of job sites are the main determinants of social integration. Hagner (1992), through qualitative research methods, demonstrated that aspects of work culture had an important bearing on the quality of the integration and work experience. A review of studies assessing social integration in employment settings between 1985 and 1995 (Hughes *et al.* 1998) suggested that social integration was affected by workplace culture to the extent that measures derived in one work setting might not be valid in another environment: 'it is unlikely that the same behaviors that are expected for a secretary, for example, would be expected for a parking lot attendant' (p.181).

Natural supports

According to Hagner and Dileo (1993, p.38), 'it is easy to be misled by the term "supported employment", because as a label for a type of service to workers with disabilities...it makes job support a professional service'. Ideas around using natural supports in workplaces have appeared in response to growing criticism of the poor integration outcomes of supported employment, and a recognition that the presence of specialist job-coaches may inhibit social relationships from developing (Nisbet and Hagner 1988).

There is an assumption that support is naturally available to supported employees in workplaces if only employment specialists can find ways to tap into it (Henderson and Argyle 1985). Mank (1996a) also suggests that tapping into this natural source of support represents a necessary and 'natural' development for supported employment's partnership with business. A contrary view has been put forward that the notion of natural supports perpetuates a 'normalisation mentality' or a tendency to expect people with disabilities to conform to societal norms (Rusch and Hughes 1996). On a more sobering note Forest and Pearpoint (1992, pp.70–71) caution against seeing natural supports as a panacea:

> Let's not romanticize the notion of...[natural] supports. When we look at people with disabilities who actually are managing in this society...we see that they are few and far between. We also see that it was blood, sweat and tears that brought them to that...and not simply good luck.

Test and Wood (1996), in reviewing the literature on natural support, found limited empirical evidence that use of natural supports was improving supported employment procedures or individual outcomes. Research has also reported supported employment staff to be generally unclear about their role in implementing natural supports (Hagner, Butterworth and Keith 1995), despite suggestions by some that natural support had become axiomatic with the implementation of supported employment (Mank 1996b).

Quality of life

Quality of life has more recently become the focus of research in supported employment (Schalock 1994). The most frequently cited quality of life dimension in the professional literature is social relationships and social inclusion. Job satisfaction is closely related to opportunities to work alongside other people (Moseley 1988). Sinnott-Oswald, Gliner and Spencer (1991) found a positive relationship between supported employment and quality of life as defined by environmental control, community involvement and perception of personal change, compared to sheltered employment outcomes. Supported employees scored higher in number of leisure activities, self-esteem, mobility, job skills and perceptions of changes in income. There are many claims that supported employment positively affects the quality of life of people with learning disabilities (King's Fund Centre 1984; McLoughlin, Garner and Callahan 1987; Wertheimer 1992).

Changes in community participation through supported employment have rarely been explored however. In support of the findings above, Knox and Parmenter (1993) established that despite positive benefits from supported employment, many individuals with disabilities remain on the periphery of the work environment – in the work setting, but not of it. Other researchers have found high levels of individual satisfaction with supported employment, including support for the assertion that it increases autonomy, individual choice and control, and that it improved opportunities for friendships (Test *et al.* 1993). However, the broader impact of supported employment on quality of life still remains fairly uncharted territory.

A qualitative research study of supported employment

A study of the impact of supported employment on the quality of life of people with learning disabilities was carried out as a doctoral thesis at the University of Edinburgh (Ridley 2000). The primary aim of the study was to explore the experience and meaning for individuals of securing a job through supported employment, particularly focusing on the reality of expected outcomes including social integration and a better quality of life as defined by individuals. It also aimed to investigate the role others, including relatives and professionals, played in determining both the expectations of supported employment and individual outcomes. While there is no consensus on the best way to tap the views of people with learning disabilities, especially about complex issues such as personal feelings and aspirations, people with learning disabilities were felt to be the most valid source of information on their experiences, particularly in respect of the quality of their lives, satisfaction with a job and the process of supported employment.

The research examined the outcomes of supported employment, particularly its impact on relationships, social networks, and individual choice and self-determination. Using 'quality of life' as a sensitising concept, the study explored the subjective experiences of supported employment and its impact on individuals' lives. This was an exploratory study using qualitative methods, an approach uncommon in the field of supported employment research at the start of the 1990s apart from Hagner's work (e.g. 1992) highlighting the relevance of understanding workplace culture. A systematic attempt was made to take in the variety of perspectives and to write about the experience from individuals' viewpoints.

The study addressed six main themes:

- the impact of supported employment on the lives of individuals with learning disabilities
- the differences between projects offering supported employment
- whether supported employment helped people with learning disabilities achieve their goals and aspirations
- the outcomes of supported employment
- whether outcomes were affected by the organisation and delivery of supported employment services
- the relevance of qualitative approaches to understanding the meanings of supported employment.

The study focused on eighteen individuals with learning disabilities who were using three different supported employment projects in Scotland. A postal questionnaire at the start of the research collected factual information about the projects, and documents such as minutes and promotional literature were gathered. A total of 104 interviews were undertaken, with project managers as well as with individual supported employees, their parents/carers or keyworkers and project workers at two points in time: before starting supported employment jobs and nine to ten months later. Over 100 hours were spent with staff in the three projects and in observations. A standard measure of vocational integration, the Virginia Commonwealth University's Vocational Integration Index (Parent, Kregel and Wehman 1992) was applied to assess the potential and actual social integration of the jobs obtained.

The research raised uncomfortable questions about the practice of supported employment and its potential to impact on individuals' quality of life, especially in relation to social integration outcomes. The major paradigm shift from 'readiness' to 'support' and the presumption of employability, especially for people with high support needs, was not evidenced in practice. There were major differences between what people with learning disabilities, their families or carers and supported employment staff sought from supported employment. The outcomes of supported employment, especially in terms of social integration, were limited.

Social integration outcomes

The study found that supported employment promised a great deal but delivered less. The outcomes for the eighteen individuals by and large did not match their aspirations, and there were significant differences between the priorities of users, carers and employment specialists. The fundamental difference between them was that users felt paid jobs were essential, whereas carers and professionals emphasised the importance of social inclusion and the intrinsic benefits of work.

Before starting supported employment the most limiting factors to users developing better social lives were lack of opportunity for social integration, as most people were attending segregated services, and lack of money. This was consistent with the findings of Jahoda, Cattermole and Markova (1990) when evaluating the social networks of people moving into community-based residential options. Participants were disappointed that supported employment did not always provide either the opportunity or the increase in income expected to change that situation.

The most common aspiration expressed was for friendship and a better social life. These were often not met, even though the majority of respondents identified 'meeting people at work' as a positive outcome of supported employment. Few friendships were formed at work over the period of the research. In common with the findings of Bass and Drewett (1997), it was found that while supported employees had friends at work, few socialised (or planned to socialise) with their co-workers outside work. That is not to say, had the research taken place over a longer period, that quite different outcomes might have been found in some cases. Work-based relationships rarely moved from the status of 'work-mates', or at best, having 'work-friends'. Often individuals were visible in their workplaces but not necessarily participating in the work culture. Neither did other employees always accept them.

Job structure, or rather the lack of it, also affected social integration outcomes in that poorly defined job roles paid only lip service to social integration as a desired outcome. Some workplaces and jobs, particularly those involving teamwork and job roles that were similar to those of other employees, provided more promising social integration opportunities. Jobs that were isolated did nothing to promote social integration and invariably resulted in job dissatisfaction. One person's job involved working physically separated from all other employees and he worked different shifts. He bemoaned the lack of contact with other people, especially as this was something he had specifically sought from supported employment. Before starting supported employment he had felt painfully isolated socially, spending most time with his parents, either at home or out socialising with them; something he was keen to change through getting a job:

> I never seem to find people that I can talk to. I thought going to work that would happen but it's not. I'm quite disappointed... I thought it might have changed a lot of things.

Because there had been no opportunities to make friends at work he was extremely disappointed with supported employment, and ultimately sought a change of job:

> It's no really changed very much if I really like to be honest. The only thing that's maybe changed is that I'm working now.

Given that employment specialists often give social integration primary importance over wages, it is noteworthy that the project with the worst record of finding paid jobs also had the lowest user satisfaction with social integration outcomes.

Supported employment appeared to do little to change the overall pattern or nature of most individuals' relationships. Very few supported employees talked about having 'real' friends at work, characterised by reciprocal actions. Relationships with co-workers were founded, in the main, on perceptions of the person as someone to be concerned about, to feel sympathy for, or as someone who needed protection from a harsh and cruel world, rather than notions of equality. That said, some individuals' aspirations in respect of making friends at work were probably unrealistic given that in reality not all workplace cultures encourage or promote the development of friendships, and that society's apparent prejudice and fear of learning disability greatly inhibits the development of equal relationships.

On the positive side, supported employment jobs offered opportunities for expanding social networks for a few people. The new relationships with Pete's (not his real name) co-workers were characterised by reciprocity in that co-workers would borrow money and grant each other favours knowing, as Pete put it, 'the favour will be returned in some way or other'. At the first interview, it was clear that Pete already had several non-disabled friends in his life, as well as family members. However, his activities were restricted through lack of money and low self-esteem. Within nine to ten months, people from work had become good friends, some of whom he socialised with on a regular basis and who had also become sources of emotional and financial as well as social support. The pattern of activities in Pete's life had changed from predominantly 'isolated activities' to activities that could be described as socially integrative. In his words: 'having a job has given me a life'. Pete was unusual however, in securing a paid job and a wage of over £100 per week.

The changes in John's life as a result of making friends at work had perhaps been less dramatic but nonetheless personally significant. The pattern of activities had changed in that he was now less involved in specialist activities, had fewer paid supporters and more non-disabled people could be counted in his circle of participation. John's family remained the main sources of social support. Nevertheless, John identified the social aspect of the job as important. He particularly enjoyed working with people and contributing through his work. Since where he worked was local, he regularly came across other employees at the shops or socialising in the local pub. Other factors, including having a young family and finishing shifts at different times to his friends, meant 'I've been meeting people at work and they've been asking me out but I've no had the chance to do that yet'.

Even where work friends had not yet become social friends, mixing with others at work of itself was beneficial in broadening social experience and increasing self-confidence in other social settings. As one individual put it:

> Before I used to be like shy and lonely, since I started working, I've kinda come oot of my shell quite a bit and got more sociable and talkative.

Quality of life outcomes

Perhaps one of the most discordant findings from the research was that supported employment had only a limited impact on the quality of life of most people. Given what is known about the ecological nature of quality of life, this should not be surprising. After all, having a job is only one life dimension, and other factors – especially where and with whom one lives, and the extent and density of one's social network – will have an equally, if not more, significant impact. It is nevertheless assumed that when one presses the supported employment button so to speak, everything else will naturally fall into place. However, not every individual in the study experienced positive benefits in their quality of life as a result of supported employment. Furthermore, the experience of supported employment itself was not always an empowering one. Not all job choices were positive: the choice was often to take a job or leave it, whether or not it fitted well with individual goals and aspirations. Not all projects worked in ways that served to enhance individuals' self-determination, but rather created dependency on professionals' expertise.

Great things are expected of supported employment, and none more so than when the person lives in supported or specialist accommodation. However, the study found stark contrast between the disability service world and ordinary workplaces, which meant any benefits derived during working hours were eliminated on re-entering disability services. Even when an individual with learning disabilities acquires skills and is perceived as competent at work, it is not guaranteed that paid supporters will adopt the same capacity approach in considering other aspects of their lives. For instance, residential support staff perceived some individuals as doing well in supported employment but did not consider them 'ready' to live independently in the community.

Individuals inhabited a 'twilight zone' straddling the non-disabled community of work and the world of disability services with different norms and values, attitudes and expectations. Consequently, rather than being life-changing, as many had hoped it would be, the experience of supported employment for some was 'compartmentalised' and restricted to the work setting. In support of the assertion by Stalker and Harris (1998), the study found that generally the places where individuals with learning disabilities live dictates the amount of choice and independence in their lives. Because some supported employees were living in specialist residential settings, the skills, status, etc. they gained through supported employment remained situation-specific while the parameters of their lives in general remained unaltered.

Lack of individual focus

A critical issue in the discussion of the 'quality' of supported employment is the extent of its individual or person-centred focus. The findings showed this to be variable. This was in relation to how vocational profiles were compiled, and how job-search and job-match activities were undertaken. It is commonly assumed that supported employment equates to or is synonymous with a person-centred focus, but there was a gulf between theory and practice. Vocational profiles were not always used to explore individuals' aspirations: one project, for example, assessed individuals' employment goals by observing individuals during group work and also basing their assessment on information received at referral. As it cannot be assumed that initial preferences will always be the product of informed choice, this was felt to be a rather limiting assumption for supported employment specialists to make.

Another project did not routinely undertake vocational profiles with all its clients with learning disabilities because when an individual had little or no work history such a strategy was felt to encourage 'unrealistic' expectations. Consequently, there were gaps in information about personal goals and aspirations, coupled with a tendency to fit people into existing jobs in both these projects. This and other evidence suggested that some projects were relying predominantly on professionals' assumptions about the current job market rather than exploring individual aspirations, and would offer placements in sheltered work settings because these were available rather than pursue integrated employment opportunities.

Although most users felt they had made the decision to take the job offered, in reality an offer typically meant take the job or leave it, not a choice between different job options. It is nevertheless impressive that many felt they had influenced the decision-making process given that other research has not been so positive (Wehmeyer and Metzler 1995). Individuals made obvious compromises in their expectations and aspirations. The challenge of determining the 'realistic' job preferences of people with learning disabilities was highlighted by two out of the three projects. They were dismissive of the notion that individuals with learning disabilities had valid job aspirations and tended to treat their opinions and preferences less seriously than those of experienced employment specialists.

Quality of supported employment jobs

The quality of supported employment jobs can leave a lot to be desired. Ridley (2000) found that the majority of jobs were part-time (many were under 16 hours per week), low status 'entry-level' positions, and low paid. This echoed the findings of earlier quantitative studies by Beyer *et al.* (1996) and Lister *et al.* (1992) of supported employment in the UK. In exploring individuals' job satisfaction in relation to the characteristics of jobs, it was found that how individuals with learning disabilities judge the meaningfulness of work is frequently in conflict with how professionals judge 'meaningful work'.

For the individuals with learning disabilities, 'meaningful jobs' were those where they perceived the tasks they performed as having meaning for them personally. Such meaning is acquired socially from other people and the culture at large (Baumeister 1991), and is not an objective quality. For example, to any outside observer and, indeed, to the supported employment project, Mike had one of the most varied and interesting jobs of the whole sample and yet he was bored and wanted to leave because in his eyes, the job lacked future career prospects. He envisaged finding 'meaningful' work in a higher status, higher paid job.

When professionals concentrate solely on achieving normative job tasks and pay little attention to individuals' perspectives, key determinants of job satisfaction, and therefore of maintaining jobs, are neglected. Supported employees valued paid jobs and were often disappointed with unpaid or low paid jobs, not because having a wage would lift them out of poverty (this is rarely the case), but because of the symbolic value of receiving a pay cheque.

It is recognised that a pay cheque or wage slip communicates a powerful message about an individual's worth and value.

Broadly speaking, the individuals in the sample reported reasonable levels of job satisfaction. Those who were dissatisfied identified problems with dull, repetitive or boring tasks, offering little, if any, opportunity for recognition or contribution to society. They were especially frustrated in poorly structured jobs or in jobs where they performed significantly different tasks to other employees. Supported employment specialists were more likely to mention performance issues as the main factor in job loss, while users identified lack of variety, meaningless jobs and poor job matches as the most significant problems. A clear link emerged between users' job dissatisfactions and reasons for job losses, confirming that job satisfaction information is of critical importance in maintaining supported employment placements.

One of the most limiting features was how individuals were generally placed in low quality jobs until something happened and jobs were lost. The absence of a career-based approach was striking. Few individuals had long-term vocational plans, drawn up in partnership with the supported employment projects. With the exception of one project, a career-based approach was not built into supported employment. As in other research, Ridley found that job placement in supported employment was often perceived as final and support as temporary, with less attention paid to long-term career plans. A few individuals actively challenged this practice by electing to leave jobs themselves in search of 'better prospects'. This confirms the earlier assertions of Pumpian *et al.* (1997), who suggested that helping people to find another job is often an afterthought in the supported employment process, with retraining being a reaction to job failure, rather than perceived as a positive event.

Conclusion: Conflicting aspirations?

Supported employment, in offering jobs with local employers at the going rate and all the benefits associated with paid work, potentially promotes the community presence and participation of people with learning disabilities.

However, as Stalker argues in Chapter 3, most people with learning disabilities will not realise these benefits: day centres continue to dominate the service landscape and there are major structural barriers such as the 'benefits trap' that deter people from taking up employment.

Although, in theory, supported employment has the potential for enhancing the community participation of people with learning disabilities, research on social integration finds rather more disappointing outcomes. Ridley (2000) found that supported employment had a more limited impact on people's quality of life than the theoretical model would lead one to expect. A major step forward then would be to acknowledge the limitations of jobs in integrated settings, in much the same way as it is now understood from research that moving into the community from long-stay hospitals is not an answer in itself. A multitude of factors including the quality and structure of supported employment jobs, workplace cultures, where individuals with learning disabilities live and so on, combine to determine whether and how an individual is or is not included at work.

Although people with learning disabilities do identify social integration as an important aspiration, the over-riding emphasis it is given in supported employment is professional-driven. In contrast, the goal of securing 'real', that is, paid regular jobs with community employers is essentially a user-driven aspiration. The model assumes that physical presence in an ordinary workplace will lead to social participation, and ultimately to acceptance of people with learning disabilities by the wider community. Emphasising social integration in this way deflects professionals' attention from important quality aspects of jobs as defined by users. That expectations are often not met, suggests this goal may be too idealistic in many of the workplaces and work cultures in the UK.

The notion of social integration is arguably over-riding other important considerations identified by users, such as the importance of securing regular paid jobs, which incidentally was emphasised in earlier formulations of the theory. Supported employment may not, therefore, move beyond achieving mere physical integration unless more systematic strategies for assessing the integration potential of jobs and intentional strategies to promote social inclusion are adopted, one of which includes creating as well as capitalising on natural supports within the workplace. It could be claimed, with a fair degree of certainty, that most other people who are not labelled as learning disabled do not seek jobs primarily to be socially integrated into society, although a social life and work friends may be a positive by-product of participating in some workforces. Why should it be assumed different for people with learning disabilities?

Clearly more weight needs to be given to ways of finding out from individuals with learning disabilities what they want from jobs and of helping them realise personal goals. Quality in day services should be more closely aligned to user requirements and a stronger focus on outcomes that contribute to improving individuals' quality of life. However challenging a prospect this may be, more weight must be given to meeting users' expectations: for example, for paid jobs. This is a concern highlighted by self-advocates in the USA who have identified among the characteristics of 'good' jobs such things as adequate pay and benefits, control of money benefits and receiving cost-of-living increases. A second aspect of 'quality' is to find jobs that are personally meaningful and satisfying to individuals. There is now a growing body of theory about using person-centred planning approaches in supported employment to enhance careers and long-term planning. There is little evidence to suggest this is currently applied in practice.

Some writers (e.g. Anderson and Andrews 1990) have recognised that the supported employment process can work in ways that actually keep people with disabilities separate from other people, even though community integration is a commonly acknowledged goal. Other studies have shown that the presence of a job coach or equivalent can be stigmatising and hinder social integration. There is a need to look more closely at the role of employment specialists, employers, co-workers and others in the person's informal social network, in supporting and facilitating social inclusion. It would be unreasonable to expect projects to be able to predict exact levels of social integration in particular work settings but practitioners could pay greater attention to evaluating strengths and weaknesses of different workplaces using any one of a number of measures or indices designed for this purpose, together with the knowledge gleaned from new insights from qualitative studies of workplace culture.

One of the key issues for future research effort, if supported employment is to fulfil its potential for people with learning disabilities, is to adopt a more fine-grained approach to researching its outcomes. The above discussion suggests that change needs to happen on a number of levels. Crude measures of quality of life and social integration taken as a measure of the success or otherwise of supported employment, tell only a partial story. Supported employment will never be a panacea for poor social networks, lack of educational opportunity, poor housing and inadequate support. A new research agenda grown out of a quality-of-life framework will need to be framed and developed in conjunction with users and families. The evidence is that such an agenda may well be a different one from the one developed by professionals.

Note

1. Dedicated to my friend and mentor Professor David Brandon.

References

Anderson, B. and Andrews, M. (1990) *Creating Diversity: Organizing and Sustaining Workplaces that Support Employees with Disabilities.* Alaska: Centre For Community Inc.

Bass, M. and Drewett, R. (1997) *Real Work: Supported Employment for People with Learning Difficulties.* Social Service Monographs. Sheffield: Joint Unit for Social Services Research, Sheffield University and Community Care.

Baumeister, R.F. (1991) *Meanings of Life.* New York: The Guilford Press.

Beyer, S., Goodere, L. and Kilsby, M. (1996) *The Costs and Benefits of Supported Employment Agencies.* London: The Stationery Office.

Beyer, S., Kilsby, M. and Lowe, K. (1994) 'What do ATC's offer in Wales? A survey of Welsh day services.' *Mental Handicap Research 7,* 1, 16–40.

Biklen, D. and Knoll, J. (1987) 'The disabled minority.' In S.J. Taylor, D. Biklen and J. Knoll (eds) *Community Integration for People with Severe Disabilities.* New York: Teachers College Press, Columbia University.

Bradley, V.J. (1994) 'Evolution of a new service paradigm.' In V.J. Bradley, J.W. Ashbaugh and B.C. Blaney (eds) *Creating Individual Supports for People with Developmental Disabilities – A Mandate for Change at Many Levels.* Baltimore: Paul H. Brookes.

Calkins, C.F. and Walker, H.M. (1990) *Social Competence for Workers with Developmental Disabilities: A Guide to Enhancing Employment Outcomes in Integrated Settings.* Baltimore: Paul H. Brookes.

Dowson, S. (1998) *Certainties without Centres? A Discussion Paper on Day Services for People who have Learning Difficulties.* London: Values Into Action.

Forest, M. and Pearpoint, J. (1992) 'Families, friends and circles.' In J. Nisbet (ed) *Natural Supports in School, at Work and in the Community for People with Severe Disabilities.* Baltimore: Paul H. Brookes.

Gold, M. (1980) *Did I Say That?* Champaign, IL: Research Press.

Greenspan, S. and Shoultz, B. (1981) 'Why mentally retarded adults lose their jobs: Social competence as a factor in work adjustment.' *Applied Research in Mental Retardation 2,* 23–28.

Hagner, D.C. (1992) 'The social interactions and job supports of supported employees.' In J. Nisbet (ed) *Natural Supports in School, at Work and in the Community for People with Severe Disabilities.* Baltimore: Paul H. Brookes.

Hagner, D.C., Butterworth, J. and Keith, G. (1995) 'Strategies and barriers in facilitating natural supports for employment of adults with severe disabilities.' *Journal of the Association for Persons with Severe Handicaps 20,* 110–120.

Hagner, D.C. and Dileo, D. (1993) *Working Together: Workplace Culture, Supported Employment and Persons with Disabilities.* Cambridge USA: Brookline Books.

Henderson, M. and Argyle, M. (1985) 'Social support by four categories of work colleague: Relationships between activities, stress and satisfaction.' *Journal of Occupational Behaviour 6,* 229–239.

Hughes, C., Kim, J. and Hwang, B. (1998) 'Assessing social integration in employment settings: Current knowledge and future directions.' *American Journal on Mental Retardation 103,* 2, 173–185.

Independent Development Council for People with Mental Handicaps (1984) *Next Steps. An Independent Review of Progress, Problems and Priorities in the Development of Services for People with Mental Handicap.* London: Independent Development Council.

Jahoda, A., Cattermole, M. and Markova, I. (1990) 'Moving out: An opportunity for friendship and broadening social horizons?' *Journal of Mental Deficiency Research 34,* 127–139.

King's Fund Centre (1984) *An Ordinary Working Life: Vocational Services for People with a Mental Handicap.* London: King's Fund Centre.

Knox, M. and Parmenter, T. (1993) 'Social networks and support mechanisms for people with mild intellectual disability in competitive employment.' *International Journal of Rehabilitiation Research 16,* 1–12.

Leighton Project, The, with Grant, S. and Cole, D. (1998) 'Young Peoples' Aspirations.' In C. Robinson and K. Stalker (eds) *Growing up with Disability.* London: Jessica Kingsley Publishers.

Lister, T., Ellis, L., Phillips, T., O'Bryan, A., Beyer, S. and Kilsby, M. (1992) *Survey of Supported Employment Services in England, Scotland and Wales.* Manchester: National Development Team.

Mank, D.M. (1988) 'Issues forum: A change in expectations.' In M. Barcus, S. Griffin, D. Mank, L. Rhodes and S. Moon (eds) *Supported Employment Implementation Issues.* Richmond VA: Rehabilitation, Research and Training Center, Virginia Commonwealth University.

Mank, D.M. (1996a) 'Evolving roles for employers and support personnel in the employment of people with severe disabilities.' *Journal of Vocational Rehabilitation 6,* 83–88.

Mank D.M. (1996b) 'Natural support in employment for people with disabilities: What do we know and when did we know it?' *Journal of the Association for Persons with Severe Handicaps 21,* 4, 174–177.

Martin, J.E., Rusch, F.R., Lagomarcino, T. and Chadsey-Rusch, J. (1986) 'Comparisons between non-handicapped and mentally retarded workers: Why they lose their jobs.' *Applied Research in Mental Retardation 7*, 467–474.

McLoughlin, C.S., Garner, J.B. and Callahan, M.J. (1987) *Getting Employed, Staying Employed*. Baltimore: Paul H. Brookes.

Moseley, C.R. (1988) 'Job satisfaction research: Implications for supported employment.' *Journal of the Association for Persons with Severe Handicaps 13*, 3, 211–219.

Nisbet, J. and Hagner, D. (1988) 'Natural supports in the workplace: A reexamination of supported employment.' *Journal of the Association for Persons with Severe Handicaps 13*, 4, 260–267.

Noonan-Walsh, P., Rafferty, M. and Lynch, C. (1991) 'The "Open Road" Project: Real jobs for people with mental handicaps.' *International Journal of Rehabilitation Research 14*, 155–161.

Parent, W., Kregel, J., Wehman, P. and Metzler, H. (1991) 'Measuring the social integration of supported employment workers.' *Journal of Vocational Rehabilitation 1*, 1, January, 35–49.

Parent, W., Kregel, J. and Wehman, P. (1992) *Vocational Integration Index: Measuring Integration of Workers with Disabilities*. Stoneham, MA: Butterworth Heinemann.

Pumpian, I., Fisher, D., Certo, N.J., and Smalley, K.A. (1997) 'Changing jobs: An essential part of career development.' *Mental Retardation 35*, 1, 3948.

Racino, J.A. and Whittico, P. (1998) 'The Promise of Self Advocacy and Community Employment.' In P. Wehman and J. Kregel (eds) *More Than A Job. Securing Satisfying Careers for People with Disabilities*. Baltimore: Paul H. Brookes.

Ridley, J. (2000) 'Mixed Fortunes: A Qualitative Study of Supported Employment and Quality of Life.' Unpublished PhD Thesis. Edinburgh: University of Edinburgh.

Rusch, F.R., Chadsey-Rusch, J. and Johnson, J.R. (1991) 'Supported employment: Emerging opportunities for employment integration.' In L. Meyer, C. Peck and L. Brown (eds) *Critical Issues in the Lives of People with Severe Disabilities*. Baltimore: Paul H. Brookes.

Rusch, F.R. and Hughes, C. (1996) 'Natural supports: Who benefits – "We" or "They"?' Invited Commentary, *Journal of the Association for Persons with Severe Handicaps 21*, 4, 185–188.

Salzberg, C.L., Lignugaris Kraft, B. and McCuller, G.L. (1988) 'Reasons for job loss: A review of employment termination studies of mentally retarded workers.' *Research in Developmental Disabilities 9*, 153–170.

Schalock, R.L. (1994) 'The concept of quality of life and its current application in the field of mental retardation/developmental disabilities.' In D.A. Goode (ed) *Quality of Life for Persons with Disabilities: International Perspectives and Issues*. Baltimore: Brookline Books.

Seed, P. (1988) *Daycare At the Crossroads*. Tunbridge Wells: Costello.

Seed, P., Thomson, M., Pilkington, F. and Britten, J. (1984) *Which 'Best Way'? A Preliminary Study of Day Services for People with a Mental Handicap in Scotland*. Tunbridge Wells: Costello.

Sinnott-Oswald, M., Gliner, J.A. and Spencer, K.C. (1991) 'Supported and sheltered employment: Quality of life issues among workers with disability.' *Education and Training in Mental Retardation*, December.

Stalker. K. and Harris. P. (1998) 'The exercise of choice by adults with intellectual difficulties: A literature review.' *Journal of Applied Research in Intellectual Disability 11*, 1, 60–68.

Steele, D. (1991) 'Survey reveals gulf between work aspirations and success.' *Community Living*, July.

Storey, K. and Horner R.H. (1991) 'Social interactions in three supported employment options: A comparative analysis.' *Journal of Applied Behaviour Analysis 24*, 2, 349–360.

Storey, K. and Langyel, L. (1992) 'Strategies for increasing interactions in supported employment settings: A review.' *Journal of Vocational Rehabilitation 2*, 3, 46–57.

Test, D.W., Hinson, K.B., Solow, J. and Keul, P. (1993) 'Job satisfaction of persons in supported employment.' *Education and Training in Mental Retardation 28*, 335–344.

Test, D.W. and Wood, W.M. (1996) 'Natural supports in the workplace: The jury is still out.' *Journal of the Association for Persons with Severe Handicaps 21*, 4, Winter, 155–173.

Wehman, P. and Kregel J. (eds) (1998) *More Than A Job. Securing Satisfying Careers for People with Disabilities.* Baltimore: Paul H. Brookes.

Wehmeyer, M.L. and Metzler, C.A. (1995) 'How self-determined are people with mental retardation? The National Consumer Survey.' *Mental Retardation 33*, 2, 111–119.

Wertheimer, A. (1992) *Changing Lives: Supported Employment and People with Learning Disabilities.* Manchester: National Development Team.

Wolfensberger, W. (1972) *The Principle of Normalization in Human Services.* Toronto: National Institute on Mental Retardation.

CHAPTER 9

Building Positive Lifestyles

The Community Option

Ann Lloyd and Angela Cole

As outlined in Part I of this book, day services for people with learning difficulties have traditionally been based in segregated, often large buildings. This has had some benefits for people but also a number of drawbacks. It is, fundamentally, a model of service provision based on social exclusion.

Numerous service reviews have shown that large numbers of people have valued going to day centres because they offer the chance to make and see friends. For many it is the *only* place where they have been able to get together with their friends during the week. Generally, people also enjoy at least some of the activities they take part in when using a centre, but service reviews have overwhelmingly shown that the things people most like doing take place outside of the buildings – in community settings (Cole 1998; Mental Health Foundation 1996; Simons and Watson 1999). People in the London Borough of Hackney (1996) said things like:

> We should be able to go out every day.

> I'd like to go to have a massage and work as a cleaner.

> I like going to college.

> I helped old people at a club. It was absolutely brilliant.

Family carers most often view day centres as services that give the person they care for positive experiences, in a safe environment, while giving them a regular break. The 'positive experiences' are, though, judged in contrast to what they would be able to offer if the person stayed at home. There is a very real fear that if the centre were not there both the users and the carers themselves would end up with a worse quality of life.

Reviews have highlighted the need to find ways of supporting people to see their friends and do things they have hitherto enjoyed at day centres while also opening up opportunities for them to do more in community settings. As a result, day services are becoming more community focused. Some have re-organised to operate through project groups, perhaps catering for 12–15 people with a shared interest such as sport and fitness activities, the arts or horticulture. Some services are looking to increase opportunities for integration by welcoming members of the public into day centres; for example, by running a café, having rooms available for meetings, aerobics, and so forth, or by making computer facilities available. Some have developed supported employment schemes or social firms for people to move into paid work.

Social inclusion inevitably means taking positive action to combat social exclusion. Ultimately, the goal must be for people with learning difficulties to be fully involved and included in their communities. Ideally, support would come not just from paid workers but from ordinary people wishing to share their time and interests with disabled people who are their work colleagues, fellow students, club members, neighbours and friends.

This chapter explores one model of service provision that was set up specifically to work towards these goals – a non-buildings based, individualised service. It is based on the authors' experiences of setting up and managing a Community Resource Service in the London Borough of Hackney.

Introducing the Community Resource Service

The service was set up as part of the day service provision run directly by the social service department. It consisted of a team of six staff, a manager and an administrative worker (shared with another team on-site). The team had an office base but no rooms for people who used the service. The expectation was that all work with people would take place in community settings.

The team had two types of staff working directly with users – community resource workers and assistant community resource workers. The former carried responsibility for planning with individuals and supporting them to do their chosen pursuits; the latter focused solely on the support function. This changed and became less rigid as the team and individual staff developed.

The manager also regularly spent time in direct contact with people who used the service. The team did not have a vehicle to transport people around in but had control of its own budget. The budget included an amount to pay for sessional support staff, to achieve flexibility, and to meet the travelling costs and expenses associated with using community facilities.

Why no base?

The service was originally conceived as another small day centre but its remit was changed before any members of staff were appointed. Following a long development period the service was actually getting off the ground during the early days of a major review of day services for people with learning difficulties in the borough. At that very early stage it was already clear that a new approach was needed. The opportunity was taken to model a different type of service, focusing on supporting each person to do things he or she personally wanted to achieve without 'day centre walls'. The service would work with people who had a wide range of support needs, and would not exclude anyone because they needed a high level of support. This was an important principle to demonstrate that all people could be supported in community settings safely, with positive advantages and benefits.

The London Borough of Hackney has a very ethnically diverse population. A more person-centred model of provision would help people of all ethnicities to feel comfortable about using the service because support and activities could be more responsive to their specific cultural needs.

Potential problems with a day-centre base

- Staff can gravitate towards it because it feels 'safer' and easier

- It may dampen creativity

- It is too easy an option to fall back on when plans go awry or the weather is bad

- It can turn into a place more for staff than people with learning difficulties, with decisions and control out of users' hands

- It removes 'ordinariness' and emphasises difference

- It can separate people from minority ethnic groups from their community and culture

- It encourages a 'getting ready' approach, but rather than being a stepping stone people often never move on

- People learn and practise skills in an abnormal environment and can find it difficult to transfer the skills to real settings

- The base can act as a buffer between carers and staff

- People are more likely to come in when they are ill and really need to be at home

- Often a lot of people are there together which is more likely to mean that some won't get on, people will irritate others, and conflict will ensue

Building positive lifestyles

It was essential to be clear about what the service was trying to support people to achieve. A key objective was to break down the barriers that lead to people with learning difficulties having less chance than most to be fully participating and contributing members of society. The service was seeking to open up opportunities and provide support for people to do things – to take on roles and responsibilities – as valuable and valued members of the community.

The borough's services for people with learning difficulties had a clear statement of purpose – to help and support people to:

- lead varied, fulfilled and ordinary lives in the local Hackney community and beyond
- have access to a wide range of opportunities
- have influence and control over their own lives
- develop knowledge, skills, interests and preferences
- be as autonomous and independent as possible
- be healthy, live comfortably and safely, and be contented
- challenge any oppression and discrimination they face.

In order to achieve these things its services would enable people with learning difficulties to:

- have a full range of opportunities and good quality support to pursue their chosen activities during the day, evenings and at weekends
- participate in activities which help them to achieve their personal goals and aspirations
- have opportunities to use local community resources alongside other citizens and become more integrated into the Hackney community and society in general
- do things with people they want to do things with
- be involved in deciding what they will personally be doing and in planning services for people with learning difficulties as a whole
- contribute to the local Hackney community.

For the Community Resource Service this meant that what people did had to be based on their personal preferences, ambitions and dreams. The support they received had to be based on a clear picture of what they needed help with so that it would be right for each person. A person-centred approach to planning was essential.

Being non-building based means that people are already where we are striving for them to be – in the community. In the community it can rain, get cold, people can wait ages for buses, people can be rude. But in the community people can also be kind, you can 'happen upon' things, you can meet new people. It is there that the widest opportunities are available, where the greatest number of relationships can be formed and where there is a rich diversity of choices to be made. Even the best day centre can only offer a limited range of opportunities and experiences, and a limited permutation of relationships.

Potential benefits of being community-based

- A limitless range of opportunities are available, and can be more easily grasped

- People can do things with people who share their culture or ethnicity

- People can build relationships with other people who aren't disabled or in a caring role

- People see that they have things in common with other local people by joining clubs and interest groups

- Staff develop their resourcefulness, creativity and a 'get on with it' approach

- Staff learn and refine their skills, especially in problem solving

- Closer links with families develop

- Everyone in the system realises what can be achieved

- People begin to change their thinking about 'day services' and start thinking about people having a lifestyle, building from where they live

- People can see their friends and do things together in ordinary places, and have a more satisfying social life

Making a community-based service work

Planning with individuals

This is the starting point: everything else flows from it.

> Developing a service to match the unique requirements of each person is…the bedrock on which services should be built. We must transform a service which expects people to fit into a limited number of activities to one which evolves a range of choices… (McIntosh and Whittaker 1998, p.67)

The team developed their own framework for discovering how people wanted to spend their time and for planning the support they needed. The way they worked was heavily influenced by person-centred planning approaches originating in Canada and the USA, particularly the 'Getting to know you' work of Brost, Johnson and Deprey (1982) and Smull and Burke-Harrison's (1992) 'Essential lifestyle planning'. An overview of different planning styles can be found in *People, Plans and Possibilities* (Sanderson *et al.* 1997). The individual planning approach used by the team was built on and developed into a person-centred planning workbook through the national 'Changing Days' project (McIntosh and Whittaker 2000).

The emphasis was on enabling people to be in control of how they spent their time. Nothing was ruled out, everything was possible. Using a person-centred planning approach was a key way that the service could empower people. It was essential that staff really got to know people's personal preferences, ambitions and dreams. It could not be a once-and-for-all approach. Many people have limited life experiences and simply do not know about things that they might enjoy. People need the chance to try things out along the way, to then build on the things they enjoy and reject those they don't. Planning with individuals has to be on-going and responsive to these changes; support must be available when people need it, which means having staff who can work flexibly.

Roles of staff

Having staff with the right approach, attitude and skills is the key to good quality service. Staff in a community-based service need to be determined, confident and prepared to act as pioneers. They need to have a strong belief in the people they serve, enjoy and value being with them, and be able to see their gifts and talents – what they can offer. They have to be knowledgeable about the local community so that they can build creatively on people's interests. Perhaps, above all, they need to have a real commitment to social inclusion.

Working in a community-based service means having to fulfil a number of roles – supporting, enabling, coaching, bridge-building, link-making.

- *Supporting* involves giving people whatever assistance they need to do the things they want to do and to participate fully. For staff in the team this ranged from very personal, hands-on help with aspects of day-to-day living (like eating, using the toilet, moving around), to accompanying someone to a class and physically helping them to take part, to speaking on behalf of someone who cannot speak for themselves.

- *Enabling* is essentially about the approach taken when assisting someone. Staff in the service needed to find ways of helping people do things for themselves, rather than doing it for them; they needed to be able to organise and plan, but also to stand back and let people get on with it.

- *Coaching* is one way of enabling people to do things themselves. It requires staff to analyse tasks and plan how to help people learn them, and then to 'walk the walk' with people until they can do it unassisted. In a community-based service this may be about someone learning a bus route so that they can get to an activity on their own; it may be about learning some parts of a job; it could be anything. Every moment is a learning opportunity – coaching and enabling are active roles that require staff to be alert and responsive to the moment.

- *Bridge-building* and *link-making* are about looking beyond the worker–user relationship to the wider society. They are both about opening doors: to new opportunities, and to new relationships. Both roles require staff to be proactive, to spot a way in, to make an introduction. More than anything people need to have the confidence to make an approach, to take the risk of a negative response, to ask for people to give their time and support. Shrinking violets need not apply!

Janet

When the team met Janet she was in her late 30s. She was living with her elderly mother and had had no contact with services for ten years, having previously been withdrawn from the day centre when she had learnt bad language. Janet was totally echolaic and spent all day in her room or watching TV. Neither she nor her mother went out. The flat they shared was in desperate need of cleaning.

The workers slowly built up a relationship with Janet and found that she was happy to go out – but this raised her mother's anxieties. The workers were also concerned that Janet's clothes were inappropriate and her personal hygiene poor, which would not help her to develop friendships. They therefore focused on rebuilding Janet's self-esteem and supported her in cleaning and decorating her bedroom. For the first time in her life Janet had nice things around her that were her own. She was supported in buying new clothes and ensuring she was on the correct level of benefits. The workers were also able to link with other services to ensure Janet got support at home around her personal care, and that her mother received services from the elders team.

With support Janet started attending college classes and also a singing group. As her confidence grew she became able to speak for herself and began to indicate what things she enjoyed, what she was worried about and what she wanted to do in the future. Janet confided in the workers that her childhood and early adulthood had been troubled and that it still bothered her. The workers secured funding from her GP to enable her to attend specialist counselling. Through this, Janet eventually revealed that she wanted to move out of the family home.

Janet was extremely worried about leaving her elderly mother on her own so the workers supported her through the long and painful process. When she finally moved into her new home Janet continued to be supported, albeit less often, by the workers. They supported her in regularly visiting her mother and adopting a new role as a caring responsible daughter.

Staff in a community-based service do not have a manager close at hand when they are out of the office, which is much of the time. They have to be able to use their initiative, manage risks and cope when the unexpected arises. Staying calm and being able to think in a crisis can make the difference between a problem resolved and a problem exacerbated.

Supporting people in the community means that staff are regularly working in public view. It is essential that they are modelling a partnership between themselves and the people they are supporting, reinforcing equal citizenship, and that decision-making lies with the disabled person. This is one way that staff can really challenge people's assumptions and pre-conceived ideas, and can help to achieve inclusion.

Ensuring consistency and continuity

It was essential that the service developed some framework documents to guide its work, and then had systems and procedures in place which supported the implementation of its policies and the achievement of its objectives. This would help to ensure that people received a consistent and reliable service, two critically important quality outcomes for a community-based service.

For people to have confidence in the service there must be an efficient system for covering work when staff are on holiday or sick. In a day centre people can simply join another group; a community-based service has to be committed to ensuring that people's planned activities happen. For family carers this is essential if they rely upon their son or daughter getting a service so that they can work or get a rest. Fundamentally, though, it is about believing that people with learning difficulties have the right to receive a quality service, and having systems and contingency plans which ensure that they do.

These may include using sessional, agency or bank workers, the manager providing back-up, or staff having set administrative time which is rotated so there is always one member of the team who can be called on. The team also found that having two named workers linked to, and knowledgeable about, each user helped to provide continuity when the lead worker was away.

Communication can be a potential difficulty with a team who are largely out and about and away from the office. A community team needs staff who can move beyond the traditional day service ethos of fixed service hours and a rigid work–home boundary. Staff in the Community Resource team understood the importance of calling each other at home if important information needed to be passed on or if cover needed to be arranged for the next day.

To achieve continuity it is also essential that people's goals and support plans are clearly recorded, with times, venues, travelling arrangements, money required, details of specific support needed, and anything else that another person would need to know to ensure not only that an agreed activity happened, but that it happened well for the person. As part of this there needs to be an analysis of risks for the person with any action planned to minimise those risks. If things are not planned out carefully and with clear objectives staff can easily gravitate towards safe options.

People using the service themselves, and their carers, need a copy of the agreed arrangements in a format that they can most easily understand so that they have the power to challenge, and complain about, the quality of the service they actually receive.

Achieving a quality service
Guiding and supporting staff

From the outset attention was paid to the training and support needs of the staff, recognising that they were the service's most valuable resource. An induction programme was specifically designed to underpin the values and objectives of the service, and to involve the team in developing some of its working procedures and systems. The aim was to develop a team with a shared purpose and an open, challenging way of working together.

Because staff of a community-based service are out and about much of the time, on-going support and guidance is imperative. The staff are thinking on their feet, adapting and changing plans when needed, sometimes dealing with difficult situations, sometimes having real successes. Staff can receive support and guidance through regular supervision sessions, team meetings, programmed office time so that people can talk to their colleagues, telephone contact, or pairing staff to work together around a person. For people who aren't located together all day there is, however, a real need to ensure that formal support mechanisms are used as effectively as possible. A problem-solving focus that involves and engages the team is both empowering and supportive. To some extent staff feeling well supported and well guided is a natural consequence of good teamwork and positive, focused leadership.

To achieve flexibility a community-based service may rely upon using sessional workers who do not have their own regular or formal support system. It is essential to ensure that they are adequately inducted into the service, understand and share its purpose, feel part of the team, and feel valued. This is a responsibility that has to be shared by all members of the team.

Support and guidance can also come, of course, from the people staff are interacting with on a day-to-day basis – the people using the service, their carers, students in their classes, colleagues at their work site. A community-based service means new ways of working and new ways of thinking about support and guidance for workers. The best person to guide staff about support is the person who is going to be on the receiving end. Carers have an important role to play too in providing information and guidance about the support needed by a person. Involving and listening to carers is essential.

Monitoring and evaluation

One way that staff in a community-based team can receive support and guidance about their practice is through on-the-job supervision. This serves a dual purpose, enabling the supervisor/manager to monitor the quality of service delivery as well as give support and guidance. A key requirement when establishing the service framework is a team commitment to open practice and accountability. Monitoring that includes the manager spending both pre-planned and unplanned time with a member of staff and user is essential. The more regularly it happens the more natural it feels and the more useful it is for everyone.

The people who see staff in action the most will not be their manager or colleagues but service users and members of the public. Creative thinking is needed to find ways to capture their views on the quality of support they have received or witnessed. This feedback is needed so that staff can continuously improve their practice and so that the quality of the service can not only be maintained but also enhanced.

The Community Resource Service did not set up a formal users' group to represent the views of people using the service. Because the service that each person received was very individualised a group approach did not seem appropriate. The focus was on getting it right for individuals, which meant finding out from those individuals and their carers whether this was being achieved. This was done as a matter of course through the individual planning process. However, the service commissioned an external evaluation after the first year of operation to help shape its future development. This involved getting the perspective of people using the service, their carers, and other key stakeholders.

Having an independent view on the service's progress, strengths and development priorities can be extremely important for a community-based service. It being a new model of service provision, there was understandable interest in whether the Community Resource Service could really help people achieve more positive outcomes than existing, more traditional services. It being a service that focuses much more on individualised responses, there were also concerns about whether it was a cost-effective service, able to achieve 'best value' from public resources. Structured monitoring and evaluation helps to answer these questions.

For the Community Resource Service it was also extremely important to monitor whether people from minority ethnic communities were being well served. The service had a responsibility to deliver ethnically and culturally appropriate opportunities and support for people – it needed to remain conscious and aware of this service objective and keep an eye on how it was doing with it. Linking with, and getting advice from, people from the different communities was essential to enable access to culturally-specific community opportunities and to learn how to deliver a better service.

The challenge of evaluation

One of the issues that the evaluation raised was about the team's role in relation to seeking out and supporting people into employment. There were two small supported employment projects in the borough and a few individuals had been referred through by the team for support. Little had changed, however, in terms of those people actually securing work. The evaluation challenged the team to see it as *their* responsibility and to take positive action themselves if a person wanted to get a job. They did, after all, know the people they were serving well and had developed a picture of each person's talents and potential contribution. This challenge was well received and led to the team supporting a number of people into part-time work.

Comparing and challenging

It can be difficult for an innovative team at the cutting edge of service delivery to know where to look for external support and advice that will help them to push forward even more. People call *them* for advice, come to visit, ask them to speak at conferences. Links with other organisations with a similar value base but who are using different ways to help develop people's lives can be helpful. The service found it particularly useful to link with supported employment agencies and the Circles Network because they challenged what the team was doing and its accepted ways of working.

Inevitably the service was compared with other services, both locally and beyond, and just as inevitably the team compared their work with that of other services around them. It was important that the service could be challenged, and that team members responded positively when it happened, modelling a commitment to quality and a concern for continuous improvement. The team's role as standard-bearers for the 'new direction' (London Borough of Hackney 1995) was very clear; but what also grew, more unexpectedly, was a watchdog role across services. The team quite naturally raised

concerns they had about the quality of service people (who they were supporting) received when using other services. This helped the organisation as
a whole to address quality problems. Team members were seen by some staff
in the more traditional day services as mavericks, and a threat. The lesson was
that having a maverick service, which stood out as different from the other
day services, challenged those services and helped to move everything
forward.

Ensuring it works for people with complex needs

It is easy for people planning services to imagine that we will always need a
different level or type of service for people with more complex needs. If
planning is at an individual level and support is arranged accordingly, with
each barrier tackled as it arises, there is no reason why people with the most
complex of needs or behaviours cannot be supported in the community.
Examples from supported employment have shown how people have responded positively to much more ordinary environments, learning from the
people around them and making a real contribution. The Community
Resource Service supported a number of people with complex needs and experienced this too. Yes, there can be some resistance from members of the
public, but most often people are accommodating and welcoming, with new
ideas about how a person could get involved and about contributions a
person could make.

Most important is that people are well supported – requiring that their
support needs are thoroughly considered at the individual service planning
stage and action is taken to address them. Having a communication profile, a
clear picture of how the person communicates (verbally, non-verbally and
with the assistance of any aids), helps interaction between a member of staff
and a user while also achieving a more consistent approach. Using graphics
and visual aids can effectively support people in making choices. Identifying
the things that a person *most* enjoys and supporting them in doing those
things regularly brings a feeling of success that will increase everyone's confidence. It is vitally important for a community-based service to engender a

feeling of trust amongst the carers of people with complex needs, and to then build on it by opening up new opportunities and experiences for people, building more positive lifestyles.

Denise

Denise was from a Jamaican family and lived with her parents. Her experience at the day centre had been quite negative. Denise, a tall woman, had a reputation for challenging behaviour and was rarely encouraged to go outside the centre as staff were worried that some of her behaviours – taking drinks from people, pouring liquid over herself – would be too difficult to support.

With one-to-one support from the community team, Denise went out regularly and developed confidence and trust. Making sure she always had access to a drink helped her to become more relaxed. Denise was happiest when busy and when practising new skills. She liked physical work, so the team supported her in securing voluntary work at a garden centre. Coaching helped her develop the necessary skills. Denise learned quickly, but staff at the garden centre were not very supportive of her being there. The worker's role alternated between supporting Denise, liaising with her parents, who were worried about Denise being away from the day centre, and negotiating with garden centre staff for Denise to stay on.

A second worker was introduced into the frame. This sessional worker was, like Denise, from a Jamaican background. It was an important step forward. This worker was able to develop a much more productive relationship with Denise's family; for example, she was able to challenge and gradually encourage them to support Denise in dressing more appropriately for her age – she had previously worn quite girlish clothes. She also enabled the mother to think about how Denise might be able to handle more of her own money. Such challenges to the family's established ways of operating may not have been so well received coming from a white worker.

With individualised and systematic teaching Denise became extremely competent at gardening tasks. The staff at the garden centre did not, however, become any more welcoming. Denise had something to offer, and it was important that it was valued. So, with her new skills and experience, the team supported her in attaining a paid part-time job with one of the council's gardening teams working at a local park.

The service found that most education classes 'for people with learning diffi-culties' were effectively closed to people with more complex needs. It looked to open classes used by all members of the public instead and succeeded in supporting some people into integrated groups. Some barriers can be posi-tively helpful when it comes to social inclusion!

Jonathan

Jonathan had lived for much of his childhood and adult life in a Surrey hospital but moved back to Hackney, to a local authority hostel, in the early 1990s. He had no contact with his family. Little was known about Jonathan's interests, likes or dislikes. He used a wheelchair and had very little speech. He went out infrequently because hostel staff were anxious about the fact that he would scream and bang his head. Before the community service got involved he had received no day services.

Through the team Jonathan was linked to two support workers who would go out with him on different days of the week. He clearly liked being out, even in bad weather, but it was really hard to get a sense of other things he liked to do. 'Going out' was in danger of losing its purpose so the workers visited the hospital Jonathan used to live in to try to get some background information about things he had done before or interests he may have had. The visit gave them few clues about his interests, but did give them an insight into his previous life on a very stark ward. It was no wonder he seemed to have no interests. They also got another important lead. When at the hospital Jonathan had had a friend, Paul, who had also moved back to Hackney. The workers arranged for Jonathan and Paul to meet up. The meeting went well and Paul indicated that he would like to see Jonathan regularly, so the team helped this to happen. Paul had an interest in fish and had an aquarium at home, and over time it became clear that the fish fascinated Jonathan. Seeing the fascination the workers supported him in buying and keeping some fish of his own. They actively helped Jonathan to build on an interest and develop a hobby of his own.

Management style and the culture of the service

In community-based services the service culture needs to be enabling and empowering. Prescriptive, directive and hierarchical management cannot work when it is essential that staff are able to act on their own initiative, take charge in a crisis and, by and large, manage their own time and work-load. Because much work is out of sight it is essential that staff have a strong investment in what they are doing. It is worth holding out for democratic decisions. The workers are the public face of the service and the quality of their support will affect people. If workers do not believe in what they are doing or that it is right for a person, if they feel alienated, unsupported or isolated, quality support will not be achieved. There must be trust.

It has been important for the team manager to spend quite a lot of time physically present in the office, available for workers to grab ten minutes when they are back at base and need advice. A priority for the manager is to nurture a team of strong, competent and effective workers; but it is essential that people are able to ask for and receive support when they need it.

A learning culture is needed. The team itself needs to feel safe, and positively encouraged, to generate, consider and implement new ideas, with members feeling responsible for the development of the service. There must be time and space for discussion of ideas, and support for people to 'give things a go'. A culture where people calculate and effectively manage risks so that people they support can try new things is the key to an innovative, person-centred service.

Some key issues

Paid worker or friend? When does work begin and end?

There are no easy answers to the question of when someone's paid work begins and ends in a community-based service. It is helpful to match up support along people's interests and passions – there is little worse for someone than being supported by a person who clearly does not enjoy the activity. It also reduces the chance of the supporter being able to help the person gain skills, make links and build on his or her interests. A member of staff who is personally keen on amateur dramatics is more likely to support someone effectively to develop an interest in drama than another staff member who has no interest in it at all. The person is more likely to know what is going on where and who might be good to link with. The experience of attending the drama group together may be mutually beneficial and enjoyable for the staff member and the person with a learning difficulty, but should the staff member continue to be paid to support the person once they have gained an entry into the drama group? Should we pay staff to support someone to go out for a meal and then on to the theatre?

Community-based services must look for long-term sustainable involvement for people. One-off activities like the trips out that many day services organise can give people a good experience but do little to build people's involvement in, or sense of belonging to, their community. Sustainable involvement means becoming a member, attending regularly, and making relationships with people. It means workers helping people to develop more natural support – deliberately supporting the person in the drama group in developing friendships and connections with people who can take on the support role. Fading the paid support is an important aim.

The impetus to develop natural support comes partly from concerns around the cost of individualised support in the context of extremely overstretched public service finances, but it is more fundamentally rooted in the desire to help people achieve social inclusion. The simple fact is that the presence of a worker can act as a barrier to real inclusion – the worker's role must be to help a person make direct connections and build relationships that make their own presence redundant.

Social support arises from at least four distinct experiences:

- feeling attached to other people who are emotionally important

- having the opportunity to engage in shared activities

- being part of a network of people who can approach one another for information and assistance

- having a place and playing a variety of roles in economic and civil life. (O'Brien and O'Brien 1992, p.27)

In a community-based service the purpose of support needs to be very clear. What is the worker trying to achieve, what goals are being pursued, how will these be reached and what is the time scale? These are difficult questions, but without the clarity staff may be left unclear as to whether they are acting as friends or as paid workers. Any team will need to agree where and how to place the boundaries. Clarity of role is important but it is a balancing act not to remove valuable flexibility and the development of positive, mutual relationships between staff and the people they support. To share a good time with someone it is essential to be able to see that person relaxed, enthused, reacting in different environments. It can change your perception of the person and their perception of you; it develops trust.

Finances and costs

Local authorities have struggled to accurately cost day services that are organised and funded as block provision. The cost per person per day has typically been worked out by simply dividing the overall service costs by the number of people using the service. This gives an inaccurate picture: it does not take into account that each person needs a different level of support. This is very much clearer in a service that has an individualised approach, but community-based services present a new challenge: patterns of service use are less likely to be centred on whole days, and support costs may be intensive at the beginning and decrease as natural supports develop. What's needed are new and different ways of costing such services and assessing their value over the long term.

The introduction of direct payments fits well with an individualised community-based service, potentially giving service recipients even more control over the support they receive. What will help even more in the future is the move towards individualised service purchasing through care management. Focusing funding on individuals, with close monitoring of the outcomes achieved for people, is totally in accord with the ethos and objectives of a good quality community-based service.

Supporting people in achieving social inclusion through an individual-ised community-based service has associated costs that cannot be ignored. Doing things in the community takes money: leisure activities, further and adult education classes, using public transport, memberships – the more people do the more it costs. For people with learning difficulties the issue is about having limited personal spending power. Most are poor and have little to spend each week. For the service the issue is about the costs for staff and supporters to be there alongside the person. A community-based service needs a strategy to address these issues. This might include giving informa-tion about costs to people so they can choose how to spend their money, benefits checks, ensuring take-up of financial breaks available to disabled people such as reduced-price leisure cards, managing charitable offers pur-posefully, and negotiating companion passes (Cole, McIntosh and Whittaker 2000). Being proactive is essential.

The risk of innovation

Community-based teams are at the forefront of a major change in thinking about day services for people with learning difficulties. There is a danger that they can feel isolated and under enormous pressure to succeed – to prove that it's a positive and successful model. It is essential to look after the innovators!

The Community Resource Service in Hackney was concerned with people's lifestyles; it was committed to inclusion. The team needed to innovate, to solve problems, to learn and develop with experience. The quality of the leadership the team received was pivotal to the outcomes it achieved with individuals. Without a leader with a clear vision and a commit-ment to tackling exclusion the service, under pressure, would undoubtedly have compromised on quality. But leaders need support too, and ensuring those in community-based teams get it has to be a high priority for organisa-tions.

In the pressure to succeed there is a real danger that services can take their eye off the ball when it comes to ensuring that people from diverse ethnic groups are being served appropriately. There is a tendency to unconscious ethnocentricity. Being community-based and focused on individuals, it is tempting to assume that this will not be an issue – but it will be unless it is regularly discussed and kept alive in the service. Staff in community-based teams must be supported and encouraged to get to know the community and the communities within it.

A community-based service needs to be set up as part of an overall strategy for improving day opportunities. Without a firm strategic foundation there is a danger that it can be seen as a luxury and quickly come under attack, particularly when initial unit costs appear high. This type of service does not offer a quick fix – it can achieve good quality outcomes for people which are person-centred and inclusive, but it needs time to do so. With the growth of community-based teams around the UK there is a pressing need for a realistic and service-appropriate costing method to be developed, as has been done with supported employment projects (see Beyer, Goodere and Kilsby 1996). Without a cost-benefit analysis that shows firm evidence of positive outcomes for individuals combined with reducing support costs, this model of provision will be vulnerable.

A community-based service cannot be formulaic. There are service features that can help, and a strong and clear framework is needed; but at the end of the day it's about whatever is right for the individuals using the service. Flexibility is the watchword; without it, a quality service will not be achieved and people will not achieve social inclusion.

Authors' Note

The views expressed in this chapter are the authors' own and not necessarily those of the Community Resource Service or the London Borough of Hackney.

References

Beyer, S., Goodere, L. and Kilsby, M. (1996) *The Costs and Benefits of Supported Employment Agencies.* London: HMSO.

Brost, M., Johnson, T.Z. and Deprey, R.K. (1982) *Getting to Know You: One Approach to Service Planning and Assessment for People with Learning Difficulties.* Madison WI: Wisconsin Coalition for Advocacy.

Cole, A. (1998) 'Stepping out in Hackney.' *Care Plan 4*, 4, 12–16.

Cole, A., McIntosh, B. and Whittaker, A. (2000) *We Want our Voices Heard: Developing New Lifestyles with Disabled People.* Bristol: The Policy Press.

London Borough of Hackney (1995) (Internal document) *A New Sense of Direction: Review of Day and Residential Services Provided by the Department for Adults with Learning Difficulties.*

London Borough of Hackney (1996) (Internal document) *Five Year Plan to Improve Day Opportunities and Day Services for People with Learning Difficulties.*

McIntosh, B. and Whittaker, A. (eds) (1998) *Days of Change: A Practical Guide to Developing Better Day Opportunities with People with Learning Difficulties.* London: King's Fund.

McIntosh, B. and Whittaker, A. (eds) (2000) *Unlocking the Future: Developing New Lifestyles with People who have Complex Needs.* London: King's Fund.

Mental Health Foundation (1996) *Building Expectations: Opportunities and Services for People with a Learning Disability.* London: Mental Health Foundation.

O'Brien, J. and O'Brien, C.L. (1992) 'Members of each other: Perspectives on social support for people with severe disabilities.' In J. Nisbet (ed) *Natural Supports in School, at Work, and in the Community for People with Severe Disabilties.* Baltimore: Paul H. Brookes.

Sanderson, H., Kennedy, J., Ritchie, P. and Goodwin, G. (1997) *People, Plans and Possibilities.* Edinburgh: SHS.

Simons, K. and Watson, D. (1999) *New Directions? Day Services for People with Learning Disabilities in the 1990s.* Exeter: University of Exeter.

Smull, M. and Burke-Harrison, S. (1992) *Supporting People with Severe Reputations in the Community.* Virginia: National Association of State Directors of Developmental Disabilities Services Inc.

CHAPTER 10

Effective Mental Health Day Services and Employment

Evidence and Innovations

Bob Grove and Helen Membrey

Mental health day services and employability

The starting point for thinking about how day services for people with mental health problems can be improved must be the question: 'What are they for?' The very term 'day services' is unhelpful. It says only that they take place during normal working hours and therefore that the people who use them are presumed to be unemployed and perhaps unemployable.

The authors' recent experience of conducting service reviews of mental health day services has been very revealing. In the course of visiting services and talking to users, staff and managers we have seen many exciting and creative projects, but in most areas the services as a whole lack coherence. There is no shared vision or service philosophy to which everyone can sign up and often – most crucially – there is no systemic way of addressing the individual needs and aspirations of the people who use them.

This is not to say that users do not value the services. When asked, people say they like their day centres – they feel safe, it is somewhere to meet their friends and they feel well supported by committed staff. However, when the questions move on to how users want their lives to be in five years' time, then the answers are different. People talk of wanting a job, a decent income and a social life not necessarily confined to the company of other service users. Unfortunately, it appears to us that the services we have visited rarely address these ambitions. All too often they are stuck at the stage of providing somewhere welcoming and safe to go and little more. We have been to day centres whose performance is judged on how many people keep coming to the building day after day, rather than on how many move on to more normal situations. Often there seems to be an implicit assumption that once a person has a diagnosis their ambitions, their belief in themselves – their individual life's journey – comes to a halt. The danger is that this can create an attitude among both staff and users that makes it a self-fulfilling prophecy.

We have found that resistance to change is justified by five highly questionable lines of argument. These can be summarised as:

- most people who use our day services are unemployable

- users share the need for structured, time-filling activity

- users are lonely and therefore feel better when in the company of people who share their mental health difficulties

- once users have found somewhere that provides the above, they lack the motivation to move on

- any talk of moving away from building-based day services will create so much fall-out among users and carers that it will be politically unacceptable.

These are serious arguments based on long and sometimes bitter experience and they need to be addressed. However, to deal with them all would take a whole book, so in this chapter we will deal with the first of these arguments – the evidence on employability. We will also deal with part of the fifth concerning the politics of change. Of course, this can only be dealt with partially, through evidence and reasoned argument; but it does need to be shown that there are alternatives that can meet people's needs for company and support and their aspirations for a normal life without trapping them in segregated, congregated service ghettos.

We chose to concentrate on employment because if it can be shown that many more people with severe mental health problems are employable than had previously been supposed and that many of the common-sense assumptions about how to help people get and keep a job are highly questionable, then all the other assumptions start to look insecure. Taking one step further – if it can be shown that there are cost-effective ways of supporting people into work who want it, then the whole edifice of generic, building-based day services starts to fall.

But do users want to work? Recent surveys indicate that users of mental health services rate the opportunity for a proper job as central to their recovery (Grove 1999). They are fearful about the risks of losing their entitlement to benefits if things don't work out, and also of other barriers that society erects to exclude them from a normal life as fully paid-up citizens. But if these can be overcome, there is overwhelming evidence that the great majority want to work when they can to improve their income and standard of living.

But is there any evidence to suggest that these aspirations are realistic? We will look first at the evidence on employability. Is it possible to assess who is likely to be able to hold down a job? Are there personal characteristics or indicators in a person's medical or social or employment history that make it possible to select those who should go into vocational programmes?

We will then look at the evidence on the effectiveness of vocational programmes. What are the programme factors that have been shown to be effective in helping people to get and keep employment, and what kind of outcomes can we expect if we use these methods? What proportion of people with mental health problems could achieve employment?

Having looked at the evidence we conclude by looking at how far day services in this country have to go to match up to evidence-based best practice and what, realistically, we can do to improve services in ways that meet the aspirations and abilities of service users.

Research findings on employability

Research in the vocational rehabilitation field over the last few decades has been predominantly American. It has largely been driven by a need to find out which service users will respond best to vocational interventions on the basis of their individual characteristics. While earlier studies have tended to explore the relationship between the characteristics of individuals with serious mental illness and their future vocational success, more recently there has been a shift towards the examination of different methodologies and approaches to vocational rehabilitation. We will explore the evidence for clinical, demographic, social and intrapersonal factors affecting employability.

Demographic factors

Most researchers have not found factors such as gender, age, education, ethnicity and marital status to have a strong effect on work outcomes for service users with serious mental illness. Some have reported a weak association between these demographic characteristics and future vocational success but, as William Anthony (1994) notes, this is related to employment participation for the general population and is not a particular feature of mental illness.

Clinical factors

There is strong evidence that a person's psychiatric diagnosis does not affect their ability to succeed in vocational programmes (Anthony 1994; Bybee, Mowbray and McCrohan 1996). Very few studies have found a link between either diagnosis or severity of impairment and employment retention. Anthony's extensive review found nine studies confirming this (1994, p.5).

On the issue of how symptoms may affect service users' ability to work there is conflicting and equivocal evidence. Some suggest that symptoms do not prevent service users participating in programmes and improving their vocational performance (1994; Drake *et al.* 1996; Mowbray *et al.* 1995; Smith *et al.* 1998). Anthony found evidence from another nine studies from the 1960s, 1970s and early 1980s all confirming that 'there appear to be no symptoms or symptom patterns that are consistently related to individual work performance' (1994, p.5). Some have argued that the more severe a service user's symptoms, the more impaired their work performance, and for that reason people are often cautious about allowing service users to work until their symptoms improve. Symptoms have been seen as predictors of social skills and work skills.

Others, however, argue that assessments of symptoms have been too generic to pick up the relationship between these different areas of functioning (Lysaker and Bell 1995; Smith *et al.* 1997). They have suggested that work performance and symptoms are distinct but inter-related areas and that there is a need to understand how specific symptoms affect particular areas of functioning (Lysaker and Bell 1995). Although more research is clearly needed to clarify this rather confusing picture, an important point about these studies of symptom effects is that ratings must be made concurrently with work activity as these are more powerful predictors than those recorded at intake to a programme. In other words, symptoms vary considerably over time (Lysaker and Bell 1995).

In addition to or instead of symptoms, researchers have looked at service users' clinical background in terms of how many lifetime hospitalisations they have had or the length and date of their most recent hospitalisation (Mowbray *et al.* 1995; Rogers *et al.* 1991). One study revealed that being recently hospitalised has an independent effect on work status: although we know that hospitalisation reduces service users' functioning levels, this is not the only way in which it impacts on vocational outcomes. However, it is impossible to pin down the nature of this relationship. Does the effect of entering a hospital in recent history diminish employment outcomes because of the stigma and disruption it causes, or is it that work lessens the likelihood of being hospitalised in the first place (Mowbray *et al.* 1995)?

Furthermore, there is some evidence that participation in work activity can have long-term beneficial effects on clinical outcomes such symptoms, medication compliance and relapse rates (e.g. Anthony *et al.* 1995; Arns and Linney 1993; Bell, Milstein and Lysaker 1993; Lehman 1995). It could be that returning to valued, adult roles has a positive impact on service users' self-esteem and their ability to manage their own illness, thus reducing symptoms.

What is clear is that the evidence does not strongly favour the use of symptom assessments, diagnosis or hospitalisation history to exclude service users from vocational programmes.

Social skills

Most studies show that social skills have only a small or non-significant relationship with vocational outcomes (Anthony 1994). While some have argued that the ability to get along with others in the workplace plays an important part in vocational success, the best way to assess these skills remains largely unresolved. There is evidence to suggest that when skills are tested generically in artificial environments the results do not translate easily to the real world and this could be one explanation why traditional measures of social skills have not been appropriate (Anthony 1994; Cook and Pickett 1994; Rogan and Hagner 1990).

However, in one study, the authors found that social skills improve significantly after as little as 17 weeks when service users are placed in real work situations. They explained this in terms of the increase in self-esteem and confidence that comes from having a productive work role, from overcoming fears of rejection, adjusting to expected social behaviours in the job site and working alongside regular colleagues (Lysaker and Bell 1995). The authors know of no other studies that have examined changes in social skills over time specifically in a work setting. As with symptoms, if social skills can be enhanced through work participation, then service users who perform poorly in this domain should not be excluded from vocational interventions.

Employment history

On the face of it the most promising predictor of future vocational performance appears to be the amount of previous work experience people have (Anthony 1994; Anthony and Jansen 1984; Bond 1992; Bybee *et al.* 1996; Drake *et al.* 1996; Xie *et al.* 1997). Although researchers have used different definitions of level of work experience (e.g. length of whole career, number of jobs over a career, length of different jobs, date of last employment), overall there is strong evidence that people with more work experience benefit more from vocational programmes than people with little or no work experience (Bond 1992). Anthony and colleagues reviewed studies showing that employment history accounted for as much as 53 per cent of the variance in vocational outcomes (Anthony, Cohen and Farkes 1990).

However, some more recent studies have incorporated newly discovered variables and, as a result of using more complex research designs, intrapersonal factors have emerged as more important than employment history. For instance, one study found that although both employment history and symptomatology were initially associated with vocational outcomes, these connections disappeared when service users' 'self-efficacy', or belief about how effective they could be in taking control of their lives was taken into account (Regenold, Sherman and Fenzel 1999).

Similarly, there is some evidence that being goal oriented is more important than how much work experience one has. Employment history did not predict outcomes in one study and the authors explained this in terms of how they had selected their research sample (Rogers *et al.* 1991). Their participants were involved in a community-based psychosocial programme, and had a vocational goal when they joined the programme. In most studies, researchers have used all hospital-based participants, whether they have employment aims or not.

The role of work history needs to be assessed carefully as a background characteristic: vocationally motivated service users should not be overlooked just because they have limited work experience (Mowbray *et al.* 1995).

Intrapersonal factors

As we have shown in relation to employment history, some more recent studies have suggested that the most significant characteristics affecting participation and success in vocational programmes are intrapersonal factors like work attitudes, work expectations, self-efficacy and motivation to work.

WORK ATTITUDES, EXPECTATIONS AND MOTIVATION

Some researchers have found correlations between work adjustment skills and vocational performance (Anthony 1994; Anthony and Jansen 1984; Bond and Friedmeyer 1987; Bryson *et al.* 1997). It has not always been clear which aspects of 'work adjustment' are critical, but some studies indicate that the most important is a 'strong feeling about the importance of work as a source of pride and accomplishment' (Blankertz and Robinson 1996; Bybee *et al.* 1996; Mowbray *et al.* 1995). However, here we have the familiar problem with direction of causality: is it that positive feelings about work accomplishments reflect a stronger motivation to gain and sustain work, or could it be that having a job heightens these feelings (Mowbray *et al.* 1995)?

In other studies, positive expectations about obtaining work made a significant contribution to participation in vocational projects (Blankertz and Robinson 1996; Braitman *et al.* 1995; Bybee *et al.* 1996; Rogers, MacDonald-Wilson and Anthony 1997; Rutman 1994).

In Alex Braitman's in-depth study of barriers to work for employed and unemployed service users, he and his colleagues found numerous factors; but the most important, particularly for unemployed service users, was motivation. They suggested that the aspects of motivation necessary to get and keep a job include having positive attitudes, being at work on time, being able to tolerate criticism, having the ability to self-start and being able to concentrate (Braitman *et al.* 1995).

One of the most crucial arguments to come out of this study is that motivation may over-ride all other barriers to work (Braitman *et al.* 1995, p.7). Although the authors highlighted a huge range of barriers including entitlements, anxiety about work and substance abuse problems, they argued that problems which have been identified by earlier research may only be significant because of the way in which they affect service users' motivational levels. The importance of pay has been recognised by several researchers (Bell *et al.* 1993; Blankertz and Robinson 1996). It will probably come as no surprise that pay is an important motivating factor – in one study the effect of returning to unpaid work placements after experiencing competitive work demotivated project participants and their work skills declined (Bell *et al.*

1993). The frequency of job loss and unsuccessful outcomes at work can also lower service users' motivation to pursue their employment goals. As with other individual characteristics, the causes of poor motivation are ambiguous – is it that repeated failures in the workplace cause poor motivation or is it that lower motivational levels reduce work skills (Braitman *et al.* 1995, p.7)?

SELF-EFFICACY

Coming back to self-efficacy, a few researchers have looked specifically at this as a predictor of future vocational performance (Arns and Linney 1993; Regenold *et al.* 1999). As a concept, self-efficacy simply refers to an individual's belief about their effectiveness or their sense of how effective they are. It has been argued that an individual's self-efficacy levels may determine whether they will initiate coping behaviour and for how long they will continue to tackle obstacles (Regenold *et al.* 1999).

Those with higher levels of self-efficacy tend to persist longer and by experiencing mastery over a situation their sense of effectiveness increases further. In contrast, those with low self-efficacy tend to avoid situations and environments that they think they can't cope with, further reinforcing their view of themselves as not possessing the necessary skills to succeed.

In another study, self-efficacy was found to be important in the long-term success of rehabilitation (Arns and Linney 1993). Changes in vocational status seemed to affect self-esteem and life satisfaction by modifying feelings of self-efficacy. Enhancing self-efficacy may therefore lead to positive vocational effects.

KEY MESSAGES ABOUT SERVICE USERS' INDIVIDUAL CHARACTERISTICS

What emerges quite strongly from this research evidence is that there is no case for discouraging service users from pursuing their vocational goals on the basis of their diagnosis, symptoms, level of social functioning or their employment history. In fact, working may actually reduce symptoms, improve social skills and reduce the likelihood of being hospitalised, while it obviously contributes to levels of work experience.

The evidence for intrapersonal factors, such as motivation and a person's sense of how effective they are, was more consistent and powerful. Interestingly, these factors are consistent with 'the recovery model' that has recently come to prominence in the American literature (Anthony 1993). In this context, recovery is seen as a process of recovering what has been lost through the experience of mental illness and becoming a patient. Ideas about recovery therefore focus on how service users can be empowered to manage their own illness in the community. This involves the development of self-awareness and coping strategies as well as both professional and community support systems (for a full discussion of this see Carling 1995).

An important point to come out of Braitman's study of work barriers was that service users who were in jobs were experiencing difficulties but they were overcoming them. They were able to work despite the side effects of medication, symptoms, anxiety and so forth. Research now needs to identify how successful coping strategies can be fostered, and what the best strategies are for developing support systems in the community.

As William Anthony argues, intrapersonal factors such as commitment to change, motivation and self-awareness can be changed through the engagement with vocational services and should not, therefore, be used to judge who is ready for employment. These individual characteristics can be enhanced by effective programmes: 'The more reasonable and less exclusionary acceptance factors may be an interested and ready individual and a relevant vocational rehabilitation intervention' (Anthony 1994, p.10).

Effective intervention: Methodologies and approaches to vocational rehabilitation

In several of the studies which set out to test service users' characteristics in relation to vocational success, researchers discovered that the different approaches of the service agencies involved seemed to play a significant part in employment outcomes (Blankertz and Robinson 1996; Bond *et al.* 1997; Drake *et al.* 1996). For instance, in one study it was found that working participants were more likely to have received direct assistance in obtaining jobs (Mowbray *et al.* 1995).

Despite this evidence, researchers have noted that most mental health programmes are not evaluated carefully enough to test the impact of specific components of their approaches (Blankertz and Robinson 1996). It has been argued by many that research should focus more strongly on the elements of different models of vocational rehabilitation rather than the service user characteristics stressed in previous research. Although there is more limited evidence for different approaches to vocational rehabilitation, what is interesting is that there appears to be a general consensus among researchers about what works.

What is emerging quite strongly is that forms of supported employment have been most effective with service users who have serious mental illness. Gary Bond and colleagues carried out an extensive review of the research in this area and found 17 studies examining the effectiveness of supported employment programmes. In each study, the advantages of particular supported employment methods were clear. In comparison with more traditional vocational interventions, participants in these programmes had higher rates of employment, longer job tenure and higher earnings (Bond *et al.* 1997). The authors reported an average competitive employment rate of 55–58 per cent for both experimental and non-experimental studies. Likewise the Back-to-Work Program in Washington DC achieved an employment rate of over 75 per cent with an average job tenure of 17 months (Abramson *et al.* 1994).

Furthermore, there has been no evidence that supported employment precipitates hospitalisation by increasing service users' stress levels (Bedell *et al.* 1998; Bond *et al.* 1997; Drake *et al.* 1994; Torrey, Becker and Mowbray 1995). Studies have found that even long-term day patients can move into supported employment programmes with positive competitive employment outcomes and with no significant negative effects (Bailey *et al.* 1998; Drake *et al.* 1996). Gary Bond and colleagues point out that 'increases in employment rates were especially marked for regular attenders of day treatment' (Bond *et al.* 1997, p.342).

Bond and colleagues' review included a number of studies examining the effectiveness of different supported employment programmes such as the Assertive Community Treatment Model and the Job Coach Model. While there is as yet no consensus about the components of supported employment for people with serious mental illness, the programmes which have the most support in the research literature share some key features. These include rapid job search with minimal pre-vocational work readiness training; the integration of clinical and vocational services; attention to service users' individual preferences; continuous assessment and ongoing support (see Bond 1998; Bond *et al.* 1997). The first two have the most empirical support. The Individual Placement and Support Model (IPS) incorporates all of these components and, therefore, emerges as the most promising programme.

A goal of permanent competitive employment

There is evidence that a single-minded focus on competitive employment is more effective in returning service users to jobs in the community, working alongside regular colleagues. Where there are sheltered workshop, day centre or clubhouse options, there are typically very low competitive employment rates and poor results in terms of moving people on.

While work attitudes, expectations and motivation levels have been found to be of key importance for positive vocational outcomes, the evidence suggests that interventions which aim to improve these intra-personal areas must occur in tandem with rapid job acquisition. What's more, most service users need direct assistance in obtaining employment: job clubs, for instance, have been found to be ineffective because they place the onus on service users to make contact with employers and find work (Bond 1998).

Traditionally, the assumption has been that improving service users' overall work adjustment and skills prior to entering the workforce is an essential first stage of vocational approaches. However, the evidence suggests that lengthy job readiness activities are unnecessary (Bond *et al.* 1997; Drake *et al.* 1996). Bond *et al.* note that 'direct approaches to finding and attaining employment, that is, place–train models, increase rates of competitive employment more than do gradual, stepwise approaches' (p.342).

For instance, several researchers have compared the employment outcomes for service users who are placed in a gradual programme with several months of pre-vocational skills training and those for service users placed in an accelerated group where they are immediately placed in a community work setting. The results are significantly better for those in the accelerated group (e.g. Bond *et al.* 1997; Drake *et al.* 1996). Proponents of this key principle believe that, although the speed at which service users get a job in the community will vary, the majority of those who express the desire to work should be able to do so, with assistance, within several months (e.g. Bond 1998; Drake *et al.* 1996).

The evidence suggests that service users are more likely to develop and change their job preferences through searching for and working at a job rather than through pre-vocational training. So experiential learning appears to be the most effective way for service users to plan their career and move forward (Becker, Bebout and Drake 1998).

The integration of mental health treatment with vocational rehabilitation into one service

There is strong and consistent evidence for integrated approaches to rehabilitation (Becker and Drake 1994; Bond *et al.* 1997; Borgeson and Cusick 1994; Chandler *et al.* 1997; Drake *et al.* 1996). Although many professionals attempt to bridge the gap between services with formal agreements and cross-training, it appears that integration is far more difficult when it involves various providers in different locations (Bond 1998).

Even when services are integrated within the same agency, there is a danger that they can become compartmentalised. Genuine collaboration between staff means shared decision-making and coordinated planning processes. Studies have shown that when there is real collaboration between mental health and vocational staff, there are fewer service users dropping out of vocational programmes and employment outcomes are significantly better

(Borgeson and Cusick 1994; Drake *et al.* 1995). Miscommunications and conflicts between clinicians and vocational specialists serving the same service user have been identified as a major barrier to job acquisition and maintenance (Rutman 1994; Torrey 1998).

Attention to individual preferences

Traditionally, providers have made choices about the pace and structure of vocational services for service users with mental illness, regardless of what they say. Studies have shown that when clients receive clear information about their choices at the point of entry into a programme, the drop-out rate is much lower (Bond 1998). They are more likely to understand and engage in the process.

Several research studies have shown that the majority of service users have a preference for the kind of job they want when entering a programme and that these are realistic and stable over time (Becker, Bebout and Drake 1998; Becker *et al.* 1996; Bond 1998). When service users obtain jobs matching their initial preferences, they are more satisfied and their job tenure is often more than doubled (Becker *et al.* 1996; Bond *et al.* 1997). Preferences extend beyond occupational choices: they include the location, hours of work, wage rate, values of the organisation, work environment and numerous other factors. Service users have also been found to favour approaches which focus on rapid job search and they prefer paid work in ordinary workplaces (Bell *et al.* 1993; Becker *et al.* 1996).

Unfortunately, most supported employment placements are in entry-level work. In the USA the most common occupations for this group are in janitorial work or food services, which accounts for between 35 and 62 per cent of jobs (Bond *et al.* 1997; Walls and Fullmer 1997). Although many service users do lack work experience and qualifications, there needs to be an emphasis on long-term career development including educational and training options (Bond *et al.* 1997). Whether service users make the transition to better jobs is unclear and there needs to be more research in this area. This may be one reason why some service users leave their jobs prematurely.

While in traditional programmes local job availability has often been the key criterion used for deciding where to place service users, this method involves fostering links with the wider business community to find more suitable work opportunities.

Continuous assessment and ongoing support in the workplace

The evidence suggests that testing employability or work readiness prior to placement in a job is not reliable. Traditional assessment approaches depend heavily on standardised tests of symptoms and skills (e.g. Bond 1998; Cook and Pickett 1994) which, as we have argued, do not have predictive validity. Although these tests can give some information about cognitive functioning or general social skills, they cannot assess a service user's ability to do a particular job in a specific work environment.

Situational assessments aim to test service users' skills in simulated work settings, using role-play for instance. As many commentators have noted, there is a myriad of different work environment characteristics that cannot be reproduced artificially (Bond 1998; Rogan and Hagner 1990). Actual work settings are the best place to assess a service user's aptitude for a particular job, whether they like the job or not and whether the environment is suited to their unique strengths, tastes, needs and experiences (Bond 1998; Cook and Pickett 1994; Rogan and Hagner 1990; Xie *et al.* 1997).

A key principle is that assessment is a continuous process which should be specific to the work culture, with implications for how to intervene and what kind of problem-solving strategies to use in work (Bond 1998).

Continuous assessment and support are clearly interrelated areas. Typically, funding mechanisms place a limit on how long professionals can work with a service user who has found employment. Closure is seen as being achieved once the service user is at the point of getting their job or after the completion of a certain number of days of employment (Bond 1998). However, the evidence suggests that the availability of on-going support is crucial to the long-term success of vocational interventions (e.g. Bond *et al.* 1997; Chandler *et al.* 1997; Cook and Pickett 1994; Lane Frey 1994;

McHugo, Drake and Becker 1998). The availability of on-going support from rehabilitation specialists has been found to predict job tenure (Xie *et al.* 1997). While there is a point at which support should be faded out or transferred on to a non-professional, there is more research needed to understand the nature and duration of supports required (Bond 1998; Marrone, Bazell and Gola 1995).

What is clear from the literature is that it is more difficult to hold on to a job than it is to get it in the first place (Storey and Certo 1996; Xie *et al.* 1997). So, although the initial goal is to maximise the fit between the service user and their job, there is an on-going need to determine the most effective way of helping them to maintain their employment (Bond 1998).

An unsatisfactory job ending is often initiated by the service user themselves, and several studies have explored why people leave their job and what might have helped them to stay (Becker *et al.* 1998; Fabian, Waterworth and Ripke 1993; MacDonald-Wilson *et al.* 1991; Xie *et al.* 1997). In one study, researchers found that unsatisfactory job terminations were associated with a huge number of different and inter-related problems arising on the job (Becker *et al.* 1998). These problems could not have been predicted by professionals in advance. The most common were inter-personal problems, dissatisfaction with the job and problems related to mental illness. The data suggest, then, that when jobs end for service users, this is largely due to unexpected events and reactions which occur once a job is in progress and that service users need help managing the intertwined areas of work, illness and inter-personal relationships.

Studies have also found that the sort of support used most often by service users is support to keep a job rather than to get it in the first place; in other words, to troubleshoot problems as they arise at work (Becker *et al.* 1998). Studies which have focused on the kinds of support used by service users once a job is in progress, have found huge variations (Becker *et al.* 1998; Fabian, Waterworth and Ripke 1993; Mancuso 1993). Service users access support for both work-related and non-work-related areas of their lives including transport, housing, benefits, medication and a whole range of other issues. Other than for simple information gathering, in one study service users most frequently looked to support staff for emotional support (Rogers *et al.* 1997). However, the conclusion here is that the type, frequency and location of supports need to be user-led, but that employment specialists must also take an active part in this process. What is important is that the support each individual needs is quickly and easily accessed at all times (Rogers *et al.* 1997).

There is some evidence that developing natural supports rather than using a job coach technique is more effective and longer-lasting (Fabian, Edelman and Leedy 1993; Hagner, Rogan and Murphy 1992; Storey and Certo 1996). Some researchers have found that the presence of a job coach may inhibit social integration at work, not facilitate it (Hagner *et al.* 1992; Storey and Certo 1996). The majority of contacts made by service users in one study were by telephone, suggesting that frequent, brief phone contacts may be more important for service users at different stages than the more intensive on-site support of the traditional job coach model (Rogers *et al.* 1997).

As a result of this there has been a shift in focus towards the development of natural supports in the workplace. This approach involves mobilising what is available in the workplace to offer support (Fabian, Edelman and Leedy 1993; Storey and Certo 1996). Employment specialists are encouraged to evaluate and improve working environments for their service users.

The characteristics of the workplace itself that promote integration and long-term job retention have not been widely researched. One of the most common barriers to work which clients themselves identify is the ignorance and prejudice of employers and co-workers (Fabian, Edelman and Leedy 1993). There is some evidence that the social characteristics of the workplace are important in long-term retention of a job, and natural support approaches might involve linking employees to existing social supports in the workplace (West and Parent 1995).

Some more recent evidence has suggested that supervisors are the 'linchpin' in successful job experiences. Sheila Akabas (1995) from the Workplace Center of Columbia has done some interesting work on this. She has found that workers who become supervisors are often unclear about their new management duties and are not given any training for this. They are often unsure about how to approach the negotiation of workplace adjustments and feel pressured to meet productivity targets rather than management ones. In some recent research, she found that most service users were both over- and inappropriately accommodated. In most cases this was due to misunderstandings between employees and supervisors. She concludes that supervisors need information and training on how to facilitate the negotiation of accommodations; they need to be monitored and helped to perform vital management roles.

Studies that have looked at which job or work environment modifications are typically required by service users have confirmed how widely this varies for each individual. In one study, 30 individuals who held 47 jobs during the study period had 231 accommodations with an average of just over 5 per job (Fabian, Waterworth and Ripke 1993). The number of accommodations per job was significantly associated with job tenure. The most frequent, however, was supervisor orientation and training to provide necessary assistance. A number of studies have found that flexible working hours is the most commonly requested accommodation in the workplace (Fabian, Edelman and Leedy 1993; Mancuso 1993; Marrone 1993).

It is not so much the characteristics of the employee that are the key to success then, but the match between the employee and the job, and some of this can be achieved by supportive work environments (West and Parent 1995).

Conclusions and implications

What, then, are the main points to emerge from the literature, and what are the implications of this evidence for day services?

We began by looking at how clients' characteristics have been investigated in order to find out who should be included in vocational rehabilitation programmes. The research literature about which client characteristics predict employability turned out be inconclusive, but suggested that intra-personal factors related to behaviour and attitudes are more promising as indicators. An important point to be made here is that these are factors that can be changed through effective rehabilitation programmes and should not therefore be used to exclude people with mental health problems.

Furthermore, there is a growing consensus that it is the service approach and not the individual service user that is the key to successful vocational outcomes. This allows us to place the onus of success or failure on the system and not on the service user (Blankertz and Robinson 1996).

Next, we looked at the strengths and limitations of different methodologies of employment placement and support. We found that whereas traditional approaches to vocational rehabilitation have been directed towards enhancing the individual to fit in with the workplace, the focus and philosophy of the most promising supported employment models place emphasis on functioning in normal adult roles, integration into the community and movement away from patient roles. In this new model, much of the responsibility for workplace and community inclusion is shifted on to professionals and employers, and clients are helped to access their own support needs. We also found that where this approach has been thoroughly tested the results in terms of employment and job tenure – even for people with severe mental health problems – are very promising. Compare the 40 to 75 per cent employment rate achieved in some programmes with the overall rate of less than 10 per cent for people for severe mental health problems in the UK according to the most recent Labour Force Survey (a quarterly survey of employment data using a sample of around 61,000 households in the UK – see Office for National Statistics 2000).

It can and will be argued that the circumstances in the USA are different – especially in respect of social welfare payments. While this is true, the fact remains that supported employment for people with mental health problems has scarcely been tried in the UK. Where it has, agencies such as Mitre in Birmingham, the Richmond Fellowship's QEST teams and Network Employment on Merseyside are reporting encouraging rates of employment placement – this despite the 'benefits trap'. Working from a philosophy of finding individual solutions, a knowledgeable support worker can find ways of mini-mising risk and enhancing income from employment. Recent changes in welfare benefits rules have also been some help and there are signs from the Government that there may be more to come.

In the UK we are in the early stages of assessing the impact of the Disabil-ity Discrimination Act, which is itself modelled on the Americans with Dis-abilities Act 1990 (ADA). Sayce (1999) argues that the ADA has been funda-mental in shifting attitudes of employers and mental health services regard-ing the employment of people with mental health problems, and that we may see the same kind of effects here.

Implications for mental health day services

The assumption that users of mental health services want and need day service provision that offers, in the main, only alternatives to employment is highly questionable. Such provision not only fails to address the rights and aspirations of service users, but also creates barriers to recovery by creating self-fulfilling low expectations and dependency. We have shown that there are effective ways of supporting individuals into employment and that if someone really wants to work, then it is likely that with the right kind of help, they will be able to achieve this ambition.

At the beginning of the chapter we reflected on our own experience of visiting traditional day services and talking to the people who use them. All the users we spoke to were clear about their priority areas of need. First, they want someone to talk to who will understand them and accept them for what they are. Second, they want something to do. These priorities emerged time and time again in stakeholder events we have attended right across the country. They have also emerged strongly in the *Strategies for Living* research report (Faulkner and Layzell 2000). Beyond that, however, the kind of things people say they need are to do with the recovery of an ordinary life. Is this going to be possible in the era of 'safe, sound and supportive' – the subtitle of the Government's policy statement *Modernising Mental Health Services* (Department of Health 1998) – and the National Service Framework? Despite the impression that is sometimes given that Government is only concerned with preventing people from harming themselves or others, there is in fact explicit support for a shift in priorities towards the kinds of services that users are asking for:

> Service users themselves believe that adequate housing and income and assistance with the social and occupational aspects of daily living are among the most important aspects of care and reduce disability... An appreciable number of service users may also need help to access employment, education and training and some at least will be able to obtain and sustain work. (NHS Executive 1999, p.46)

There are, in addition, a number of mainstream policy initiatives that will support service users in accessing employment. We have already mentioned the Disability Discrimination Act, which explicitly includes people with mental health problems within its remit. The New Deal for Disabled People, and the requirement for local authorities to draw up Joint Investment Plans (JIPs) on Welfare to Work for Disabled People by 2001, will also focus the minds of planners and commissioners and provide incentives for joined-up thinking and working.

But what about the other things people say they want – someone to talk to, something to do? Here there is emerging evidence that professionals do not need to be directly involved in providing front-line social support and that service users themselves can organise and lead services if given the resources. Needless to say, if most people are at work or similarly engaged during the working day, then the social support is likely to be needed at weekends or evenings when professional workers are often unavailable. User-led out-of-hours services are operating effectively in a number of London boroughs. In Newham a local user group has received substantial funding to take over the freehold of a community centre, from which they will provide services not only for people with mental health problems but for the whole community.

But policy initiatives alone will not bring about change, nor will the creation of innovative projects that are simply bolted on to a system which is based on an entirely different philosophy. We believe that for change to take place there will need to be a paradigm shift in the assumptions on which day services are based. In this chapter we have suggested that an employment focus based on individual placement and support is likely to be effective in meeting the needs and aspirations of service users, and can play a vital role in helping them recover a normal life. The IPS principles involving individual support and removing barriers to participation can be applied equally to education, creative and leisure activities.

So are we anywhere near articulating a unifying philosophy for day services? At the beginning of the chapter we looked at five implicit assumptions on which traditional day services have been based and challenged their validity. To bring about a paradigmatic shift we propose five principles on which day services of the future should be based. Services should:

- address the needs, aspirations and rights of individuals to recover those aspects of an ordinary life that are lost through mental ill health

- emphasise individual support, the development of self-confidence, self-efficacy and coping mechanisms

- make no prior assumptions about an individual's employability and support those who want a job in obtaining and keeping paid work by the most direct route

- provide more support for self-organised work, support services and creative activity

- move away from segregated, congregated settings towards real-life settings and investment in practical support rather than buildings.

Further research is needed, especially in the UK. Some of this might be usefully directed at how people with long-term psychiatric illness manage their symptoms while working, and what reasonable accommodations in the workplace would enable them to work to their full potential. Other studies might look at adjustments and support in education. However, a vital area for the immediate future is to look at the effectiveness of user-led services and how such developments can be encouraged and supported. For addressing all these questions there will, in our view, need to be trained researchers with experience of using mental health services who can participate in the design of studies and take a lead in carrying them out. This will not only improve the quality of the work by bringing in expertise gained from experience, but will also ensure that disabled people benefit financially from participating in research. But that is another chapter.

References

Abramson, L., Chuck, J., Ripke, B. and Schweitzer, K. (1994) 'Strategies to increase job tenure for people with psychiatric disabilities: An overview of the back to work programme.' *American Rehabilitation 20*, 4, 13–17.

Akabas, S.H. (1995) 'Supervisors: The linchpin in effective employment for people with disabilities.' *Journal of the California Alliance for the Mentally Ill 6*, 4, 17–18.

Anthony, W.A. (1993) 'Recovery from mental illness: The guiding vision of the mental health system in the 1990s.' *Psychosocial Rehabilitation Journal 16*, 4, 11–23.

Anthony, W.A. (1994) 'Characteristics of people with psychiatric disabilities that are predictive of entry into the rehabilitation process and successful employment outcomes.' *Psychosocial Rehabilitation Journal 17*, 3, 3–14.

Anthony, W.A., Cohen, M.R. and Farkas, M.D. (1990) *Psychiatric Rehabilitation.* Boston, MA: Boston University Center for Psychiatric Rehabilitation.

Anthony, W.A. and Jansen, M.A. (1984) 'Predicting the vocational capacity of the chronically mentally ill.' *American Psychologist 39*, 537–544.

Anthony, W.A., Rogers, E.S., Cohen, M. and Davies, R.R. (1995) 'Relationships between psychiatric symptomatology, work skills and future vocational performance.' *Psychiatric Services 46*, 4, 353–358.

Arns, P.G. and Linney, J.A. (1993) 'Work, self and life satisfaction for persons with severe and persistent mental disorders.' *Psychosocial Rehabilitation Journal 17*, 2, 63–80.

Bailey, E.L., Ricketts, S.K., Becker, D.R., Xie, H.Y. and Drake, R.E. (1998) 'Do long-term day treatment clients benefit from supported employment?' *Psychiatric Rehabilitation Journal 22*, 1, 24–29.

Becker, D.R., Bebout, R.R. and Drake, R.E. (1998) 'Job preferences of people with severe mental illness: A replication.' *Psychiatric Rehabilitation Journal 22*, 1, 46–51.

Becker, D.R. and Drake, R.E. (1994) 'Individual placement and support: A community mental health center approach to vocational rehabilitation.' *Community Mental Health Journal 30*, 2, 193–213.

Becker, D.R., Drake, R.E., Bond, G.R., Xie, H., Dain, B.J. and Harrison, K. (1998) 'Job terminations among persons with severe mental illness participating in supported employment.' *Community Mental Health Journal 34*, 1, 71–82.

Becker, D.R., Drake, R.E., Farabaugh, E. and Bond, G.R. (1996) 'Job preferences of clients with severe psychiatric disorders participating in supported employment.' *Psychiatric Services 47*, 11, 1223–1225.

Bedell, J.R., Draving, D., Parrish, A., Gervey, R. and Guastadisegni, P. (1998) 'A description and comparison of experiences of people with mental disorders in supported employment and paid prevocational training.' *Psychiatric Rehabilitation Journal 21*, 3, 279–283.

Bell, M.D., Milstein, R.M. and Lysaker, P. (1993) 'Pay and participation in work activity: Clinical benefits for clients with schizophrenia.' *Psychosocial Rehabilitation Journal 17*, 2, 173–177.

Blankertz, L. and Robinson, S. (1996) 'Adding a vocational focus to mental health rehabilitation.' *Psychiatric Services 47*, 11, 1216–1222.

Bond, G.R. (1992) 'Vocational rehabilitation.' In R.P. Liberman (ed) *Handbook of Psychiatric Rehabilitation*. New York: Macmillan.

Bond, G.R. (1998) 'Principles of the Individual Placement and Support model: Empirical support.' *Psychiatric Rehabilitation Journal 22*, 1, 11–23.

Bond, G.R., Drake, R.E., Mueser, K.T. and Becker, D.R. (1997) 'An update on supported employment for people with severe mental illness.' *Psychiatric Services 48*, 3, 335–346.

Bond, G.R. and Friedmeyer, M.H. (1987) 'Predictive validity of structural reassessment at a psychiatric rehabilitation center.' *Rehabilitation Psychology 32*, 99–112.

Borgeson, N.J. and Cusick, G.M. (1994) 'Outreach and interagency collaboration: A deterrent to drop-out from vocational rehabilitation.' *Psychosocial Rehabilitation Journal 18*, 2, 95–98.

Braitman, A., Counts, P., Davenport, R., Zurlinden, B., Rogers, M., Clauss, J., Kulkarni, A., Kymla, J. and Montgomery, L. (1995) 'Comparison of barriers to employment for unemployed and employed clients in case management programme: An exploratory study.' *Psychiatric Rehabilitation Journal 19*, 3–8.

Bryson, G., Bell, M.D., Lysaker, P. and Zito, W. (1997) 'The Work Behaviour Inventory: A scale for the assessment of work behavior of people with severe mental illness.' *Psychiatric Rehabilitation Journal 20*, 4, 47–55.

Bybee, D., Mowbray, C.T. and McCrohan, N.M. (1996) 'Towards zero exclusion in vocational opportunities for persons with psychiatric disabilities: Prediction of service receipt in a hybrid vocational/case management service programme.' *Psychiatric Rehabilitation Journal 19*, 4, 15–27.

Carling, P.J. (1995) *Return to Community – Building Support Systems for People with Psychiatric Disabilities*. New York: Guilford Press.

Chandler, D., Meisel. J., Hu, W., McGowen, M. and Madison, K. (1997) 'A capitated model for cross-section of severely mentally ill clients: Employment outcomes.' *Community Mental Health Journal 33*, 6, 501–516.

Cook, J.A. and Pickett, S.A. (1994) 'Recent trends in vocational rehabilitation for people with psychiatric disability.' *American Rehabilitation 20*, 4, 2–12.

Department of Health (1998) *Modernising Mental Health Services*. London: HMSO.

Drake, R.E., Becker, D.R., Biesanz, J.C., Torrey, W.C. and McHugo, G.J. (1994) 'Rehabilitative day treatment versus supported employment. I. Vocational outcomes.' *Community Mental Health Journal 30*, 5, 519–532.

Drake, R.E., Becker, D.R., Biesanz, J.C., Wyzik, P.F. and Torrey, W.C. (1996) 'Day treatment versus supported employment for persons with severe mental illness: A replication study.' *Psychiatric Services 47*, 10, 1125–1127.

Drake, R.E., Becker, D.R., Xie, H. and Anthony, W.A. (1995) 'Barriers in the brokered model of supported employment for persons with psychiatric disabilities.' *Journal of Vocational Rehabilitation 5*, 141–150.

Fabian, E.S., Edelman, A. and Leedy, M. (1993) 'Linking workers with severe disabilities to social supports in the workplace.' *Journal of Rehabilitation 59*, 29–33.

Fabian, E.S., Waterworth, A. and Ripke, B. (1993) 'Reasonable accommodations for workers with serious mental illness: Type, frequency, and associated outcomes.' *Psychosocial Rehabilitation Journal 17*, 2, 163–172.

Faulkner, A. and Layzell, S. (2000) *Strategies for Living: A Report of User-led Research into People's Strategies for Living with Mental Distress.* London: Mental Health Foundation.

Grove, B. (1999) 'Mental health and employment: Shaping a new agenda.' *Journal of Mental Health 8*, 2, 131–141.

Hagner, D., Rogan, P. and Murphy, S. (1992) 'Facilitating natural supports in the workplace: Strategies for support consultants.' *Journal of Rehabilitation 58*, 1, 29–34.

Lane Frey, J. (1994) 'Long-term support: The critical element to sustaining competitive employment: Where do we begin?' *Psychosocial Rehabilitation Journal 17*, 3, 127–134.

Lehman, A.F. (1995) 'Vocational rehabilitation in schizophrenia.' *Schizophrenia Bulletin 21*, 645–656.

Lysaker, P. and Bell, M.D. (1995) 'Work performance over time for people with schizophrenia.' *Psychiatric Rehabilitation Journal 18*, 3, 141–145.

MacDonald-Wilson, K.L., Revell, W.G., Nguyen, N. and Peterson, M.E. (1991) 'Supported employment outcomes for people with psychiatric disability: A comparative analysis.' *Journal of Vocational Rehabilitation 1*, 3, 30–40.

McHugo, G.J., Drake, R.E. and Becker, D.R. (1998) 'The durability of supported employment effects.' *Psychiatric Rehabilitation Journal 22*, 1, 55–61.

Mancuso, L. (1993) *Case studies on reasonable accommodations for workers with psychiatric disabilities.* Washington Business Group on Health.

Marrone, J. (1993) 'Reasonable accommodations for workers with serious mental illness: Type, frequency, and associated outcomes.' *Psychosocial Rehabilitation Journal 17*, 2, 163–172.

Marrone, J., Bazell, A. and Gold, M. (1995) 'Employment supports for people with mental illness.' *Psychiatric Services 46*, 7, 707–711.

Mowbray, C.T., Bybee, D., Harris, S.N. and McCrohan, N. (1995) 'Predictors of work status and future work orientation in people with a psychiatric disability.' *Psychiatric Rehabilitation Journal 19*, 2, 17–28.

NHS Executive (1999) *National Service Framework for Mental Health.* London: DoH.

Office for National Statistics (2000) *Labour Force Survey.* London: Office for National Statistics. www.ons.gov.uk

Regenold, M., Sherman, M.F. and Fenzel, M. (1999) 'Getting back to work: Self-efficacy as a predictor of employment outcome.' *Psychiatric Rehabilitation Journal 22*, 4, 361–367.

Rogan, P. and Hagner, D. (1990) 'Vocational evaluation in supported employment.' *Journal of Rehabilitation 56*, 1, 45–51.

Rogers, E.S., Anthony W.A., Toole, J. and Brown, M.A. (1991) 'Vocational outcomes following psychosocial rehabilitation: A longitudinal study of three programs.' *Journal of Vocational Rehabilitation 1*, 3, 21–29.

Rogers, E.S., MacDonald-Wilson, K. and Anthony, W.A. (1997) 'A process analysis of supported employment services for persons with serious psychiatric disability: Implications for programme design.' *Journal of Vocational Rehabilitation 8*, 3, 232–242.

Rutman, I. (1994) 'How psychiatric disability expresses itself as a barrier to employment.' *Psychosocial Rehabilitation Journal 17*, 3, 15–36.

Sayce, L. (1999) 'From the Supreme Court to the British Mental Health Service: New opportunities for social inclusion.' *A Life in the Day 3*, 4, 5–12.

Smith, T.E.. Rio, J., Hull, J.W., Hedayat-Harris, A., Goodman, M. and Anthony, D.T. (1997) 'Differential effects of symptoms on rehabilitation and adjustment in people with schizophrenia.' *Psychiatric Rehabilitation Journal 21*, 2, 141–143.

Smith, T.E., Rio, J., Hull, J.W., Hedayat-Harris, A., Goodman, M. and Anthony, D.T. (1998) 'The rehabilitation readiness determination profile: A needs assessment for adults with severe mental illness.' *Psychiatric Rehabilitation Journal 21*, 4, 380–387.

Storey, K. and Certo, N.J. (1996) 'Natural supports for increasing integration in the workplace for people with disabilities: A review of the literature and guidelines for implementation.' *Rehabilitation Counseling Bulletin 40*, 1, 63–76.

Torrey, W.C. (1998) 'Practice guidelines for clinicians working in programmes providing integrated vocational and clinical services for persons with severe mental disorders.' *Psychiatric Rehabilitation Journal 21*, 4, 388–393.

Torrey, W.C., Becker, D.R. and Mowbray, C.T. (1995) 'Rehabilitative day treatment vs. supported employment: II. Consumer, family and staff reactions to a programme change.' *Psychosocial Rehabilitation Journal 18*, 3, 67–75.

Walls, R. and Fullmer, S. (1997) 'Competitive employment: Occupations after vocational rehabilitation.' *Rehabilitation Counselling Bulletin 41*, 1, 15–25.

West, M. and Parent, W. (1995) 'Community and workplace supports for individuals with severe mental illness in supported employment.' *Psychosocial Rehabilitation Journal 18*, 4, 13–24.

Xie, H.Y., Dain, B.J., Becker, D.R. and Drake, R.E. (1997) 'Job tenure among persons with severe mental illness.' *Rehabilitation Counseling Bulletin 40*, 4, 230–239.

The Contributors

Chris Clark is Senior Lecturer in Social Work and Head of Department at the University of Edinburgh. His research and teaching interests cover professional ethics, community care and voluntary action. Recent publications include *Social Work Ethics: Politics, Principles and Practice* and contributions to *The Blackwell Encyclopedia of Social Work* (edited by Martin Davies) and *Critical Practice in Social Work* (edited by Robert Adams, Lena Dominelli and Malcolm Payne).

Angela Cole is a freelance consultant with more than 20 years' experience in human services. Her experience includes direct support work, social work, lecturing, service management and commissioning. She now undertakes review and development work around the country and has supported numerous services trying to help people achieve more ordinary lifestyles. She has a keen interest in person-centred planning and community inclusion and is active in her local community alongside people with learning difficulties as well as in her work. She has an MSc and is the author of numerous publications.

Anne Connor is Project Manager for the Partners in Change programme, based in Scottish Human Services. Partners in Change promotes involvement in the health and related services through shared learning and capacity-building for activitists and workers. Previous work includes managing the Allies in Change programme, social work research at the Scottish Office, work as lead commissioner for mental health services at Lothian Health Board and as a freelance consultant. Her publications include co-editing of two Research Highlights volumes: *Mental Health and Social Work* (with Marion Ulas) and *Performance Review and Quality in Social Care* (with Stewart Black).

Abi Cooper is a freelance consultant and qualified social worker with 12 years' experience in the homelessness and mental health sectors. She was formerly Researcher for the National Day Centres Project of the National Homeless Alliance where her work included visiting over 70 day centres nationwide, training and policy work. She wrote *All in a Day's Work: A Guide to Good Practice in Day Centres Working with Homeless People* and *Better by Design*, which addresses design issues in day centres.

Bob Grove is Director of the Employment Support Programme at the Institute for Applied Health and Social Policy at King's College, London. He works as a consultant and researcher with Government departments and health and social care agencies in the public and voluntary sectors. Previously he worked in the voluntary sector, developing and managing a wide range of employment schemes for disabled and disadvantaged people. He is author of *The Social Firm Handbook* and editor of the mental health journal *A Life in the Day*.

Susan Hunter is Lecturer in Social Work at the University of Edinburgh. She has a particular interest in the implications for vulnerable adults, including older people and their carers, of the recent changes in community care.

Ann Lloyd is a Commissioning Manager with the London Borough of Newham. With A Chance to Work she supported people with severe learning difficulties and complex needs into real jobs. As a staff development officer she helped staff gain skills needed to support the moving-on process during the closure of a large hospital for people with learning difficulties. In 1995 she led a team in setting up Hackney Community Resource Service – a community-based team supporting people in realising ordinary goals. Publications include chapters for *Days of Change* and *Unlocking the Future* (both edited by McIntosh and Whittaker).

Helen Membrey is a Research Associate at the Centre for Mental Health Services Development, London. She is currently working on a two-year project researching the support and barriers to employment for people who use mental health services. Helen has successfully completed an MSc in Social Research Methodology.

Jo Moriarty is a Research Fellow at the National Institute for Social Work. Her research interests include support for carers and services for people with dementia. She has written books on the subject of respite care, including *Better for the Break* (co-authored with Enid Levin and Peter Gorbach) and on the use of community services by people with dementia (co-authored with Sarah Webb). She is currently working, with colleagues from NISW and the REU (formerly the Race Equality Unit) on a project looking at the quality of life and social support for people from minority ethnic groups.

Julie Ridley is a Senior Research with Scottish Health Feedback. She has worked for many years in research posts in both the voluntary sector, with MIND and the British Association of Social Workers, and in local government Social Work Departments in Scotland. In 2000, she graduated with a PhD from Edinburgh University, with a study of the impact of supported employment on the quality of life of people with learning disabilities. Her research work has been broad-based, most recently including work on young people's perceptions of health, aspects of healthy eating, the future of hostels for homeless people, the involvement of patients and the public in health services, defining 'personal care' and direct payments to mental health service users.

Kirsten Stalker (BA, PhD, CQSW) is Senior Research Fellow at the Social Work Research Centre at the University of Stirling, where she has worked for most of the past ten tears. Much of her research has been about support to people with learning disabilities and to disabled children. Her current work focuses on risk and uncertainty in community care. Among other publications, she is editor of two *Research Highlights* volumes – *Developments in Short Term Care: Breaks and Opportunities* and, with Carol Robinson, *Growing Up with Disability*.

Susan Tester is Senior Lecturer in Social Policy at the University of Stirling, where she specialises in community care, ageing and comparative social policy. She is currently a principal investigator for a project exploring perceptions of quality of life of frail older people, within the Economic and Social Research Council Growing Older Research Programme. Her publications include *Community Care for Older People: A Comparative Perspective* and *Caring by Day: A Study of Day Care Services for Older People*.

Glenda Watt is a strategic manager in the Department of Corporate Services, City of Edinburgh Council. She has responsibility for implementing 'A City for Ages' – the city's plan for the development of services to older people. Prior to this she was a Planning and Commissioning Officer, Services for Older People with the council's social work department. She has nursing qualifications and a Diploma in Social Work from Stirling University.

Subject Index

Author Index